*Gender and discourse: language and
power in politics, the Church and organisations*

REAL LANGUAGE SERIES

General Editors:

JENNIFER COATES, University of Surrey, Roehampton

JENNY CHESHIRE, Queen Mary and Westfield College,
University of London, and

EUAN REID, Institute of Education, University of London

Gender and discourse:

language and power in politics, the Church and organisations

Clare Walsh

Longman

An imprint of **PEARSON EDUCATION**

Harlow, England · London · New York · Reading, Massachusetts · San Francisco · Toronto · Don Mills, Ontario · Sydney
Tokyo · Singapore · Hong Kong · Seoul · Taipei · Cape Town · Madrid · Mexico City · Amsterdam · Munich · Paris · Milan

Pearson Education Limited

Head Office:
Edinburgh Gate
Harlow CM20 2JE
Tel: +44 (0)1279 623623
Fax: +44 (0)1279 431059

London Office:
128 Long Acre
London WC2E 9AN
Tel: +44 (0)20 7447 2000
Fax: +44 (0)20 7240 5771
Website: www.history-minds.com

First published in Great Britain in 2001

© Pearson Education, 2001

The right of Clare Walsh to be identified as Author
of this Work has been asserted by her in accordance
with the Copyright, Designs and Patents Act 1988.

ISBN 0 582 41892 5

British Library Cataloguing in Publication Data
A CIP catalogue record for this book can be obtained from the British Library

Library of Congress Cataloging-in-Publication Data
Walsh, Clare.
    Civilizing discourse : women in politics, the Church, and the environmental movement
/ Clare Walsh.
        p. cm. — (Real language series)
    Includes bibliographical references and index.
    ISBN 0-582-41892-5
    1. Feminism.   2. Women in politics—Great Britain.   3. Women and religion.
4. Ecofeminism.   5. Persuasion (Rhetoric)   I. Title.   II. Series.

HQ1176.W35   2001
305.42—dc21   2001029980

10   9   8   7   6   5   4   3   2   1

Set in 10/12pt Janson by Graphicraft Limited, Hong Kong
Produced by Pearson Education Asia Pte. Ltd.
Printed in Malaysia, VVP

The Publishers' policy is to use paper manufactured from sustainable forests.

Contents

To Stuart

Transcription Conventions

I have employed broad transcription conventions, whereby normal punctuation, other than the use of capital letters for proper nouns, is omitted. Line numbers are included for ease of reference:

{Responding}	Curly brackets are used to enclose paraphrases of questions asked by the interviewer.
. . .	Three consecutive dots indicate where short sections of the tape have been omitted.
(indeciph)	This is used to signify speech that is indecipherable.
[laughs]	Square brackets are used to describe marked prosodic features, such as tone of voice, and any non-verbal behaviour perceived to be relevant.
italics	Italics are used for emphatic stress on particular words.
and~and	The tilde character (~) is used to indicate where words run into one another, often in instances of build-up repetition.
↑	The up-arrow symbol is used where the speaker employs a marked questioning intonation.

List of Figures

Acknowledgements

I would like to thank Sara Mills for her constructive criticism, support and encouragement at every stage throughout the course of the research for this book. I would also like to thank all of my informants who generously took time out of their busy schedules to be interviewed by me.

1

Aims and General Theoretical Issues

The aim of this book is to develop an analytical framework that will combine the insights of critical discourse analysis (Fairclough 1989, 1992, 1995b; Chouliaraki and Fairclough 1999) and a range of feminist perspectives on discourse as social practice. The intention is to employ this framework in an investigation of women's participation in a number of 'communities of practice' (Eckert and McConnell-Ginet 1992) previously monopolized by men. The question to be addressed is whether women uncritically accept pre-existing discursive practices, whether they contest and seek to change them, or whether they shift strategically between these two positions, depending upon what is perceived to be appropriate at any given time. Comparisons will also be made with women's involvement in organizations where they are in a majority and where a feminist ethos prevails. According to Cameron (1997: 34), the potential advantage of grounding analysis in specific linguistic communities is that 'it leads away from global statements, and the stereotypical explanations that frequently accompany them, towards a more "local" kind of account that can accommodate intra- as well as intergroup differences'.

Following Freed's (1996) insight that certain spaces, settings and domains may be gendered as either primarily masculine or feminine, I will argue that historically the minority status of women within public sphere institutions, such as Parliament and the established Church, means that the dominant discursive practices which circulate in these domains are those associated with white middle-class male speakers. Through habitual use, these masculinist[1] discursive norms have assumed the status of gender-neutral *professional* norms, as have male-orientated patterns of behaviour and association. I will suggest that, as a result, women's public rhetoric is more likely than men's to be fractured by competing, often contradictory, norms and expectations and that this fact, in turn, has implications for the way in which women are perceived and judged by others, as well as for the roles they are assigned within the public sphere. In particular, I will argue that, over and above the normal expectation that women should be professionally competent, they are also expected to civilize male-gendered spaces. At the very least, this expectation imposes an additional burden on women who occupy public sphere roles, and, in many instances, it conflicts with the predominantly masculinist view of professionalism alluded to above.

With reference to selective transcripts of in-depth structured interviews with women in each of the domains under investigation, I will suggest that the complex negotiations in which women engage in order to manage these competing norms cannot easily be accommodated within a dichotomous model of gendered linguistic styles. Nonetheless, this is precisely how their linguistic behaviour is often 'fixed' and evaluated by others. In other words, there is what I will term a 'metadiscursive gap' between how gender is practised by individual women in everyday talk and professional contexts, and the stereotypical standards by which their linguistic behaviour is judged. I will make reference to a wide range of texts from a variety of sources in order to illustrate the role that the media, in particular, play in *mediating* the perception of women's involvement in the public sphere and in (re)producing normative gender ideologies.

A central thesis of this book is that both the institutional constraints with which women have to negotiate and the stereotypical evaluations of their performance of public sphere roles have contributed to a process of discursive restructuring. One effect of this has been that the gendered nature of the public–private dichotomy has been reproduced *within* the public sphere. The public sphere is in danger of becoming an asymmetrical two-tier system in which women's subordinate status is institutionalized. However, women are not passively positioned in relation to the institutional and other discursive constraints that operate on them. I will suggest that they, in their turn, have helped to promote a counter-tendency whereby the discursive boundaries between the traditional public and private spheres are becoming increasingly weakened and permeable.

Walter (1998) urges feminist activists to shift their attention away from what she perceives to be an unhealthy and unhelpful preoccupation with women's private sphere identities, to concentrate instead on securing greater equality for women within public sphere roles. Although I will suggest that such a wholesale shift would mask the many parallels between the two spheres in terms of gender asymmetry, in a recent reader comprising essays on language and gender (Coates, ed., 1998), women's involvement in the public domain was reflected in only one section, which seems to indicate that this is a relatively under-researched area. In particular, little research of a specific-ally linguistic nature has been carried out into women's engagement in the type of institutional discourses of the state that are the subject of three of the case studies in this book – namely, those on women in party politics and in the established Church (see Chapters 3, 4 and 6 respectively). Likewise, although there is a general perception that women are particularly active in the micropolitics of new social movements (McRobbie 1994; Fairclough

1995a), little detailed work has been undertaken into the distinctive discursive strategies, if any, they employ. These will be examined in the third case study (see Chapter 5) based on a comparison between the London-based Women's Environmental Network (WEN) and a number of mainstream environmental groups, notably Friends of the Earth (FoE).

1.1   The concept of 'communities of practice'

Eckert and McConnell-Ginet (1992) adapted the concept of 'community of practice' (abbreviated by them to CofP), from the work of the social learning theorists, Lave and Wenger (1991), who developed it in their study of traditional apprenticeships. Eckert and McConnell-Ginet (1999: 186) offer the following definition of the concept: 'A CofP is an aggregate of people who, united by a common enterprise, develop and share ways of doing things, ways of talking, beliefs, and values – in short, practices'. This emphasis on 'practice' is important, since it means that interest is not confined to issues of language, but extends to the whole range of discursive competencies by which members of a given community of practice construct their individual and collective identities, including their gendered identities. In her study of a community of practice comprising a group of Asian American adolescents, Eckert (1989) stresses the complex ways in which gender is co-constructed with other aspects of identity, including age, ethnicity and social status. Eckert and McConnell-Ginet (1999: 186) acknowledge that these practices can arise out of common enterprises that are more or less informal, and/or more or less institutionalized. Although they do not elaborate on this point, it would seem to raise the crucial issue of the extent to which practices are normatively imposed by a few members of a community of practice, or consensually agreed by all its members.

This issue is addressed to some extent by the idea that some members of a given community of practice are deemed to be more 'core' than others. Coreness is based on the degree to which individuals align themselves with the shared interests, activities and viewpoint(s) of the community as a whole. The concept of coreness is likely to prove useful in explaining differences between women (and men) within a given community of practice. For instance, the degree to which women accommodate themselves to prevailing masculinist discursive practices may depend on their feminist orientation, from pro-feminist to anti-feminist, with a wide range of possible positions in between, including those based on different kinds of feminist affiliation. Since individuals co-construct their identities along a number of different axes simultaneously, this may on occasions lead them to assume contradictory subject positions.

I will argue that in male-dominated communities of practice an element of dissonance is introduced into women's membership by virtue of their gender identity alone. Yet, attempts to define the concept of a community of practice, as opposed to other sociolinguistic concepts such as 'speech community' and 'social network', tend to foreground consensus as an ideal. This is implicit in a comment made by Holmes and Meyerhoff (1999: 176): 'The basis of . . . variation lies in how *successfully* an individual has acquired the shared repertoire, or assimilated the goal(s) of the joint enterprise, or established patterns of engagement with other members' (my italics). However, in mixed-sex communities of practice, dominated by masculinist discursive practices, conflict is as likely to occur as consensus, especially since, as Cameron (1998: 447) notes: 'Women and men are now in competition for the same kind of power and status as opposed to taking up complementary roles.'

I will suggest that the social meanings attached to the discursive norms and practices adopted by individuals within a community of practice are not always those they intend to convey. Cameron's (1998: 449) observation that 'speaker intention is not the final guarantor of interactionally produced meaning' holds equally true for other semiotic modes, such as non-verbal behaviour, sartorial codes and so on. For this reason, it is necessary, as Bergvall (1999: 282) notes, 'to consider and clarify the force of the socially ascribed nature of gender: the assumptions and expectations of (often binary) ascribed social roles against which any performance of gender is constructed, accommodated to, or resisted'. This entails moving beyond the local accounts of discursive practices afforded by a focus on specific communities of practice to a consideration of the beliefs and ideologies about gender that circulate in the wider society. According to Bergvall (1999: 284), the uni-directional power of media discourse, whereby the roles of producer and inter-preter do not alternate, make it a particularly potent cultural site for the reproduction of normative gendered identities and relations. This view is supported by the current study of media coverage of women's participation in a wide range of civil and public sphere roles. Nonetheless, I will suggest, that (some) media institutions also function as sites of discursive *struggle* in the ongoing debate about 'appropriate' gender roles and behaviour, rather than simply reproducing conservative gender ideologies.

1.2   Negotiating masculinist discursive norms

There is no doubt that women in the West are increasing their role as active citizens, participating in political debate and public opinion formation – most visibly in central and devolved institutions of the state formerly dominated by men, and also in grassroots movements, including women-specific groups. Yet, as Cameron (1997) notes, there is a need to account for differences *between* women, as well as between women and men, since not all women in civil and public sphere roles respond in the same way to the masculinist discursive norms they encounter. I intend to outline a number of possible strategies available to women who enter traditionally male-dominated communities of practice and to consider the potential risks and advantages of each, both from the point of view of the career interests of individual women, and from the point of view of the broader feminist goal of eradicating inequalities based on gender.

1.2.1 The accommodation model

One strategy, advocated by Lakoff (1975), is for women to embrace existing masculinist discursive practices that have become normative within the majority of communities of practice in the public sphere on the grounds that these are perceived as powerful, whereas those associated with women's speech are perceived as weak and powerless. Although subsequent empirical work has called into question many of the claims made by Lakoff about so-called 'powerless' features of women's speech (O'Barr and Atkins 1980; Holmes 1984; Cameron et al. 1989; Coates 1996), Lakoff's views have remained influential in both feminist theory and praxis. The strategy of accommodation she advocates is illustrated in practice in a study conducted by McElhinny (1995: 221), which revealed that female police officers defeminize their language and behaviour 'in order to reconcile others and themselves to their presence in the police department'. Yet, as Coates (1998: 295) points out, even wholehearted and uncritical conformity to implicitly androcentric professional norms on the part of women can lead to negative evaluations of their speech:

> But women who successfully adapt to characteristically male linguistic norms run the risk of being perceived as aggressive and confrontational, as unfeminine – in other words, there is a clash between what is expected of a woman and what is expected of a person with high status in the public sphere.

This claim is borne out by empirical evidence summarized by Crawford (1995: 65). It would appear, then, that the strategy of accommodation to androcentric norms can be counter-productive, leading to negative evaluations of women's performance of public sphere roles. A number of feminists have argued that the uncritical acceptance of this strategy is, in any case, fundamentally inimical to the feminist goal of promoting gender equality, since it helps to reify a situation in which masculinist norms are legitimated, while women's speech is constructed as a 'problem'.

1.2.2 The critical 'difference' model

A second strategy is for women to challenge the unproblematized status of masculinist norms, promoting in their stead the more cooperative discourse style which extensive empirical research reveals tends to be favoured by women in a wide range of cultural contexts (see, for instance, Holmes 1995). With regard to the performance of public sphere roles, this strategy is illustrated by Coates's (1995) account of studies on women's involvement in a number of occupational contexts. Again, there are risks associated with this approach, since evidence suggests that the mismatch between the discursive choices made and those that are deemed 'professional' means that women are often judged to be weak and ineffectual (Holmes 1995; Tannen 1996). More fundamentally, some feminist linguists have criticized this approach as naively apolitical. Cameron (1992: 76), for instance, says of masculine and feminine speech styles: 'However we value the two styles morally . . . it is evident that instrumentally they have political consequences.' By embracing feminine norms, she claims, women help to reify the traditional gendered nature of the public–private dichotomy, 'constructing women to function best in the private domain and men in the public one' (ibid.).

Evidence from my research would suggest, instead, that the value some 'difference' feminists attach to cooperative discourse strategies in the workplace may, in practice, have contributed to the creation of a gendered split *within* the public sphere, by reinforcing the prevailing view, even among some women, that they are naturally suited to relatively low status roles. These include such roles as 'soft' portfolios (party politics), pastoral work (the Church) and fund-raising and administrative activities (the environmental movement). In her review of Holmes's book on linguistic politeness, MacMahon (1998: 279) is concerned that the advocacy of women-orientated norms in occupational roles may lead to a 'Stepford Wives scenario in which women direct all their energies into being as blandly pleasant as possible'. Interestingly, this echoes very closely the widespread perception of the majority of the Labour Party's female MPs, the so-called 'Blair's babes', who gained their seats in the 1997 general election – a perception of blandness that has been fuelled by largely hostile media coverage.

Yet this underestimates the ability of feminist-identified women to influence the norms and structures that prevail in the communities of practice in which they participate. For instance, I will argue that women have contributed to the increasing 'conversationalization' of the public sphere, noted by Fairclough (1992, 1994, 1995b), among others, whereby interpersonally orientated discursive practices are displacing purely transactional ones. Cameron (1995b: 199) acknowledges that feminine speech styles coincide with those increasingly favoured in certain workplace contexts:

> What is happening, at least in theory, is a shift in the culture of Anglo-American corporate capitalism away from traditional (aggressive, competitive and individualistic) interactional norms and towards a new management style stressing flexibility, team-work and collaborative problem-solving, which is thought to be better suited to changing global economic conditions.

In its most politicized or *critical* guise, the 'difference' approach stresses that it is not women who should change their discursive style, but rather it is men who should adopt the norms associated with women's speech on the grounds that these are both morally and instrumentally preferable (Holmes 1995: 209ff). This view was echoed recently by the editor of the magazine *Management Today*: 'If men want to be successful at work they must behave more like women' (the *Guardian* 27 September 1999). In this context, the advocacy of linguistic strategies preferred by many women no longer seems like wishful thinking.

Cameron's view that '*gender is a problem, not a solution*' (1995a: 42, italics in the original), seems to assume that the promotion of traditional feminine speech styles in the public domain will inevitably lead to the reaffirmation of normative ideologies about gender. However, the very fact of connecting them to public sphere contexts is likely to increase their status and instrumental value. Cameron's other major concern appears to be that an undue focus on issues of language can be a distraction from 'tackling the root cause of women's subordinate status' (1995b: 205). Yet, if the sort of 'verbal hygiene'[2] practices promoted by feminist linguists, such as Holmes (1995) in particular, can be shown to effect structural changes that lead to greater equality in the workplace, then this objection is no longer valid. Indeed, Holmes's approach would seem to answer Toolan's (1997: 89) call for a *more critical* discourse analysis, one that seeks to change, correct and minimize 'inequity, hegemony and control'.

This study will, however, call into question any *simple* equation between the cooperative discursive style favoured by many women, and increasingly promoted in a number of public sphere domains, and more inclusive and egalitarian practices in the workplace. It will be argued that the meanings this style carries depend on the purpose for which it is used and the co(n)text in which it occurs. For instance, whatever the intention of the text producer, it may be perceived and evaluated by addressees as patronizing, insincere or even, I will suggest, as directive, rather than inclusive (see page 50). Swann and Graddol (1995: 144) make the point that this type of style can serve to disguise the operation of power, since it, 'can be used to give the appearance of democratic participation while being well designed for the manufacture of consensus and consent'. Likewise, in her recent book about verbal hygiene practices in the service industries, Cameron (2000) argues that the rhetoric of empowerment is used for coercive ends, often to the disadvantage of female workers in particular. I will argue that the connection between linguistic practice and the gendered identities and relations it helps to constitute needs, therefore, to be evaluated in a highly context-sensitive way.

A more fundamental objection put forward by Cameron (1995a) to the 'difference' model is that the polarized nature of gendered discourse styles it identifies is as much a product of the empirical research carried out by sociolinguists as something 'discovered' by it. Cameron (1990) also expresses her scepticism about the equation of quantitative methods of data collection and the 'truth' about linguistic behaviour. In this instance, the implication is that researchers end up interpreting their data in ways that will confirm their *a priori* assumption about gender duality. However, study after study, using a wide range of sophisticated and context-sensitive modes of data analysis, as well as less reliable ones, have revealed remarkably similar patterns of linguistic behaviour among women in a range of cultural and institutional settings (Brown 1980; Tannen 1989; Holmes 1995; Wodak and Benke 1996). This does not mean that such behaviour should be interpreted as part of an unchanging female essence. Indeed, far from relying on essentialist notions about gender, many 'critical difference' feminists assume that men can and should shift their gendered linguistic behaviour in the direction of feminine norms (see Holmes 1995: 209ff). That the linguistic variables that correlate with women's speech are, in many instances, preferred norms is evident from women's groups and organizations where they have become normative and where they do tend to coincide with egalitarian structures (see Chapters 4, 5 and 6).

More problematic are the views of those political theorists whose ideas rely on essentialist ideas about women's speech. For instance, in the concluding chapter of her book, *Public Man, Private Woman*, Elshtain (1993) answers her initial question about the sort of public language feminists should begin to speak by calling for 'values and language which flow from "mothering"' (ibid.: 336). It remains unclear whether she is referring here to the institution of mothering or the latent potential in the majority of women to mother. Either way, by emphasizing 'womanly' values of care, community, selflessness and so on, and by linking these to natural sex difference, Elshtain helps to re-produce the discourse that defines them as such. This discourse is itself a political construction that serves to sustain a gender hierarchy in which women are likely to be perceived as naturally suited to subordinate roles within the public sphere. As Cameron (1995a: 43) points out, the goal of feminist theory is not to reify existing gender relations, but to 'open up the possibility of challenge and change'. This, I would suggest, is what 'critical difference' feminism does.

1.2.3   The performative model

The uncritical acceptance of pre-existing masculinist norms, or the active promotion of alternative norms associated with women's speech, are not the only strategies available to women who enter public sphere domains. A third solution, identified in more recent ethnographic work, is the conscious shifting between masculine and feminine norms (see, for instance, Hall and Bucholtz 1995; Bergvall et al. 1996). This presupposes a performative[3] view of gender as something that can be deployed strategically. My data indicate that this type of style shifting is routinely practised by women in traditionally male-dominated institutions. Thus a number of my respondents said they invest in ideals of femininity for strategic purposes in certain circumstances, while in others they align themselves with masculinist professional norms with equally strategic, but different, ends in view. However, I will suggest that this type of gendered style shifting is not without risks, since the hybrid nature of the resulting discursive style can lead to accusations of inconsistency and insincerity, accusations that are prevalent in media coverage of high profile women. In addition, I will call into question the belief that such strategic shifts in linguistic behaviour are invariably radical, either in intent or effect.

It has become a truism among poststructuralist feminists that performative shifts further the goal of promoting greater gender equality, since they are said to deconstruct polarized beliefs about gender, or, in this instance, about masculine and feminine speech styles (Butler 1990, 1993). Yet, as Cameron notes, 'Playing with the codes only keeps the codes in play' and paradoxically may even reify them in their 'most exaggerated and dichotomous forms' (1997: 32). The former British prime minister, Margaret Thatcher, is a case in point. She switched between a confrontational masculinist style and a self-consciously exaggerated and stylized version of feminine speech and behaviour (Fairclough 1989: 182ff; Webster 1990). I will suggest that, in many instances, such shifts in style are, in any case, less a matter of political calculation and more a pragmatic means of managing the competing, often contradictory, expectations that operate on women in public sphere roles. I will also argue that the poststructuralist assumption that identity can be performed strategically is too rational and intentionalist and ignores the personal and emotional investment individuals have in aspects of self-identity, including those constituted by the linguistic choices they make. As Tannen (1996: 131) points out, speech styles are not, 'hats you can put on when you enter an office and take off when you leave'.

1.2.4   The concept of 'appropriacy'

A performative theory of language and gender relies implicitly on an appeal to the concept of 'appropriacy'. Thus in her research on the style shifting of female engineering students, Bergvall concludes, 'The trick is to know when to behave appropriately' (1996: 180). However, judgements about the appropriacy or otherwise of an individual's behaviour are usually outside her or his control. Indeed, Bergvall's own findings illustrate this point. She makes it clear that even where assertive female students employ strategies, such as self-deprecating laughter, to mitigate the perception of their power, they were often negatively assessed by peers. Despite their attempts to engage in a complex set of negotiations with conflicting role expectations, they remain caught in an evaluative double bind, 'When the women are assertive, they are resisted by their peers; when they are facilitative, their work may be taken for granted and not acknowledged' (Bergvall 1996: 192). When Bergvall says of her respondents, 'Most often, however, they operate outside the limiting norms that would define them on the basis of predetermined, binary, oppositional categories' (ibid.), I would argue that this is as much an instance of wishful thinking, as an interpretation extrapolated from her data, since no such discursive space in fact exists.

Like Cameron (1995b), I am suspicious of appeals to 'appropriacy', which is often viewed by linguists as a panacea for all those ill-informed and damaging appeals to 'correctness' made by 'shamans' (Bolinger 1980). Cameron (1995b: 234) deftly exposes the equally subjective bases for most judgements about what is appropriate. As noted above, the question remains: Who decides, and on what basis? The answer is that such decisions remain the privilege of the powerful, and, I would suggest, of the increasingly powerful mainstream media. The criteria employed are often stereotypical, drawing upon folk-linguistic ideas about the connection between gender and linguistic behaviour. It could be argued that there is no reason why the concept of appropriacy could not be extended to include the 'affective' dimension of speech – in other words, its ability to forge and sustain interpersonal relationships or to promote collaborative, rather than confrontational, interaction. Yet, appeals to 'appropriacy' tend not to be ideologically creative, but rather lead to judgements that are politically conservative, hence Cameron's point that they serve to 'reify the norms we currently have' (1995b: 234).

Feminist praxis demands other criteria: not simply whether speech is appropriate to its context of utterance, but whether it presents a challenge to existing unequal relations of power; not whether it accords with the advice from a training manual on 'how to get the most from your staff', but whether it is sincere and consistent with one's actions. Tannen (1996) argues that women managers tend to praise staff more than male peers, but unless this praise is consistent with their general managerial style – in other words, unless it is perceived as more than purely strategic – then it is likely to induce cynicism rather than motivation. Montgomery (1999) refers to this as the 'performative paradox' and cites Scanell in support of this view, 'If a person's behaviour is perceived by others *as* a performance, it will be judged to be insincere, for sincerity presupposes, as its general condition, the absence of performance' (Scannell, cited in Montgomery 1999: 9).

The contingent and subjective nature of validity criteria such as 'sincerity' and 'consistency' mean, of course, that there will be no universal agreement about them. For instance, there may well be some who will have judged Mrs Thatcher as sincere when she celebrated the superior virtues of domesticity for women when addressing them, but there are others who will have been all too aware of the gap between her rhetoric, on the one hand, and her policies and lived experience, on the other. Since all judgements about discursive style are therefore both subjective and contested, including judgements about appropriacy, it is necessary to make a persuasive case for those which seem to be in keeping with feminist goals. Thatcher's style fails on these grounds for many feminists, however competent and stylistically flexible she may have appeared.

Montgomery (1999: 12) argues that, 'The emphasis on validity claims adds a hitherto neglected dimension to the systematic study of language and communication'. I would suggest that the importance of validity claims has been seriously underestimated by those who advocate a performative approach to language and gender. If one accepts that identity is constituted intersubjectively through language, then the response to one's use of language by others is crucial. Nor do judgements about the validity of an individual's speech rely exclusively on linguistic evidence. Equally important factors are accompanying prosodic, paralinguistic and kinesic traces and cues. Montgomery (1999) illustrates the central role played by these factors in his analysis of the different evaluations of the verbal tributes offered by Tony Blair, the Queen and Earl Spencer, respectively, in the aftermath of the death of Diana, Princess of Wales. He concludes his analysis by claiming that sincerity has shifted from being a private sphere virtue to a virtue expected of public figures. He explains this shift by linking it to 'the changing ways in which broadcasting configures modalities of communication' (ibid.: 29). I would argue, however, that its importance has increased in all public sphere domains in direct proportion to the emphasis placed on image consultancy and what Fairclough (1992: 9) refers to as the 'technologization' of language in these domains. Those in public sphere roles ignore its importance at their peril.

1.3   Theorizing gender

Cameron (1996: 33–4) argues that work in sociolinguistics needs to theorize the social, and, in particular, gender, in a more sophisticated way, since it 'has turned out to be an extraordinarily intricate and multilayered phenomenon – unstable, contested, intimately bound up with other social divisions'. She believes that feminists have a responsibility not to operate with reductive and misleading definitions of gender, since their 'research findings have been taken up in popular media, and applied institutionally for practical purposes' (ibid.: 34). This is certainly borne out by my research into media coverage of women in public life, which reveals that media producers frequently operate with reductive gender stereotypes.

1.3.1   Gender: one variable among many

Cameron claims that the complex mapping of the intersection between gender and other variables is 'probably the greatest theoretical change in feminist linguistics over the past twenty years' (1997: 33). Given the focus of this book, the main emphasis will be on the way gender intersects with institutional 'habitus' (Bourdieu 1977) and status, as well as with the gender politics espoused by individual women. However, I will suggest that other identity criteria intersect with gender in a way that often doubly disadvantages women. Thus the minority of women priests who are black and/or lesbian seem to attract particularly discriminatory responses from parishioners. This double/triple 'otherness' appears to be too much of a threat to the status quo, especially in a climate of backlash against so-called political correctness, a climate that I would argue has helped to re-legitimize overt sexism, racism and heterosexism. More generally, and especially in the media, allusions to class and age often function to undermine women's credibility in public sphere roles in a way that appears to be less true for male colleagues.

While it is important to acknowledge that the isolation of gender as a variable in relation to linguistic behaviour has led to a distorted view of its importance and mode of operation, it is more difficult to avoid 'bolting on' other variables in a tokenistic way. This is something that black women in particular find suspicious, hence, the w(e)ary reaction of high-profile black women, most notably the veteran Labour MP, Diane Abbott, who declined to be interviewed by me. To some extent the influence of other axes of identity is less marked in the case of women's participation in the institutions investigated in this book, since implicit identity criteria of whiteness and middle-classness and, to a lesser extent, heterosexuality and middle-agedness, continue to operate as *de facto* entry credentials to what remain essentially conservative institutional spaces. For instance, there are only two black women MPs and few black women priests, despite the relatively high proportion of black people in the Church of England. One might assume that the more radical credentials of the environmental movement would make it more open to participation by black people, yet, significantly, those who set up the Black Environmental Network (BEN) say they felt compelled to adopt a separatist policy in order to have their voices heard in a white-dominated movement (in the *Guardian* 17 March 1999).

1.3.2   Pluralizing masculinities

Just as intragroup differences between women need to be acknowledged, so too do those between men. Thus Hearn (1992: 4) makes the point that 'not only do men dominate women, but also different types of men dominate other men – able-bodied over men with disabilities, heterosexual over gay, and so on'. This is illustrated in the Church's long-standing ruling on gay priests, whereby they are denied the right to practise their sexuality openly. In the introduction to a collection of essays on language and masculinity Johnson and Meinhof (1997) suggest that inequalities between men could be reflected in the use of 'masculinities' in the plural. A number of essays in the collection stress the variability of linguistic behaviour among men (Kiesling 1997; Pujolar 1997), while others call into question the assumption that men eschew interactive strategies based on cooperation (Hewitt 1997; Cameron 1997). Hewitt, for instance, points out that the competitive displays in which men often engage require all participants to submit to the operation of consensual rules. A number of the studies on which the essays are based underline the importance of language as a resource for establishing and maintaining homosocial bonds between men. However, I will argue that these cooperative strategies among men function to exclude women and gay men, and therefore constitute an important mechanism for ensuring the continuing marginalization of both women and homosexual men within public sphere institutions. Threadgold (1997: 33–4) alludes to the even more pervasive power of a presupposed male homosocial audience. I will also explore this phenomenon, especially in relation to the way in which mediatized public discourse[4] covertly genders its ideal addressee as male.

Johnson (1997: 12) argues that the disproportionate focus on women's speech means that men's speech has retained its status as the 'default mode' for both sexes. As a corrective to this, in my case study on the London-based Women's Environmental Network (WEN) in Chapter 5, I intend to analyse the linguistic practices of both men and women within the same frame of reference, by comparing WEN with male-dominated environmental groups, such as Friends of the Earth and Greenpeace. The virtual exclusion of feminine norms from many public sphere institutions and organizations, until relatively recently, makes it difficult to accept Johnson's account of feminine and masculine norms as mutually dependent constructions in a dialectical relationship (Johnson 1997: 22).

However, I agree with Johnson's view that the neglect of close attention to men's linguistic behaviour has served to obscure the considerable common ground that exists between the speech of women and men, something that is not surprising, given that they are drawing on the same linguistic resources. Evidence from my data indicates that the commonalities are, if anything, increasing. Not only are the discursive strategies associated with women's speech increasingly employed by both women and men in the public sphere, but women in public life are also encroaching on traditionally male-orientated linguistic domains, such as swearing (see also de Klerk 1997). In addition, the willingness of women to talk openly about issues that have traditionally been treated as taboo among men, such as menstruation, breast cancer, pregnancy and so on, poses a challenge to the idea that women's language is more likely than men's to be marked by euphemism.

1.3.3   Sex and gender: collapsible categories?

The title of an earlier book in this series, *Rethinking Language and Gender Research: Theory and Practice* (edited by Bergvall et al. 1996), indicates their view that the essays in the collection represent a new departure in the field, and more specifically in the conception of gender which they feel ought to inform the theory and practice of linguistic research. Following Butler (1990), Bergvall and colleagues make the radical, and in my view untenable, claim that sex, like gender, is a constructed category. This leads them to confuse and conflate the two terms, sex/gender, thereby effectively erasing a distinction that many feminists have found to be theoretically useful. This is evident in the following, where they employ the terms designating sexual identity, female–male, where feminine–masculine would normally be employed:

> Individuals who fail to fit the strict female-male dichotomy are either ignored or subject to boundary policing . . . Thus, assertive women may be nudged back into their approved roles by being labelled *aggressive bitches*, and nurturing men may be reminded of their deviance by being labelled *wimp*, *sissy*, *fay* or *pussy-whipped*.
>
> (Bing and Bergvall: 1996: 6–7; italics in the original)

I would argue that this offers an account of the policing of gendered, rather than sexual, identities. In any case, my work on sacerdotal ministry in the Church of England suggests that gender-crossing behaviour is differentially evaluated for men and women, whereas Bing and Bergvall seem to imply that they are equally penalized for such behaviour. It would appear that the instances they cite, where sexual identities seem to be at stake, are not sufficiently widespread to merit collapsing the traditional feminist formulation whereby sex is seen as a biological category and gender as a socially constructed one. The fact that such instances trouble the sex/gender dichotomy does not mean that this dichotomy is no longer theoretically useful; it simply means that they are exceptions to a general and generalizable rule. I remain unconvinced by their claim that 'the idea that female and male bodies are fundamentally different is relatively new' (ibid.: 7) since the historical evidence they cite is selective and patchy.

Equally unconvincing is the attempt made by Butler (1990: xx) to generalize about how people 'do gender' from the marginal practice of male/female drag artists. As Cameron (1997: 32) points out, in many cases 'the femininities they enact are exaggerated stereotypes, fakes'. Far from furthering a feminist agenda, such caricatured performances of femininity are often perceived as insulting by women. How can one explain the insult, unless there is something in traditional modes of femininity that many women seem anxious to defend? It suggests that women invest in some aspects of femininity which they view as positive markers of self-identity, as well as those which would be deemed by some feminists as reactionary. This perhaps offers a timely reminder that not all aspects of the ideology of femininity, including those traditionally associated with linguistic behaviour, are incompatible with feminist goals. To argue that they are ignores the fact that, as active though socially constrained agents, women themselves have helped to shape the conception of gender, including gendered linguistic behaviour, that circulates at any given time in a given society.

The main argument put forward by Bing and Bergvall (1996) is for an approach that does not involve the bringing of preconceived ideas to bear on the study of language, sex and gender; yet it is clear from their introductory chapter that they are already committed to a way of thinking about both which emphasizes diversity, rather than dichotomy, as though diversity were in itself a good thing. This may well be true, but a political case needs to be made for such a view. This is symptomatic of the poststructuralist tendency to privilege discursive plurality, yet as Cameron (1996: 43) points out, the value of different linguistic styles is contingent upon the context of use and the mechanisms by which they are evaluated. Yet I am persuaded by the arguments of feminist linguists, such as Coates (1995) and Holmes (1995), that some speech norms favoured by women at least have the potential to be ethically and instrumentally preferable to the masculinist speech norms that currently assume the guise of professional norms in the public domain. The promotion of this critical difference view, far from leading to the co-optation of feminist research on language and gender, can in fact constitute a radical challenge to the status quo.

Equally paradoxical is Bergvall's (1996) commitment to deconstructing gender as a category, while at the same time urging women to recognize it as a ready-made identity marker by which they can assert their common experiences. She insists that, in the case of her respondents, a failure of empathy with other women 'fuels the conflicts they experience' (ibid.: 193). She develops this point further: 'The anti-feminist stance of many of the women, reinforced by the conservative campus climate, leads them to be naively apolitical, depriving them of any common ground upon which to work together to contest limiting gender stereotypes' (ibid.: 193). Yet, this is precisely where her theoretical commitment to the deconstructing of *both* sex and gender polarities inevitably leads.

1.3.4   Gender, a flexible and fixed category

The approach to gender that informs this book is one that views it as both a flexible and a fixed category. On the one hand, it will be argued that gender does not simply reflect a pre-existing identity, but helps to constitute, maintain and transform that identity in everyday situations via talk and the paralinguistic behaviour that accompanies it. On the other hand, the metadiscursive control exercised by others, and especially by the media, constrains this process of ongoing identity formation. This is because the metadiscursive gap alluded to earlier (see p. 2) means that, however fluid the enactment of gendered identities by individual women may be, the schemata[5] by which their behaviour and speech are evaluated often remain fixed and persistent, and for this reason it is important that feminists should not simply dismiss folklinguistic assumptions:

> Although folklinguistics is often dismissed by linguists as unscientific and inaccurate (both of which it is), it is certainly not without interest for a feminist linguistic theory. Feminists must pay attention to beliefs about male and female speech, because prejudice is often more powerful than fact.

> (Cameron 1992: 54)

I would argue that this is especially true for understanding the different ways in which the speech of men and women in public sphere roles is evaluated. Folklinguistic ideas are also important for understanding women's self-perceptions of their own linguistic practices and the ideological and symbolic work that such practices perform. This book will attempt to map out the complex ways in which interpretative constraints and self-perceptions interact.

The theory of gender as both flexible and fixed is shared by Crawford (1995), but she sees the political potential of 'doing gender' as *radically* circumscribed. She creates the impression that conversational humour, largely restricted to private sphere interaction, is one of the few discursive spaces that permit women to exercise the linguistic licence to 'do gender' in ways that transgress conventional gender expectations. Butler (1990) betrays the opposite tendency of overemphasizing the constitutive nature of discourse, while ignoring material constraints. I agree with Threadgold's view that her work betrays a confusion between the metaphorical and the real:

> Her metaphor/narrative of performing gender is seductive and productive in her writing, but the gendered body which performs does so in fictions, again in a place apart from the material and institutional constraints on real bodies . . . it may well be that it is only those with a certain level of cultural and economic capital and the right colour skin whose lives as discursive practices are really open to interventions or resignification of this theoretical kind.

> (Threadgold 1997: 83–4)

As Fairclough (1992: 66) points out, subjects are socially pre-constituted; there is no simple 'free play of ideas in people's heads'.

Unlike Butler, Dorothy Smith recognizes the institutional constraints that operate on women's identities. She argues that there is a constant tension between women's freedom to make choices within discourse and the regulatory practices which function to limit these choices and determine how they are perceived. For instance, in her discussion of the textually mediated discourse of femininity, she points out that, while women are subjected to disciplinary regimes embedded in texts, 'Behind appearance and its interpretation is secreted a subject who is fully an agent' (Smith 1990: 193). Following Smith, I will argue that 'women actively work out their subject positions and roles in the process of negotiating discursive constraints' (ibid.: 86). More specifically, I will suggest that by exploiting this dialectic between structure and agency, women have been able to effect both discursive and structural change in a number of communities of practice within the public sphere.

1.4   Theorizing masculinist hegemony

The term 'patriarchy' is problematic since it implies a monolithic and totalizing system of oppression in which all men dominate all women. This obscures the differences between women, noted above, as well as differences between men. The term's original meaning, 'the rule of the fathers', carries connotations of paternalism that do not capture the subtle and varied ways in which women continue to experience discrimination in a range of public domains. This is not to deny that residual aspects of this paternalism can still be found. For instance, it manifests itself in systems of patronage and mentorship, whereby powerful older men help to foster the careers of younger male colleagues, incidentally sidelining the career chances of women. Likewise, Threadgold (1997) identifies a persistent public discourse of 'care and protection' that seeks to contain and control both women and members of ethnic minorities. However, I will suggest that two of the main ways in which gender inequality is perpetuated are through the operation of impersonal masculinist discursive practices that have become normative, as well as through concrete fraternal networks that transcend the boundaries of institutional discourses.

I will argue that the operation of masculinist hegemony is diffuse; it is embedded in impersonal discursive practices and institutional structures that are historically associated with men. Foucault's concept of 'orders of discourse'[6] allows for an understanding of discourses as masculinist in their expression. He claims that certain institutional discourses maintain their dominance because they are organized around practices of exclusion, often involving speech rituals: 'Religious, judicial, therapeutic, and in large measure also political discourses can scarcely be dissociated from the deployment of a ritual which determines both the particular properties and the stipulated roles of the speaking subjects' (Foucault 1984: 121). Also, in the definition of what he terms 'societies of discourse', he highlights their ability to position those outside as excluded 'others': '... [they] function to preserve or produce discourses, but in order to make them circulate in a closed space, distributing them only according to strict rules, and without the holders being dispossessed by this distribution' (ibid.). It is this insight that will be developed further in my analysis of women's exclusion from, marginalization within, and challenges to, a range of masculinist institutional discourses which position them as 'outsiders within'.

Although the social theorist Sylvia Walby (1990) retains the term 'patriarchy', her work is useful in that she avoids the economistic tendency which dominates many discussions of the operation of masculinist hegemony. Instead, she suggests that there are many dimensions of power (economic, political and cultural) that form a complex matrix of power relations, often with institutional bases. Walby's major insight, which is central to this book, is that, whereas private patriarchy operated on the basis of exclusionary tactics, denying women access to participation in the public sphere, public forms of masculinist power have the effect of segregating and subordinating women once they enter the public sphere. As mentioned earlier, this study will suggest that the asymmetrical power relationship which underpinned the traditional public/private dichotomy is therefore being reproduced *within* public sphere institutions. In particular, I will argue that women in the public eye continue to be seen and judged by male colleagues and by the media in terms more appropriate to the private domain. Hearn (1992: 175) observes: '. . . of special interest is the occurrence of sexual harassment, which is often at high levels when women enter what are traditionally men's domains and occupations'. This practice, together with more covert means of segregating and marginalizing women, has the effect of undermining their claims to authority in public sphere roles.

A number of feminist theorists (e.g. Sedgwick 1985; Pateman 1989) have suggested that the nature of masculinist power itself has changed in that it has become less top-down, and more horizontal in its operation. For instance, Sedgwick (1985) argues that the interdependence and solidarity between men, what she terms 'homosocial bonding', is one of the mechanisms by which masculinist norms become reproduced in the public sphere:

> . . . in any male-dominated society, there is a special relationship between male homosocial (*including* homosexual) desire and the structures for maintaining and transmitting patriarchal power; a relationship founded on an inherent and potentially active structural congruence.
>
> (Sedgwick 1985: 25; italics in the original)

The form this takes is, she claims, culturally contingent. It can range from hierarchical forms of homosociality, made manifest in bonds based on competitive mastery and subordination, to more egalitarian forms that rely on an ideology of brotherhood which transcends differences of social class. The latter seem to be particularly relevant to the operation of institutional discourses in the West as we enter the new millennium and have been labelled collectively and variously as 'the old boys' network', 'the boys' club' and 'cronyism' in everyday parlance, and as 'viriarchy' (Waters 1989) and 'fratriarchy' (Remy 1990) by social theorists. Even Coward (1999), who has expressed scepticism about the systematic nature of current forms of gender discrimination against women in the West, acknowledges that such networks continue to be detrimental in their effect: 'Networking and men's narcissistic interest in each other often cut women out of positions of power. Sexual attitudes are often denigratory. Male hostility to women is still a significant fact' (Coward 1999: 212). I will suggest that women's entry into previously male-dominated environments has, in some instances, led to a defensive strengthening of fraternal networks and that a 'thickening' effect occurs because these networks often cut across the boundaries of different communities of practice.

In order to counter the masculinism they confront in many public institutional spaces, some women have developed their own counter-networks. The potential power of such networking has been emphasized by many feminists who have achieved positions of prominence in public sphere institutions. Thus, in an article in *Everywoman* (September 1995, p. 11) Mary Robinson, then President of Ireland, highlighted:

> . . . the kinds of structures that are evolved by women, for example, the capacity to link an informal grouping together in very supporting and helping ways. I think that this way of networking, and networking in a way that links grassroots organizations into systems, is very important.

I will suggest that the linking of 'grassroots organizations into systems' is an important feature of women's networking in all of the communities of practice investigated in this study. Yet the relatively recent history of this type of networking among women means that its ability to transform public sphere institutional structures is often contained by the far more potent power of male homosocial bonds which are deeply embedded in public sphere discourses. As Macdonald (1995) points out, popular media representations of the concept of sisterhood have meant that it is often equated with sentimentalism – a charge which Elshtain argues was justifiably levelled against suffragist public rhetoric (Macdonald 1995: 359). Macdonald also suggests that the inevitable reduction of sisterhood to a matter of emotional bonding undermines its radical potential. This was strikingly evident in media reports of the period that followed the signing of the Northern Ireland peace settlement (4 April 1998). The comment, reproduced in a wide range of broadcast media, was that, 'Everyone felt very emotional, *especially the women of the Northern Ireland Women's Coalition*' (my italics). This comment was underscored by images of the women crying uncontrollably and hugging one another. The question arises: Why has male homosocial bonding not been subject to the same kind of reductive treatment in the media? The common-sense view of male homosocial bonds is that they are rational and strategic. This may be symptomatic of the common phenomenon whereby the discursive strategies employed by women invariably become downgraded.

It is important to acknowledge that gender inequality is not only reproduced by the activities of men. Male-identified women, like Margaret Thatcher, pride themselves on being seen as offering no special favours to women, which almost inevitably means that they end up discriminating against them, as Thatcher did. She did little to promote the careers of other women, thereby safeguarding her reputation as an exceptional woman, even being worthy of the title 'honorary man'. A very different problem is the fact that women, whether consciously or not, often have an investment in their own subordinate status. For instance, members of the organization Women Against the Ordination of Women seem to have derived reassurance from the paternalistic authority wielded by male priests. On the basis of in-depth interviews, Coward (1992) suggests that some women respond to the competitive and often hostile environment of the workplace by returning to the familiarity of the domestic realm. A legitimate feminist goal is surely to make this environment less alienating and I will argue that one way in which critical difference feminists have sought to do this is by promoting more woman-friendly discursive norms, as well as by seeking to change institutional structures.

1.5   The discursive restructuring of institutional and societal orders of discourse

The political philosopher, Carole Pateman (1989), argues that masculinism has been intrinsic to the bourgeois public sphere since its inception in the seventeenth century. Hearn (1992), for instance, provides a detailed historical account of the ways in which the objectifying discourses associated with public bureaucracies have evolved in conjunction with hegemonic forms of masculinity. I will suggest that one effect of women's entry into traditionally male-dominated domains has been to make explicit the implicitly masculinist nature of the beliefs, norms, values and practices that masquerade as gender-neutral professional norms within these communities of practice. Most men are less likely to find themselves at odds with these norms, since they accord more readily with their socially ascribed roles. By contrast, some women have felt so alienated from them that they have elected to develop alternative communities of practice, based on women-orientated discursive practices. A central thesis of this book is that a process of discursive restructuring is currently taking place within the institutional order of public sphere discourse, whereby the gendered nature of the public–private dichotomy is being reproduced *within* the public sphere, with women occupying a dispro- portionate number of subordinate roles.

The somewhat crude, but influential, critical mass theory espoused by Dahlerup (1988) assumes that it is only when women constitute a substantial skewed minority of about 30 per cent or more that they are likely to be in a position to contest the dominant discursive practices that prevail in tradi- tionally male-dominated institutions. However, my research suggests that even relatively small numbers of women can make a difference within a community of practice, if they manage to develop critical difference strat- egies which ensure that their 'interactional power' (Mills 2000) exceeds their institutional power and status (see especially Chapter 4). On the other hand, the mere presence of substantial numbers of women, in itself, offers no guarantee that the masculinism that pervades many institutions and organ- izations in the civil and public spheres will be called into question, unless some, or all, of these women unite to promote the goal of gender equality. Even where this occurs, I will suggest that the efforts of feminist-identified women can be undermined by a range of factors, including the operation of fraternal networks both within, and, more significantly, *between*, commun- ities of practice. Such networks are not necessarily cooperative; they are often productively competitive and may only incidentally marginalize and/or exclude women. Yet, if it is true, as Hearn (1992: 20) suggests, that the public identities of men and the homosocial relations between them are now more likely to be forged covertly through interaction in private spaces – 'clubs, chats in saunas, behind closed doors . . . "fixes" in pubs and snugs, in locker rooms' – then this makes them even more difficult to contest.

The institutionalization of gender inequalities has been exacerbated by the operation of certain 'colonizing' discourses at the societal level of dis- course. Habermas (1989) defines 'colonizing' discourses as types of discourse that have particular salience in late capitalist society and which expand their functions across institutions. His thesis is that communicative discourse types that are orientated to interpersonal goals are being colonized by strategic discourse types that are orientated to instrumental goals. Although Habermas does not say so explicitly, these goals are at odds with, or even hostile to, the discursive norms which empirical evidence suggests are often favoured by women. One such strategic discourse, alluded to above, is the discourse of professionalism which purports to be gender-neutral, but which in reality emerges from a long tradition of male monopoly of the norms associated with professional life, and which is expanding at the expense of more vocational discourse types (see especially Chapter 6).

Perhaps *the* most salient colonizing discourses in post-industrial society, however, are those associated with commodification. As Fairclough (1994: 253) points out, these have the effect of weakening the boundaries 'between on the one hand the discursive practices of the market in the more traditional sense, and on the other hand the discursive practices of politics, public services like health and education, Government and other forms of public information, and even the arts'. I will suggest that commodified discourses have had contradictory effects on women's access to, and participation in, the public sphere. Walby (1990: 181) notes that market forces helped to bring women into the public sphere, but I will suggest that the resulting preoccupation with the image of public figures has had a particularly detrimental effect on women in public sphere roles. On the other hand, social movements like the Women's Environmental Network have been able to translate the lip-service paid to the 'power of the consumer' into genuine power for many women who would otherwise be denied a political voice on important issues concerning the links between the environment and health, such as the current controversy surrounding the production of genetically modified foods (see Chapter 5).

It is my contention that the increasingly mediatized nature of public sphere discourse has also had contradictory effects on women who perform public sphere roles (see also Talbot 1997). This is not surprising, since a number of feminist analysts have pointed out that a masculinist culture prevails in the majority of mainstream media institutions (van Zoonen 1994; Macdonald 1995). The narrow elite of accessed voices remain predominantly male and male journalists remain in a majority, especially when it comes to reporting so-called 'hard news' stories. The assumption of an ideal reader who is gendered as male means that media producers continue to construct women as 'other' and/or trade on the concept of 'women-as-group' (Fowler 1991: 103). Chouliaraki and Fairclough (1999: 104) introduce the concept of 'media capital' to refer to the advantage that accrues to certain events, individuals, groups and so on if they attract extensive coverage in the media. I will suggest that women's media capital is sometimes perceived as so low that their public sphere activities are not deemed newsworthy and are seldom, if ever, reported. Where women *are* included as represented subjects, gender stereotypes abound, including those which dichotomize the sexes in crudely antagonistic terms, something that chimes well with the news values of 'negativity' and 'conflict between people', referred to by Bell (1991: 156). However, Fairclough's (1989: 51) view that 'the media operate as a means for the expression and reproduction of the power of the dominant class and bloc' does not offer an adequate account of the complex workings of media texts. His more recent work on media discourse challenges the tendency to view news-making practices as homogeneous and stable (Fairclough 1995a). I will suggest that contradictions manifest themselves in the hybrid nature of media texts which both function to expose overt sexism, yet often reproduce it in covert forms.

The picture outlined above is further complicated by the fact that other 'colonizing' discourses appear to have led to a process of destructuration whereby the discursive boundaries *between* the spheres have become weakened and permeable. Fairclough (1992: 110), for instance, describes what he terms the 'conversationalization' of public sphere discourse:

> a more general translation of public language . . . into private language: a linguistic shift which is itself part of the rearticulating of the relationship between the public domain of the political (economic, religious) events and social agents, and the private domain, the domain of the 'lifeworld', of common experience.

He does not specify who the agents of this change are. I will suggest that the presence and activities of women in public sphere roles has, at the very least, contributed towards this discursive shift. Other feminist analysts have made this link explicit, hence van Zoonen's (1998) designation of this process in the media as the 'feminization' of the media. However, as with other discursive strategies associated with women, this process has recently been denigrated as a process of 'dumbing down' by influential male gatekeepers (Humphreys 1999). I will argue that if the mainstream media have been 'feminized' to some extent, this has been achieved in a way that reproduces a reactionary discourse of femininity which disguises what Dorothy Smith (1990: 159) terms, 'The cracks, seams, varieties, contradictions in the multiple sites and modes of being a woman'. I will therefore suggest, with Macdonald (1995), that the conversationalization of public discourse has, at the very least, been contradictory in its effect for women who participate in the public sphere. Finally, I intend to explore the various ways in which feminist-identified women have actively contested the boundaries between the public, civil, and private spheres, often by taking advantage of independent changes occurring at the institutional and societal levels of discourse.

1.6   Structure of the book

Chapter 2 sets out in detail the framework for approaching feminist critical discourse analysis to be applied to the data in the four case studies that follow. The methods of data collection and analysis employed in the case studies is also discussed briefly, in the light of feminist debates about the relative merits of the various methodological procedures available to researchers.

The first case study, in Chapter 3, focuses on women who enter British parliamentary politics. The 'glass ceiling effect' is difficult to account for in a political party like the Parliamentary Labour Party which, theoretically, seems committed to equal opportunities for men and women. It becomes more explicable when it is recognized that the institutional orders of masculinist political discourse and the equally masculinist discourse of the print media operate through fraternal networks to segregate and subordinate women once they have entered the arena of party politics. However, this needs to be set alongside the changes that have resulted from women's increasing presence in the House of Commons, notably in the wake of the 1997 general election. Particular reference is made in that chapter to a feminist rereading/rewriting of Foucault's (1984) work, and to the work of feminist political theorists, including Pateman (1989) and Walby (1990).

Chapter 4 considers the gendered implications of the recent trend towards secessionism in UK politics. The considerable impact that women have made thus far on the policy priorities and structures of the Scottish Parliament would seem to lend support to the argument that devolution as a political process should be welcomed by feminists. However, a consideration of the treatment by both her political colleagues and the media of one female minister in the Welsh Assembly makes it clear that the mere presence of a high proportion of women in a community of practice is no guarantee of a woman-friendly ethos. By contrast, despite its status as one of the smallest and newest political parties in the Province, and despite having to confront entrenched sexism, the Northern Ireland Women's Coalition has managed to accrue to itself considerable interactional power, which it has used to ensure that the new Northern Ireland Assembly is responsive to the interests and needs of women. The remainder of the chapter explores in detail the contribution made by the Coalition to the Talks process leading to the formation of the Assembly, as well as the way in which this contribution has been framed in the media. The chapter includes a critical evaluation of the usefulness of the concept of gendered news frames (Norris 1997) in accounting for the complex and contradictory ways in which the media represent women's involvement in public sphere roles.

Chapter 5 shifts the emphasis away from women's involvement in state institutions to a consideration of their activities in grassroots organizations. A number of feminist political theorists have suggested that new social movements (NSMs) constitute sites of political participation that are particularly open to women. This is supported by my study of the activities of the London-based Women's Environmental Network (WEN) which has sought to exploit women's role as primary consumers in order to expand their role as active citizens. However, a comparative study of the preferred discursive practices of WEN and other non-gender-specific environmental groups, notably Friends of the Earth, helps to foreground the masculinist ethos that pervades these groups. The constructive role the media are said to have played in helping to reinvigorate the civil sphere (McRobbie 1994) needs to be qualified in the light of the often trivializing coverage of WEN's campaigns. Particular reference is made in that chapter to a feminist rereading/ rewriting of Habermas's (1989) work on the bourgeois public sphere.

The focus of Chapter 6 of the study is on women's participation in the Church of England in the period before and since their ordination as priests. Such a study affords opportunities for comparing women's role as campaigning 'outsiders' and their relatively recent and, for some, grudgingly-granted role as 'insiders', in what is obviously a liminal period in the Church's history as an institution. The pre-ordination campaign created an ideal opportunity for proponents to construct a coherent set of oppositional discursive practices designed to challenge masculinist definitions of the priestly role. However, the ability of women priests to promote these alternative norms in the post-ordination period has been hampered by their continuing institutional sub-ordination within the Church's structures, a situation that is sanctioned by canon law. That chapter will make particular reference to Butler's (1990) performative theory of gender to account for the range of, sometimes contradictory, subject positions women priests have occupied in their attempts to satisfy socially ascribed and, in particular, media-generated expectations that they will perform their role as priests in a distinctive way. It will conclude by suggesting that women's entry into the priesthood *has*, nonetheless, made a difference to both Church structures and modes of ministry.

In the concluding chapter of the book (Chapter 7) I will suggest that my case studies point to the need for a more socially situated theory of language and gender to account for the complex interplay between the choices women make within discourse and the broader social-structural constraints within which they have to operate. A focus on local communities of practice within the public sphere helps to illuminate the wide range of ways in which women have chosen to negotiate with the masculinist discursive norms they continue to confront, whether they are involved in institutions of the state or grassroots organizations. However, a comprehensive account of the construction of gendered identities and gendered relations in contemporary society also requires an investigation into the expectations and stereotypes that circulate in the society as a whole and exert a powerful influence on the subject positions available to women who enter the public domain. This book suggests that one means of accessing these global ideologies of gender is by undertaking a critical analysis, such as I propose in Chapter 2, of the contradictory ways in which women's public identities are represented in the media.

Notes

1. The term 'masculinist' is used here, and throughout the book, to refer to discursive practices that have evolved historically in conjunction with hegemonic forms of masculinity and have often become deeply entrenched in institutions within the public sphere. Unlike the term 'patriarchal', it does not assume that these practices are either coherent or intentionally designed to deny women equality of access or status, though this is often their effect. Women can, of course, choose to adopt, rather than contest, such practices.

2. The term 'verbal hygiene' was introduced by Cameron, in her book of that name (1995b), to cover a wide range of practices which entail some form of linguistic engineering. She is at pains to point out that such practices are not, in themselves, reprehensible; instead, their efficacy, or otherwise, should be assessed in terms of the uses to which they are put. Her central argument is that all language use is value-laden and that individuals and groups need to 'focus critically on the particular standards and values being invoked and to propose alternatives' (ibid.: 115). As a case in point, Cameron argues *against* accepting a narrowly instrumental view of language as the basis for teaching English in schools (ibid.). However, she admits that she remains personally unconvinced by the arguments of some feminist linguists who claim that the discursive style preferred by women is inter-actionally superior to men's and should, for this reason, be promoted in workplace contexts (ibid.: 208).

3. The performative theory of gender was developed by Judith Butler in her influential book, *Gender Trouble* (1990). Butler denies that gender is a foundational identity category, and instead stresses that it is constituted by a series of performative acts. As such, she argues that it is open to interven-tion and resignification. For instance, she celebrates drag performances for denaturalizing the constructed nature of all gendered identities and advoc-ates the promotion of parodic practices 'that disrupt the categories of the body, sex, gender, and sexuality and occasion their subversive resignification and proliferation beyond the binary frame' (ibid.: x).

4. Fairclough (1995a: 176) refers to the 'order of mediatized political dis-course' as a means of capturing the role the media play in structuring political discourse. In particular, he suggests that one of the functions of the institutions of the mainstream media is to literally *mediate* between the official discourse of politics and the lifeworld discourse of viewers/listeners/readers. The media do not transparently report events, but select and frame official voices in various way, often translating them into a more accessible lifeworld idiom. I suggest that this *mediating* function is not confined to party politics, but extends to all civil and public sphere discourse types.

5. Mills (1995: 187ff) defines 'schemata' as frameworks, which are often stereo-typically gendered, and which represent an intermediate stage between language and ideology: 'These structures are well-trodden pathways, which because of their familiarity take on an air of commonsense knowledge. It is only by describing these seemingly commonsense structures that we begin to expose their constructed nature and at the same time their pernicious-ness' (ibid.: 197).

6. Fairclough (1992: 68ff) adapts the concept of 'orders of discourse' from Foucault's essay of that name (1984) to refer to configurations of discourse practices. These can occur at different, often interdependent, levels: the immediate situational level, the institutional level and the societal level.

2

Towards a Feminist Critical Discourse Analysis

I will begin this chapter by explaining why I feel there is a need for a distinctly *feminist* approach to critical discourse analysis (CDA) and will then go on to suggest how such an approach might manifest itself in an analytical model for the critical study of discourse. CDA draws on a Foucauldian view of discourse as inextricably bound up with the social and, more radically, as *constitutive* of social identities and relations (Fairclough 1989, 1992, 1995b; Chouliaraki and Fairclough 1999). However, a number of approaches to CDA, including that of Fairclough, marginalize the importance of specifically gendered identities and relations and the social inequalities to which these contribute. While accepting that power relations are not reducible to class relations, Fairclough (1989: 34) nonetheless privileges class above other determinants of power:

> . . . it is not acceptable to regard gender, race and so forth as simply parallel to class. I shall regard class relations as having a more fundamental status than others, and as setting the broad parameters within which others are constrained to develop, parameters which are broad enough to allow many options which are narrowed down by determinants autonomous to the particular relation at issue.

This economistic tendency to treat gender-based inequalities as derivative of capitalism serves to disguise the operation of *cross-class* fraternal alliances which have supported the exclusion of women from a number of public and civil sphere domains and activities. It also downplays the significance of other aspects of women's subordination. For instance, feminist theorists have shown that class relations are experienced differently by women and men (Skeggs 1997), and by women and men of different racial and ethnic groups (McClintock 1995; Threadgold 1997). Finally, and perhaps most significantly, it fails to acknowledge that class is itself a highly contested site.

As a feminist discourse analyst, I am primarily interested in contemporary social struggle that centres on the production, maintenance and transformation of gendered identities and relations. Such a focus is intended to remedy the class bias in existing work in CDA, rather than seek to claim a privileged place for gender among other determinants of power. Indeed, I hope to illustrate the complex ways in which gender intersects with other variables, including class, race and age. I will argue that the stance individuals adopt *vis-à-vis* gender politics and their own gendered identities is also important, since, as I made clear in Chapter 1, gender is an increasingly contested aspect of self-identity in late modernity.

Poststructuralist feminists have argued that the inherent instability of gender as an identity category has rendered problematic all feminist approaches that rely on an overarching metalanguage. The metalanguage I will propose, however, is contextually constrained and localized, rather than abstract and universal in its application. Nor is it exclusively linguistic, since it is based on a recognition of the permeability of the boundaries between linguistic and other semiotic phenomena. The aim, then, is to connect the insights of linguistic and social semiotic theory with an analysis of wider discursive and social changes relevant to the analysis of gender.

No approach to the critical study of texts is entirely bottom-up, however, since the analyst brings an understanding of these wider changes to bear on her or his linguistic analysis. This understanding is also likely to influence the types of texts scrutinized. In my case, I am interested in looking for textual traces of shifts in gendered identities and relations that occur in periods of rapid discursive and institutional change. One needs, of course, to be alert to the dangers of tautology, but my intention in this book is not simply to use texts to *describe* these changes, but to help to *explain* them in a more nuanced way than would be possible in the absence of close attention to linguistic analysis. This, in turn, is intended to facilitate a feminist critique of the changes currently taking place in gendered identities and relations in the civil and public spheres in order to establish whether these changes have helped to promote more equal relations between men and women. If not, the explicit political goals of a feminist approach to CDA are to provide a basis for challenging those textually mediated social, political and economic inequalities that continue to exist, as well as to suggest alternative discursive practices that are likely to prove more egalitarian.

2.1   Discourse, power and discursive change

Unlike much of Foucault's own work, feminist work in the field of discourse analysis has stressed the creative dialectic that exists between structure and agency (Smith 1990; Mills 1995; Threadgold 1997). As Mills (1995: 2) states:

ideologies of gender are not solely oppressive, and they are not simply imposed on women by men. Women and men construct their own sense of self within the limits of these discursive frame-works, and build their pleasures and emotional development, often in conscious resistance to, as well as in compliance with, these constraints.

I will argue that *intertextual* analysis, in particular, can help to foreground traces of the type of hybridization that occurs when new and old gendered paradigms coexist in tension with one another. Indeed, I will suggest that women's public identities are discursively produced by this clash of competing norms and expectations. However, with Threadgold (1997), I will argue that such a dynamic view of discourse does not preclude the existence of an underlying stability in public discourse which serves to (re)produce gender inequality.

I do not, however, share Threadgold's (1997) emphasis on an embodied feminist practice. Her preoccupation with the corporeality of traces in texts appears to be motivated by a desire to write back into poststructuralist theory the gendered nature of the subject. It is also linked to her critique of theorists 'who see ideology as the result of a failure of *intellectual* labour' (ibid.: 98; italics in the original). Although at one point she refers to 'embodied consciousness' (ibid.: 50), there is little reference thereafter to consciousness. Granted, she attempts to bridge the gap between bodily habit and belief by appealing to Bourdieu's (1977) concept of 'habitus'. However, the overwhelming impression emerges of female subjects as reducible to their bodies, which in turn implies only a limited and crudely materialist view of human agency. With Elshtain (1993: 277), I believe that 'a rich view of the human subject' is a prerequisite for an adequate feminist social theory. More specifically, I believe that a theoretical approach that seeks to promote and facilitate intellectual labour is a sound basis for a feminist politics, since such a view is perfectly compatible with safeguarding our bodily selves.

2.2   The role of the analyst

As the name suggests, the goal of the critical discourse analyst is the overtly political one of encouraging interpreters of texts to develop a critical awareness of the way linguistic choices often have ideological effects, and in particular the contribution they make to the unequal distribution of power relations in society. There are some who have argued that overt political commitment, whatever its complexion, is incompatible with objective text analysis. For instance, Widdowson (1995: 169) claims that such commitment leads the critical discourse analyst to select 'those features of the text which support [her/his] preferred interpretation'. This is a criticism that feminists are, of course, accustomed to answering, not least by pointing out that *no* theoretical or methodological approach is politically neutral and that *all* readings of texts are invariably selective. The difference is that critical linguists, including those working from a feminist perspective, openly acknowledge their political aims, and are committed to promoting alternative and resistant subject positions to the dominant ones encoded in texts. By contrast, in his re-reading of a text about antenatal care analysed by Fairclough (1992: 170–1), Widdowson (1996) obligingly takes up a compliant subject position. He offers an analysis that he suggests 'is more cooperative than conflictual, which invokes no hegemonic struggle, and which is rather more favourable to the medical profession' (1996: 68). One of the claims of critical discourse analysis is that such readings contribute to the maintenance of existing relations of social inequality, in this instance between medical experts and female patients, whereas resistant readings can cumulatively contribute to their transformation.

In a somewhat different criticism of critical discourse analysis, Cameron expresses her scepticism about the expert status to which the critical discourse analyst appears to lay claim (1995b: 233). From a feminist perspective, in particular, this assumption would seem to introduce an unwelcome hierarchical element into the analysis of discourse. To some extent this is offset by the type of self-reflexive approach adopted in this book. Yet, what of Cameron's claim (ibid.) that ordinary readers are well aware of the connections between language, power and ideology? While this offers an antidote to the tendency to view readers as passive, it nonetheless ignores the fact that a good deal of interpretative work in everyday situations is based on 'slack' (Wicomb 1994), as opposed to close, reading. A feminist approach to critical discourse analysis aims to offer readers the analytical tools to recognize the 'subtler and hence more insidious discriminatory and exclusionary discourses that abound' (Toolan 1997: 94). This does not mean neglecting instances of overt sexism[1] altogether, and although these may be easy to identify (Mills 1998: 247), this does not mean that they are always easy to contest. Indeed, I would suggest that the backlash against political correctness has opened up a discursive space for the re-emergence of overt sexism. Such sexism has even been justified on the dubious grounds that 'if men oppress each other, why should women complain?' (Johnson 1997: 20).

2.3   Gender and reader positioning

In common with other approaches to critical discourse analysis, I begin with the theoretical premise that all natural linguistic and semiotic communication rests upon the possibility of choice or selection from a set of alternatives, albeit within certain constraints. Mills (1995: 31) outlines a feminist model of text that specifies the various production and reception regimes that operate on texts to constrain the choices both text producers and interpreters can make – regimes that are, she suggests, often implicitly gendered. As well as the constraints imposed by the linguistic system itself, these include norms and expectations about rhetorical conventions, the affiliations of the text producer and the assumptions she or he makes about the implied audience. For instance, feminist critical discourse analysts have demonstrated that 'the reader in a wide range of texts is positioned as predominantly male' (Mills 1995: 67). One aim of a feminist approach to CDA is to encourage listeners/readers to read back into texts elements presupposed at the production stage and to recognize formal and semiotic features that promote preferred, often male-gendered, readings.

It is assumed, therefore, that the choices text producers make are not random, but are motivated, often by a desire to position listeners/readers as compliant subjects. Such choices impose constraints on the process of interpretation by acting as traces and cues which promote certain readings, while seeking to suppress others. In this way, they can serve to reinforce or challenge dominant conceptual frames, including those involved in the reproduction of normative gendered identities and gendered relations. Listeners/readers construct hypotheses about the preferred meaning of texts on the basis of the traces and cues they perceive to be present 'in' the texts, as well as on the basis of their own, often gendered, assumptions about the communicative event. Interpreters are not passive, then, but active, since they often have to do a good deal of inferential work to make connections that are not always made explicit in a text. As Gee (1990: 86) points out, 'the choices and guesses we make may be *more or less conscious* and *more or less conventionalized* (routinized, a matter of habit)' (italics and parentheses in the original).

To have ideological effects, textual traces and cues do not need to be conscious; they may be the relatively unconscious products of common-sense assumptions, often based on stereotypical ideas. Fairclough (1989: 84) points out that only those common-sense assumptions that help to sustain unequal relations of power are ideological. Mills (1998: 237), for instance, notes that feminist ideas have become part of the common-sense knowledge presupposed in texts, especially those aimed at young women readers. Yet, I would agree with Coward (1999) that the version of feminism that tends to circulate as common sense in popular and media texts is often reductive and/ or distorted and should not remain immune from a feminist critique. However, while Coward argues that what she terms 'womanism' disadvantages men, especially working-class men, I will argue that popularized versions of feminism are just as likely to disadvantage women. This is because the selective appropriation of feminist theories that stress women's supposed difference from men often helps to rationalize their continuing marginalization and subordination in civil and public sphere roles. Of course, the preferred readings cued by texts, popular or otherwise, are not always accepted by readers and may well be resisted, or even rejected. The type of textual and intertextual negotiations which such resistant readings entail are just as likely to have implications for the identities, relations and beliefs of listeners/readers as more compliant readings. Indeed, one of the central aims of a feminist critical discourse analysis is to promote such resistant and oppositional readings in order to call into question normative gender ideologies.

2.4   Gender and genre

Work in feminist stylistics has encouraged readers to recognize that so-called ideal generic conventions are often far from ideal since they tend to be gendered in stereotypical ways (see, for instance, Mills 1995: 159ff). In their analysis of Martin Luther King's 'I have a dream' speech, Gill and Whedbee (1997) point to the text's uncritical acceptance of the generic convention, sanctioned by a long intertextual history, whereby political speeches address a citizenry gendered as male. As this study will demonstrate, other non-literary genres, such as the genres of political debate and religious sermons, are also being subjected to feminist scrutiny, with the result that the conventions that characterize these genres are currently undergoing a process of challenge and change. What is needed is an understanding of genre that permits a degree of negotiation between socially sanctioned generic norms and individual, or in the case of feminist challenges, collective, agency.

For this reason, the definition of genre adopted in this study is one that views it as entailing socially ratified uses of language modelled in the *minds* of individual producers and interpreters of texts. As such, genres are linked to, and indeed draw upon, cultural scripts and other larger schemata that operate across the boundaries of discourse types, and that likewise reflect dominant ideologies about gender (see also Mills 1995: 187ff). In the absence of more concrete information from the fields of cognitive linguistics and artificial intelligence, the precise mechanisms by which genres, scripts and schemata function remain, however, largely a matter of speculation. As Cameron (1998: 442) notes, as discourse analysts 'we can only use what people say as a basis for the construction of inferences about what they intended'.

2.5   The interface between text and co(n)text(s)

By adopting a narrow definition of discourse as 'text and talk', socio-cognitivist theorists such as van Dijk (1998) are obliged to expend a good deal of intellectual effort theorizing not only the relationship between text and social context, but also the relationship between written/verbal text and any accompanying visual material. The more multi-modal approach to discourse advocated by Toolan (1996), Kress and van Leeuwen (1996) and Kress et al. (1997), and also developed in this study, means that cues from a range of semiotic modes, including the visual, are already incorporated into a complex understanding of what I will call *texture*. However, I would dispute the view of Kress et al. (1997) that words and images are generally read as a *single* text. The example they use to illustrate their contention is a two-page spread from a Brazilian magazine featuring a profile of a conservative politician on the left hand page and an advertisement for a car on the right hand page (1997: 276ff). Although the juxtaposition of the two texts *may* have been vetted by the advertisers of the car, it seems far-fetched to suggest, as Kress and van Leeuwen (1997) do, that most readers will perceive them as a single textual unit. I would argue that one of the reasons why the same text gives rise to variable interpretations is precisely because individuals vary in what they perceive as relevant cotexts and intertexts.

2.6   The micro-level of feminist critical text analysis: an integrational approach

As noted above, from the point of view of a feminist critical discourse analysis, any attempt to devise an overarching and globally applicable metalanguage based on a closed set of linguistic items is likely to prove misguided. This is because *any* linguistic item or structure has the potential to become ideologically charged, depending on the way it is coloured by the surrounding cotext and/or by the context of production and consumption in which it occurs. In his provocative defence of the regulation of what he terms 'hate speech', Fish (1994: 106) makes the point that 'every idea is an incitement to somebody, and since ideas come packaged in sentences, in words, every sentence is potentially, in some situation that might occur tomorrow, a fighting word and therefore a candidate for regulation', and, I would add, for critical analysis. What is needed, therefore, is a framework that is flexible enough to attend to the *local* specificities of the text/context interface. Yet if a feminist approach to critical discourse analysis is to be replicable, it is nonetheless important to set out some form of framework – albeit broad and contingent – for analysing discourse critically at the textual level. In particular, the aim is to devise a framework that will help to foreground the tension between the identities women in public sphere roles fashion for themselves and those ascribed to them by others, especially the media.

The corollary of the radically co(n)text-dependent view of language advocated in this study is that the boundaries between linguistic levels, and indeed between linguistic and extralinguistic phenomena, become extremely permeable. This renders problematic a traditional metalanguage which emphasizes the linear ordering of autonomous linguistic elements. According to Toolan (1996: 132), 'language in all its diversity and contextual embeddedness cannot reasonably be characterized as a closed system of endlessly iterable fixed signs'. As Lee (1992: 26) points out, the structuralist orientation in language studies derives from Saussure's segmental metaphor where linguistic elements are treated as discrete homogeneous categories. Such an approach assumes that meaning resides in individual lexical and grammatical components, whereas an integrational approach stresses that meaning is negotiated in context (Harris 1996; Toolan 1996). More specifically, Toolan's (1996: 3) central thesis is that interpretation is not analytical and decompositional, but rather integrational and compositional.

Halliday's (1994) systemic functional grammar would appear to offer a multidimensional model of the relationship between language and co(n)text. For instance, he notes that 'there are rarely any sharp lines in language, since it is an evolved system and not a designed one' (1994: xxv). Despite this, his chief concern in *An Introduction to Functional Grammar* seems to be the mapping of functional categories onto traditional linguistic structures. Feminist approaches to critical text analysis also tend to accept conventional structural categories as a point of departure. For instance, Mills (1995) organizes her book, *Feminist Stylistics*, in terms of a tripartite analytical framework comprising word and phrase/sentence levels respectively, together with a third more functionally orientated level of discourse. This approach leads to a number of anomalies. To take just one example, generic pronouns are discussed at the level of the word yet, like all personal pronouns, they are effectively *empty* categories whose meaning depends on the recoverability of antecedents in the surrounding co(n)text. Thus in order to illustrate their pseudo-generic nature, it is necessary to make reference to their co(n)text of use. Even full lexical items have very different meanings in different contexts. In her discussion of the connotations of the word 'girl', Mills (1995: 98) acknowledges 'the importance of context, and . . . the need not to assume that sexism resides within individual language items'. Yet, I would argue that any approach which relies on formalist categories as a point of departure tends to obscure, rather than illuminate, such differences in use.

There is, then, in such frameworks a constant tension between treating language as an object of description and a stated commitment to developing a more dynamic model that accounts for the way language functions in specific contexts of use. I will argue that it is more productive to view texts in terms of lexicogrammatical networks of relations, whose meanings are determined in specific contexts of use, rather than as comprising discrete and autonomous levels. This shift in perspective, which contests the linguistic/semiotic boundary, leads to a view of language as a multilayered meshing of texts, contexts and histories. On this reading, attention to the linear ordering of linguistic elements remains a necessary, but not a sufficient, basis for the analytical framework I am developing here.

Toolan (1996: 259) likewise suggests that a preoccupation with syntactic sequencing may lead linguists to overlook other associative connections: semantic, intonational, kinesic and the interrelations between them. Furthermore, in both spoken and written texts the paradigmatic axis may be as important as the syntagmatic one. Thus each item chosen can be set against choices that were *not* made, leading to a focus on structured absences from texts. Gaps in syntax, for instance, may be ideologically significant, because readers/listeners are invited to infer connections left implicit. It would be difficult to account for the ideological effects of structured absences in Toolan's (1996) approach, since he does not allow for the existence of predictable structures. In my proposed framework, however, these structured absences from texts will be accounted for by reference to the operation of highly conventionalized (inter)textual networks. In other words, I view language as a fluid code, rather than rejecting a code-view of language altogether.

In my proposed framework, I extend the textual to include any element in, or presupposed in, the co(n)text that contributes to texture. Such elements may be realized by *implicit* (inter)textual traces which account for the ways in which readers/listeners interpret a text as a coherent, as opposed to a cohesive, whole. This extended definition of the (inter)textual also includes the interplay between textual cues and other interpretative cues present in the co(n)text. The latter might comprise extralinguistic cues, signalled by accompanying visual material, such as photographs, cartoons and so on, and, in the case of spoken interaction, by paralinguistic features such as facial expressions and body language. Such cues are often used by addressees to establish the validity, or otherwise, of given speech acts. However, I will argue that the way in which validity criteria are applied is contingent on the gender of the text producer. For instance, I will suggest that the criterion of 'sincerity' is likely to be applied more stringently to evaluations of women's performance of public sphere roles, than to men's (see Chapter 3). This multifunctional view of the textual, or rather the (inter)textual, is in keeping with the recent work of Kress et al. (1997: 257) who view language 'as one representational element in a text which is always multi-modal, and [which] has to be read in conjunction with all the other semiotic modes of that text'.

Rather than assuming, however, as many text linguists do, that texts are produced and perceived as both cohesive and coherent, in keeping with Fairclough's more recent work (1995a), I will suggest that close critical analysis often reveals them to be riven with tensions and contradictions. Indeed, the primary focus of this study will be on this discursive *heterogeneity* and more specifically on the way public sphere discourses are fractured by competing, and often contradictory, ideologies of gender. According to Cameron (1998: 445):

This reflects the fact that there is currently a degree of conflict, especially in modern middle-class communities, about the respective roles, rights and obligations of women and men. Such conflict does not only (or always) position women and men on opposite sides. It can be just as marked, or more marked, between women of different generations or classes. Because of the conflict of *interest* it represents, however, it is likely to be felt as most salient when it arises in male–female interaction.

Although texts are inherently ambivalent, the combination of linguistic and other (inter)textual traces and interpretative cues nonetheless function to promote dominant readings, including readings that reify normative gendered identities and relations. This may not, of course, be their effect on individual readers who may (choose to) misread the cues and/or may choose to read 'against' them. Given the asymmetrical power relations that continue to exist between men and women, Cameron (ibid.: 447) suggests that male interlocutors in particular are likely to engage in 'strategic' misreadings.

To offset some of the problems with the approaches discussed thus far, the analytical model adopted in this study will take functional categories as *a point of departure* for analysis. The basic premise is that language serves two fundamental functions, the interpersonal and the ideational, and, in the sections that follow, an attempt is made to set out an inventory of (inter)textual forms and sociosemantic categories by which these metafunctions are realized. The aim is to explore patterns of habituated use that function to reproduce normative gendered identities and relations. Although the meaning attached to these forms and categories in *specific* contexts is contingent on the interpretative assumptions that interlocutors bring to the speech situation, I intend to suggest that the *range* of meanings attached to given (inter)textual traces and cues *is* predictable. I will also explore some of the factors that are likely to give rise to variable interpretations.

One of the major contributions of feminist sociolinguists has been their insistence on the centrality of the interpersonal metafunction in language, and, in particular, on its role in forging intimate relationships between women (see, especially, Coates 1996). This has been asserted often in the face of dismissive claims that such uses of language are trivial and/or of little value outside the private sphere. The interest feminist sociolinguists have in establishing how gendered linguistic norms arise have also led them to focus on the ways in which linguistic norms are implicated in the constitution of gendered identities. As Mills (1997: 150) points out, this aspect of language has generally been neglected: 'Linguistics has largely ignored questions of the role of language in the constitution of subjectivity and selfhood.' Where it has been addressed, it has often been treated in a superficial way. Thus Threadgold notes that Halliday's initial formulation of the interpersonal as 'an exchange of meanings or goods and services' (cited in Threadgold 1997: 96) is an extremely reductive one.

Fairclough's solution to Halliday's less than satisfactory conception of the interpersonal is to propose two separate metafunctions, the 'relational' and the 'expressive', which refer respectively to the social relations and social identities enacted via texts in discourse. Following Voloshinov's (1986) work on intersubjectivity, I will suggest that these are best viewed as two facets of the one interpersonal metafunction, since identities are always formed and transformed through a never-ending process of sociolinguistic interaction with others, and/or with texts. As Pearce (1994) points out, Voloshinov's approach stresses the role of power and conflict in determining the nature of the utterance. This compares favourably with Habermas's (1984, 1987) theory of communicative action which relies on a utopian concept of an ideal speech situation in which participants have symmetrical rights. Empirical research has shown that this is far from true of cross-sex interaction, where men employ strategies, such as interruption and non-response, as prerogatives of power (Zimmerman and West 1975; Fishman 1983; Holmes 1995). Likewise, my own research points to the considerable power the media have in constructing and maintaining normative gendered identities and relations, identities and relations which are often at odds with those that women and men construct for themselves.

The second metafunction in my framework, the *ideational*, is closer to Halliday's initial conception, since it subsumes the expressive and evaluative aspects of language, as well as knowledge and beliefs. This seems more satisfactory than Fairclough's decision to assign them to two separate metafunctions, since I would argue that the distinction between them is difficult to sustain. This point is also stressed by Poynton (1990: 251–2):

> The attachment of feeling to representation is of particular importance to the circulation of ideologies, because it involves a virtual physical attachment of people to beliefs and values, thereby ensuring a fierce commitment to those beliefs and values and resistance to attempts 'to take them away' by means of argument.

Threadgold (1997: 13) identifies what she regards as a preoccupation among male linguists with the ideational stripped of its evaluative and emotive dimensions as symptomatic of a more general masculinist and technicist orientation in work produced in the field of systemic linguistics. In addition, a number of feminist linguists have argued that this has led analysts to overlook the interpersonal functions of a range of linguistic and pragmatic features, such as hedges, intensifiers and pragmatic particles (Coates 1989; Holmes 1995). This study will suggest that a foregrounding of the ideational at the expense of the interpersonal also characterizes the traditional discursive strategies associated with professionalism in a wide range of institutional domains, as well as the persuasive rhetoric produced by male-dominated environmental groups (see Chapter 5).

Although both metafunctions should be regarded as operating *simultaneously* in discourse, I would agree with Threadgold that the interpersonal should be regarded as the 'driving function' of language (Threadgold 1997: 13). This view is not exclusive to feminist (socio)linguists since Toolan (1996: 2) also regards what he terms 'orientedness to others' as the pre-eminent function of language. The increasing conversationalization of public sphere discourse types, noted by Fairclough (1992: 204), means that this is now just as true of public sphere interaction as it is of interaction in the private sphere and is, in fact, contributing to the blurring of the boundaries between the private and public spheres noted earlier. For instance, phatic interaction, with little or no ideational content, plays a central function in cementing relations between intimates, workmates and strangers in everyday situations, whereas texts with little or no interpersonal orientation are restricted to a number of technical or highly specialist domains. This is because the majority of linguistic choices related primarily to the ideational also have implications for the way the identities of participants, and the relationships between them, are enacted via texts. Thus the ideas, beliefs and attitudes that producers encode in texts obviously say a good deal about their own social identities and their attitudes towards addressees. Since text producers are likely to frame these in a sympathetic way, framing devices act as interpretative cues, encouraging listeners/readers to take up compliant or resistant subject positions which, in turn, helps to shape *their* identities. The decision to assign linguistic and pragmatic phenomena to separate metafunctional categories is therefore purely for the purpose of analysis, yet it can be justified on the grounds that in any given utterance a particular function or subfunction is likely to be primary (see also Holmes 1995).

2.6.1   The interpersonal metafunction

There are a number of different kinds of identity and relation enacted via texts, including those of/between any represented individual(s), the text producer, and the assumed reader (see Fig. 2.1). However, the primary focus of this study is on the tension between how individuals in the public eye choose to construct their own identities – a process that is, in any case, always subject to material and discursive constraints – and the representation of these identities by others, notably the media. I will suggest that the performative choices made by women in public sphere roles are constrained not only by institutional and societal norms, but by the investment they themselves have made in aspects of discursively produced femininity. I will argue, therefore, that individual women negotiate with gendered linguistic norms in ways that are complex and contradictory, which is in stark contrast to the media tendency to construct gendered identities for them which ignore these complexities and serve to locate them within a preconceived binary frame. However, I will illustrate ways in which these same media texts bear traces of women's resistance to the public identities being constructed for them.

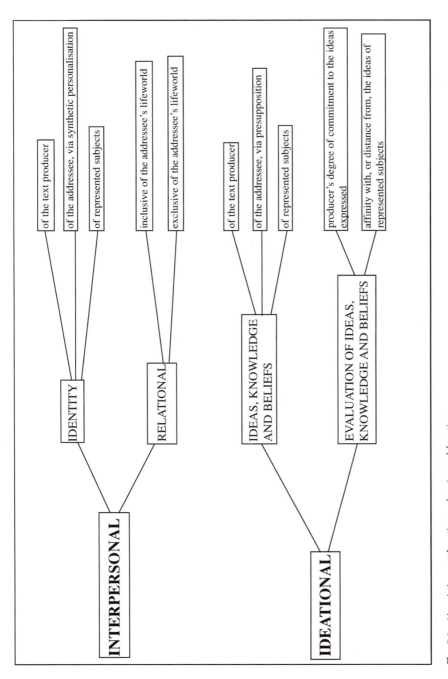

Fig. 2.1 Linguistic metafunctions, showing subfunctions

Interestingly, it would seem that one effect of women's entry into public sphere roles has been to heighten men's sense of their own gendered identities. Coward (1999: 98–9) goes so far as to suggest that 'probably the key aspect of feminism's success is this displacement of men from [a] position of neutral authority, the ungendered space, against which women as gendered subjects were always measured'. I will argue, however, that women's presence in traditionally male preserves has led to a new defensive version of traditional male networking, a phenomenon known as 'boundary heightening' (Powell 1993: 114) and, in some cases, to an exaggerated performance of macho masculinity (see also Faludi 1992: 308). I will also suggest that, outside the academy and a limited number of sites of popular culture, such as men's magazines, women are still much more likely to be constructed *primarily* as gendered subjects than their male counterparts and that this has the effect of underlining an apparent lack of fit with their exercise of public and professional roles. Likewise, there is a persistent tendency among institutional discourses of the public sphere to gender their listeners/readers as male, thus discursively excluding women from their address. The gendering of readers is one element in a process of what Fairclough (1989: 62) terms 'synthetic personalization', whereby text producers simulate a relationship of intimacy with addressees. It is my contention that the producers of the majority of media texts are more likely to employ a mode of address that is inclusive of the lifeworld of *male* readers.

As noted above, the interpersonal metafunction can be divided into the identity and relational subfunctions, although once again it must be stressed that they are closely interrelated. The identity subfunction is largely concerned with the way subject positions are created in discourse, while the relational subfunction focuses on degrees of affinity and/or social distance between participants. The question that I intend to answer in detail in this section is how the interpersonal metafunction is realized (inter)textually in ways that are relevant to the production, reproduction and transformation of gendered identities and gendered relations. Subsequent chapters will investigate the different implications these realizations have in the specific 'habitus' (Bourdieu 1977) which prevails in each of the communities of practice under investigation. It is important to stress that the areas identified in the sections that follow are intended to be representative, rather than exhaustive.

2.6.2   The identity subfunction

Naming practices

The constraints of the linguistic system of naming in English mean that women have to confront and negotiate issues around self-naming practices that men do not have to consider. This means that they not only have to represent their femininity to themselves (see Black and Coward 1990), but they also have to represent their gender politics to others. Whether they like it or not, their gender and gender politics become salient categories in the perception of their public identities. Thus whereas both men and women in the public sphere might have to decide whether to use or dispense with a title such as 'Dr', only women have to decide *between* the titles 'Miss', 'Ms' and 'Mrs'. The choice of 'Miss' or 'Mrs' has come to be perceived as signalling disidentification with feminism and an identification with more traditional discourses of femininity. 'Ms', on the other hand, is usually assumed to signify a statement about one's gender politics in that it is equated with a feminist stance. In reality, the situation is likely to be more complicated than this, since some of the women interviewed for this study choose to eschew the title 'Ms', and the label 'feminist', for strategic reasons, even though they regard themselves as pursuing feminist goals. This is because they feel themselves to be operating within institutions that are hostile to feminism. Given the widespread media backlash against 'political correctness' (Faludi 1992), women who let it be known that their preferred title is 'Ms' may attract hostile coverage for this reason alone, especially in the tabloid press. At the very least, the assumption of an 'I *am* a feminist, but . . .' stance lays women open to the charge of inconsistency, whatever their underlying motive may be for assuming such a stance. This is also true of feminist-identified women who nonetheless choose to take their husband's surname on marriage. Potentially this can be remedied by the revival of a 'maiden' name, as in the case of high profile women, such as Hillary Rodham Clinton and Cherie Booth Blair, but such a strategy may well be viewed as revisionist, and therefore suspect. This highlights the potential metadiscursive gap that can exist between the strategic intentions of speakers and the perception and evaluation of the linguistic and other discursive choices they make by others, and, in the case of public figures, by the powerful institutional force of the media.

Diminutive forms of first names, even where self-selected, appear to carry different connotations for women and men. Thus the Labour Cabinet Minister, Mo Mowlam, had to think long and hard about whether to adopt her full name, Marjorie, when she entered politics, because she felt that a self-chosen diminutive might be interpreted as signifying a lack of authority in a female politician (cited in the *Guardian* 6 July 1999: 7). By contrast, the current Prime Minister's choice of 'Tony' over 'Anthony' is sanctioned by a long and honourable tradition among (male) MPs in the Parliamentary Labour Party (PLP). Indeed, this decision is more likely to have increased his status and credibility as a politician with leadership pretensions, carrying as it does connotations of solidarity with ordinary Labour voters. It would seem, then, that whereas for men in public life the differential power/solidarity meanings associated with full/diminutive names are generally compatible, for women they are often in tension, partly because of their greater insecurity in male-dominated institutions. The dilemma this poses is evident in an article in the *Daily Mail* bearing the headline, 'The name is Margaret, not Maggie' (1 July 1994). The alleged resistance of the then Deputy Leader of the PLP, Margaret Beckett, to accept the use of the diminutive form of her name is taken as 'evidence' of her relative formality and distance when compared to the ex-Prime Minister, a view reinforced by the visual cues in juxtaposed photographs of a smiling Thatcher and an unsmiling Beckett.

Lexical and collocational patterns

Naming practices obviously go beyond preferred titles and first names. Women in the public eye also have to decide whether they are comfortable with the gender marking of non-gender specific names for occupational roles, as in 'woman politician' and 'woman priest'. The fact that 'male politician' and 'male priest', unless used in a specifically contrastive co(n)text, are still largely regarded as tautologies suggests how far these roles are still seen as the preserve of men. The ex-Conservative MP Edwina Currie made her views on this issue very clear: 'I think that Margaret Thatcher and I would both say that we're not women MPs. We're MPs. I don't represent women; I represent 76,000 people' (cited in the *Express on Sunday* 3 March 1985). This statement provides a trace of the way some women in public life feel the need to resist the widespread media practice of employing naming practices that prioritize their gender over their professional status. In other words, however women in public life may wish to name themselves, it is as stereotypically gendered subjects that their identities are reproduced in the media. Fowler views this as symptomatic of a widespread practice whereby the concept of 'women-as-group' is traded in discourse (1991: 103). Despite traces of women's resistance to this practice, its ubiquity in media texts serves cumulatively to naturalize and reproduce normative gendered identities.

Fairclough (1995b: 102) notes that 'Collocations are often a good place to look for contradictions in texts'. Dysphemistic collocations such as 'lipstick feminists' and 'career feminists' provide traces of a perceived tension between feminist-identified women and the public sphere roles they occupy. Such collocations presuppose that the collective political goals of feminism are fundamentally incompatible with the image consciousness and competitive individualism that are, it is implied, needed to attain high-profile institutional roles. Such presuppositions afford feminists little discursive space in which to construct coherent subject positions for themselves. If they attempt to reconcile high status institutional roles and the subject position of 'feminist', they are liable to the charge, often levelled by other feminists, as well as by colleagues and the media, of a lack of integrity. A counter strategy among feminists has been to call into question normative assumptions about 'the best *man* for the job'. This is true in all the domains investigated in this study, but is particularly striking in the case of the Northern Ireland Women's Coalition which has sought to contest the near-exclusive equation of 'politician' and 'hard *man*' in the Province's political life. For instance, in its campaign literature, the Coalition renders these 'hard men' discursively, if not materially, redundant by dismissing them as 'dinosaurs'.

Media representations of women in the public eye often include trivializing collocations. An infamous example is the caption 'Blair's babes' which accompanied an inset photograph of the PLP's record 101 female MPs in the 1997 General Election (*Daily Mail* 8 May 1997). The use of the genitive implies that they 'belong' to Blair, and the connotations of 'babe' simultaneously infantalize and sexualize their identities. This is reinforced by the cues in the accompanying photograph which ostensibly celebrates their approximation to a 'critical mass' (Dahlerup 1988), yet by locating Blair at their centre, it transforms their story into a visual narrative of masculine control (Fig. 2.2). This collocation has since been recycled in numerous media texts, although it is sometimes used in a more tongue-in-cheek way.[2] As Fairclough (1995b) notes, a range of alternative subject positions is open to media producers. If the reader assumes that the role of entertainer, rather than that of serious analyst, is to the fore in this instance, she or he may interpret the collocation 'Blair's babes' in the spirit of postmodern irony. Irony, can, of course, disguise an ideological stance. I will argue that the collocation 'Blair's babes' imposed a homogeneous synthetic identity on Labour's new women MPs, an identity that has made it difficult for them to be taken seriously as politicians of conviction.

This tendency to sexualize women's identities is also evident among hostile male colleagues who exploit the polysemy of words and phrases to introduce sexual innuendo into supposedly asexual organizations and institutional spaces. A vivid instance of the undermining effect of such verbal harassment is provided by Joan Ruddock, MP, who recalled an early experience of speaking in the Commons: 'I was speaking once in an army debate eh talking about strip searching and one of the Tory men said I'd like to strip search *you*' (Trans. II: 120–1).[3] Verbal sexual harassment is, of course, a contested site of meaning and some women may not feel offended by such behaviour. Those who make their displeasure clear, by contrast, often find themselves being labelled as 'humourless feminists' for 'not properly handling "normal" sexual attention' (Powell 1993: 126). Tannen (1996: 260) argues that, 'being female is in itself "faultable" – a term used by Erving Goffman to capture the sense in which someone can be embarrassed or made to feel in the wrong because they have a particular characteristic'. She contrasts this with what she claims is men's very different relationship to their sexual identities, 'many men regard their sexual prowess as a form of power, not vulnerability' (ibid.: 261). According to Hearn (1992), the impulse to humiliate women through sexual innuendo stems from a fear of women's sexuality which in turn interferes with men's homosocial workgroups. In some institutional contexts, women's sexuality is not only regarded as anomalous, but as 'tainting', as will be evident in Chapter 6 on women in the Church.

Fig. 2.2   Photograph of 'Blair's Babes' that appeared on the front page of the *Daily Mail* (8 May 1997)

Thematic structure

Evidence from this study suggests that both familial roles and appearance continue to be thematized for women, often in text and/or utterance initial 'dossier' epithets,[4] while their academic and professional qualifications tend to be backgrounded. It is not uncommon for their identities to be reduced to sartorial metonyms, as in the article accompanying the *Daily Mail* photograph of Blair's babes:

> The women *frothed* out of Church House, Westminster, in a multi-coloured tide. It was like the Chelsea Flower Show meets the Girl Guides, as the fuschia suits loved by the likes of Margaret Beckett (No. 83), and Barbara Follett's glittering emerald green (No. 74), mingled with more sombre browns and beiges.
>
> (*Daily Mail* 8 May 1997: 40; my italics)

The use here of the trivializing verb 'frothed' encourages the view that what Labour's women MPs offer is a superficial 'splash of colour' on the previously dull Westminster political scene. Lakoff (1995: 45) points out that the disproportionate focus on women's appearance is effectively a form of silencing, since it deflects attention away from what they are actually *saying*. Ward's (1984) observation that this is true whether the woman in question 'defies or exemplifies a popular stereotype' (cited in Lee 1992: 111) is supported by my research. Indeed, despite the wide range of images and sartorial codes adopted by women in public life, they tend to be portrayed either as 'femmes' or 'frumps', signalling to them that they are women in a male-dominated environment.

In her recent book, Faludi (1999) argues that men are now just as likely to be evaluated in terms of their surface appearance, including in terms of their heterosexual attractiveness. While this may well be true of such popular icons as Sylvester Stallone, and perhaps of certain high-profile political leaders such as Bill Clinton and Tony Blair, there is less evidence that this holds true for the majority of men in male-dominated institutions and organizations. It could, of course, be argued that this places women at an advantage, since they are likely to stand out among the drab grey suits. This, in turn, could be said to give them a disproportional amount of media capital relative to their minority status, hence the headline in the *Financial Times* (4 May 1997) after the gains made by women in the 1997 general election, 'Women start to beat back pinstripe hordes'. But those who actively invest in modes of femininity often find themselves at odds with the normative requirements of the professional role that most men fulfil with a minimum of effort.

(Inter)textual traces and cues

The perceived mismatch between women and the public sphere roles they occupy can often be deduced from the intertextual resonances of the terms used to describe them. A vivid example occurred in a recent profile of the former Shadow Home Secretary, Ann Widdecombe, which appeared in the *Guardian* under the telling headline 'Out of this world'. She is described by journalist, Simon Hattenstone, in the following terms:

> Her head is tiny, trapped inside the jet-black basin cut, her legs non-existent and she walks on a giant bosom. Her face is somehow not human. Not inhuman, just not human. She looks as if she could have been created by Stephen Spielberg as a companion for ET . . . I'm beginning to think Ann Widdecombe is from Planet Pod.

(the Guardian 21 June 1999)

This lends support to Puwar's (1997) argument that women – and black people – in Parliament and the Civil Service are seen as 'space invaders'. The extreme misogyny evident in this particular description provoked an angry response in the 'Letters' page from, among others, the feminist campaigner and writer, Claire Rayner, indicating that readers often read against such sexist texts. As will be evident in the chapters that follow, this example is not untypical of the many metaphors and other intertextual references that are used to refer to women in public sphere roles in order to signal their anomalous position as 'outsiders within'.

The tendency among women themselves, most notably in the Church and the environmental movement, is to discuss the performance of their public and professional roles in terms that seem calculated to stress the *complementary* nature of their private and public identities. Thus some women frame their experience of the latter by employing familial and bodily tropes. In the light of the media tendency noted above, this discursive strategy may inadvertently help to contribute to the widespread perception that women are particularly suited to a narrow range of usually subordinate public sphere roles. Faludi (1992) argues that the media all-too-readily embrace women's appeals to their special nurturing and domestic management skills, 'marking women as "special" slips easily into placing limits on them. "Special" may sound like superior, but it is also a euphemism for "handicapped"' (ibid.: 360). A more productive strategy, employed by Margaret Thatcher, with the help of the public relations firm Saatchi and Saatchi, was to exploit the productive *clash* of stereotypically gendered subject positions as housewife, nanny and dominatrix, with masculinist roles of technocrat and 'toughocrat' (Webster 1990). Whereas this undoubtedly furthered her personal political ambitions, it did little to further the feminist goal of promoting greater equality for *all* women in public sphere institutions.

Fairclough (1995b) argues that one of the functions of media discourse is to mediate between public sphere discourse types and the lifeworld discourse of readers. In the case of the genre of the media interview, this mediatizing role generally results in the production of hybrid texts which emphasize the public and private identities of the public figures interviewed (ibid.: 189). I will suggest that the genre of the media interview is gendered in the sense that the balance of this coverage varies, depending on the gendered identity of the interviewee. When women in public life are pro-filed in the media there is a relative *absence* of references to their public sphere roles and a disproportionate focus on their private sphere identities. Of the 101 potted biographies which accompanied the photograph of 'Blair's babes' in the *Daily Mail* (8 May 1997), only eight omitted any reference to the marital status of the MP concerned. Likewise, in the profile of Widdecombe referred to above, central to the interviewer's construction of her as an alien is his obsessive foregrounding of her childless state. In a mock-sympathetic tone, he invites the reader to 'imagine how lonely life must be for her with no partner, no kids and just a mouthful of crooked teeth for company' (the *Guardian* 21 June 1999). Thereafter, he records her response to no fewer than three separate questions as to why she did not want to have children. By contrast, profiles of women in public life who *do* have children often bear traces of interrogative strategies which foreground the alleged 'problem' this poses for the fulfilment of their occupational roles.

2.6.3   The relational subfunction

Naming practices

The media are under no obligation to accept the self-selected titles of women in the public eye, creating a rich resource for variable representation not available to them in the case of men. The titles and names they choose can signal a number of meanings, including ideological distance or affinity with the individuals represented. For instance, the *Guardian* and the *Independent* are the only papers which use Mo Mowlam's preferred title, 'Ms'. She is referred to as 'Miss Mowlam' in *The Daily Telegraph*, despite the fact that she is married, while *The Times* employs the more formal and respectful aca-demic title, 'Dr'. Fowler (1991) makes some interesting observations about the asymmetrical patterns of naming for men and women in the print media, although he stresses the fact that they need to be analysed in a context-sensitive way. He illustrates this by reference to the different meanings asso-ciated with the diminutive form of first-name-only used in relation to the former prime minister, Margaret Thatcher:

> [It] is the standard reference . . . in the right-wing popular press, and in that particular context it signifies a friendly intimacy; used in the *Daily Mirror*, however, which claims to represent the interests of the Left, it might connote casualness or disrespect.
>
> (Fowler 1991: 99)

The rather clear-cut ideological division he draws between different news-papers is no doubt somewhat crude, but cotextual cues can clearly function to promote preferred meanings for the naming practices used within specific newspaper articles. Fowler also notes that it is 'more difficult to apply last names alone to women, with different significance' (ibid.). The unequal personalization of men and women in this respect may provide a trace of media producers' greater respect for women, but it also indicates a lack of easy familiarity when discussing female actors in public sphere roles. By contrast, the practice of using last-names-only for men can carry connota-tions of solidarity, through its association with this pattern of use in the British public school system.

This study supports the view that women in public life tend not to mark the difference between their professional roles and their personal relation-ships. One way in which this manifests itself is in their tendency to minimize status distinctions between themselves and addressees by inviting first name use. However, a number of interviewees reported the pattern also noted by Mills (1995: 110) that people *presume* that they can address them in this way, whether or not they have sanctioned this pattern of naming. It would seem that assumptions about gender override issues of asymmetrical power relationships in this respect, a pattern also noted by Tannen (1996: 264) in relation to interaction between patients and women doctors. An alternat-ive reading, however, might be that there is a general shift to less formal marking of status differences in public sphere discourse types (see Fairclough 1995b), a shift that women's increasing presence may have helped to reinforce.

Lexical and collocational patterns

By choosing to employ informal lexis, a text producer can establish a relation-ship with the implied addressee as a 'co-member of the world of common experience, the lifeworld' (Fairclough 1995b: 137). More specialist vocabulary can position the speaker as expert, and listeners/readers as receivers of information. The question that will be explored in this study is whether women in public life consciously employ more informal and accessible lan-guage than male peers. There would seem to be some empirical evidence to lend support to this view. For instance, a comparative study by Frances Smith (1993) of sermons delivered by ten male and four female trainee preachers on the same biblical text revealed that the men were much more likely to assume an expert 'stance' in relation to their listeners by interpret-ing the text in question for them. This was also the strategy adopted by one of the women, despite the fact that the sermons were delivered to fellow students. Two of the other women, however, 'translated' the text into a more accessible and contemporary register, while the fourth employed a number of other linguistic devices in order to construct and maintain a 'low-profile' stance (cited in Tannen 1996: 173–5). The female Anglican priests interviewed for this study likewise claim to employ a consciously accessible rhetorical style when preaching in order to avoid the sort of remote language and authoritative tone that they feel characterizes the preaching style of many male priests.

Obviously the question of intended audience is crucial here. For instance, there is some ambiguity in Frances Smith's (1993) study, at least as reported by Tannen, about whether the trainee preachers were invited to *simulate* an address to an intended congregation. If not, then the decision of one woman to speak 'as if she were telling a story to a group of children' (Tannen 1996: 174–5) could, with some justification, have been viewed as patronizing by her fellow trainees. In other words, whatever the speaker's intentions, an accessible style might be perceived as more patronizing by listeners/readers, than a specialist one that positions them as knowledgeable, even if not wholly comprehending, subjects. There is, in any case, some evidence from my study that the relative insecurity that women experience in male-dominated institutions and organizations leads some of them to employ even more professional jargon than their male colleagues, especially when interacting with these colleagues in committees and public forums. The sense that women have to outdo men at their own game is evident in the views expressed by a number of female MPs interviewed by Puwar (1997: 4): '[women] have to work twice as hard to be considered half as good' and 'we will have succeeded in getting equality for women when women can be as mediocre as the men'. Given that women in woman-orientated organizations are freed from these constraints, do they eschew such jargon? My comparative study in Chapter 5 of the very different campaigning styles adopted by female- and male-orientated environmental groups considers the question in some detail.

Pronominal choices

Mechanisms for establishing relations between text producers and readers/ listeners include the rich resource of pronominal reference. Van Dijk (1998: 203), for instance, claims that 'there are few words in the language that may be as socially and ideologically "loaded" as a simple *we*'. The interpersonal meanings of pronouns will be considered here, while their ideological functions will be considered in the section below which relates to the ideational metafunction. The structured absence of personal pronouns, often achieved by the sustained use of passive constructions and nominalizations, and/or the use of exclusive 'we', can lead to an impersonal and/or authoritative address. By contrast, as the name suggests, the use of *inclusive* 'we' presupposes common ground between text producers and assumed readers/listeners. Yet, I will demonstrate that in media texts, and numerous other texts associated with institutional discourse types, this so-called inclusive use of 'we' is often implicitly gendered as male. By assuming a commonality of beliefs and values with their ideal male addressees, such texts contribute to positioning women as members of an 'out group'. This raises an important general point that is often downplayed, especially by feminist linguists: language orientated to others can serve an *exclusive* as well as an inclusive function (see Fig. 2.1).

In her discussion of the relationship between pronoun choice and speaker claims to authority, Tannen (1996: 137) suggests that, 'It is not uncommon for many men to say "I" in situations where many women would say "we".' She goes on to imply that this tendency to share credit with others by eschewing the use of the first person pronoun may affect women's prospects for promotion since their individual achievements may go unrecognized. However, this ignores the fact that inclusive 'we' does not unambiguously signal solidarity with listeners/readers in all co(n)texts of use, and in some cases can be used to lay claims to authority in relation to addressees. For instance, Fairclough (1995b: 181) notes an ambivalence in Thatcher's inclusive uses of 'we': 'On the one hand they claim solidarity by placing everyone in the same boat, but on the other they claim authority in . . . claiming the right to speak for the people as a whole.' Another instance of this potential ambivalence can be found in an example cited by Coates, in order to support her claim that women doctors mitigate their directives to patients by using 'we' rather than 'you': 'Maybe what we ought to do, is stay with the dose of di(avameez) you're on' (1995: 26). Yet it could be argued that the patient might perceive this use of 'we' as directive, or even infantalizing, rather than inclusive. This alerts us to the need to be sensitive to co(n)text immanent factors when judging the relational meanings conveyed by pronominal use.

Relational modality choices

Holmes (1995) cites an impressive body of empirical evidence in support of her claim that women are more sensitive then men to the face needs of addressees. One way in which this sensitivity manifests itself is through their use of a high density of affective modality markers, including hedging devices, often expressed by modal verbs and adverbs; facilitative tags, like 'aren't they?' and pragmatic particles, such as 'I mean' and 'you see'. They are also more likely to employ deontic modality markers which serve to mitigate, rather than strengthen, the illocutionary force of utterances. It is not surprising then that many of the women interviewed for this study claim to find themselves at odds with the confrontational norms that prevail in previously male-dominated institutions and organizations. In some instances, this has led them to be openly critical of these norms and to call for the implementation of alternatives. Whatever their commitment, in principle, to a more collaborative style, this study would suggest that the institutional constraints that operate on women in public sphere roles often lead them to employ hybrid speech styles, marked by mixed, often contradictory, modality choices. By contrast, women who belong to groupings and organizations with a feminist ethos, such as the Northern Ireland Women's Coalition and the London-based Women's Environmental Network, have developed structures in which egalitarian and collaborative rhetorical styles not only prevail, but have in their turn become normative (see Chapters 4 and 5).

There is, of course, a danger that, as well as meeting all the other requirements of their public sphere roles, women will carry the additional burden of being expected to civilize male institutional spaces. For instance, the editorial in the *Daily Mail* (8 May 1997) said of Labour's newly elected women MPs, 'May they breeze like a long overdue breath of fresh air through its [the House of Commons'] Victorian corridors'. The view that the presence of women can make a difference is implicit in the claim made by Holmes (1995: 194) in her book on linguistic politeness: 'despite their lack of social power, women have considerable social influence: their linguistic behaviour determines the overt and publicly recognized norms of polite verbal interaction in the community'. However, one consequence of this socially ascribed expectation is that those who fail to conform to norms of politeness are likely to be judged even more harshly than male peers. Thus Cameron (1992: 209) notes that Thatcher's speech style attracted a disproportionate amount of hostile comment. More recently, Mo Mowlam's reputation for swearing was used to call into question her suitability for the job of Northern Ireland Secretary (the *Guardian* 20 July 1999), whereas this pattern of linguistic behaviour by a male politician is unlikely to attract comment. Again, this suggests that the speech of men and women in public life is often evaluated according to different criteria.

Speech acts and relational meaning

Halliday (1994: 68) suggests that the inherently dialogic nature of speech acts means that they should be thought of as speech 'interacts'. The relationship between participants in any given situation can be signalled by the sort of speech acts text producers feel themselves entitled to accomplish. Van Dijk (1998: 209) argues that it is in this way that the 'social position, power and control of social members can be exercised, opposed, mitigated or emphasized'. A number of linguists have argued that once again gender is a key factor in determining the preferred speech acts and deontic modality markers used by text producers (Coates 1995; Holmes 1995; Tannen 1996). In particular, it is claimed that women are more likely to use mitigating devices to offset potentially face-threatening acts. For instance, in her comparative study of the speech acts favoured by male and female academics, Kuhn (1992) suggests that female academics tend to avoid issuing unmitigated directives to express what they require from students at the beginning of a course. Whereas male colleagues used bald directives such as, 'I require X', women tended to emphasize the institutional origin of regulations, employing the nominalization, 'the requirements are Y' (cited in Tannen 1996: 175). But, Lee's work (1992) alerts us to the danger of assuming that mitigated forms are invariably less coercive. He argues that they are often mitigated precisely because they are more likely to threaten the negative face needs of those addressed, whereas 'the bare imperative is used when the action is perceived as being in some sense to the benefit of the reader' (Lee 1992: 150). Attention to the specific co(n)text of use is therefore required before the illocutionary force of a given speech act can be established.

The assumption that men are less sensitive about threatening others' face appears to be borne out by reference to the speech acts they favour when addressing each other. However, in her study of the speech of young adolescent males, Cameron (1997) argues that it is a mistake to regard speech acts such as ritual insults as purely competitive linguistic behaviour, since they also serve an important solidarity-building function: 'Participants in a conversation or other speech event may compete with each other and at the same time be pursuing a shared project or common agenda (as in ritual insult sessions)' (ibid.: 59). In other words, ritual insults constitute both verbal duelling *and* an instance of cooperative talk. They represent an integral part of a stylized performance of heterosexual masculinity, whereby participants affirm their identity as members of an in-group, at the expense of those positioned as outsiders. In this instance, the homosocial bonds affirmed between participants were achieved by identifying homosexual men as an out-group. In mixed-sex organizations and institutions, such behaviour is likely to position both gay men and women as excluded others, since there is some evidence that women may experience such behaviour as alienating (Holmes 1995: 153; Tannen 1996: 76). Cameron's essay is important, therefore, not only because it casts doubt on the competitive/cooperative dichotomy that underpins a good deal of feminist research, but because it highlights the fact that cooperative discursive strategies can serve an exclusive, as well as an inclusive, function, something noted above in relation to the pronominal choices speakers make.

As well as differences in the speech acts preferred by men and women, there is some evidence to suggest that there are differences in the types of speech act used when addressing both sexes. For instance, in her New Zealand data, Holmes noted, 'a clearly observable tendency for women to be complimented on their appearance more often than men' (1995: 131). She goes on to assert (ibid.) that:

Provided it is not sarcastic, a compliment on someone's appearance such as *you're looking wonderful* is difficult to interpret as anything other than a positively polite utterance. An appearance compliment is clearly an expression of solidarity, a positively affective speech act.

Despite her stated commitment to the context-dependence of meaning, Holmes largely ignores questions of context here. She does make reference to the relative status of participants when she observes that 'males are even more likely to compliment women of higher status than women are' (ibid.: 135). Yet, I would argue that the context of situation in which compliments occur is at least as important as the question of the relative status of those involved. In professional contexts, for instance, even compliments between equals can function to personalize the relationship between complimenter and recipient in a way that may be perceived as inappropriate. This was certainly the overwhelming response to this practice among the women interviewed for this study, all of whom had examples of occasions when compliments on their appearance made by male colleagues had, they felt, drawn unwelcome attention to their sexual identities, when they were hoping for the focus to be on the content of their talk. In other words, in the majority of cases, my respondents did not perceive compliments as *positively* affective speech acts, but as *negatively* affective speech acts, establishing the wrong sort of relationship between themselves and the colleagues who addressed them in this way. Once again, this is a situation that lends itself to strategic misunderstanding, as Uchida (1992: 558) notes:

> Against the addressee's charge of insult or harassment, the addresser can justify himself by saying that it was only a compliment; he was trying to be nice and friendly; and no, of course he had no intention of dominance!

Holmes (1995: 143) also notes that men appear to perceive compliments as 'more referentially orientated evaluative utterances'. This may be due less to their differing perceptions of these speech acts, as she suggests, than to the fact that they are more likely than women to be complimented on their competence rather than on their appearance.

In relation to speech acts where the function is to give advice, I will suggest that alternative media produced by women-orientated groups and organizations challenge the tendency evident in the mainstream media to position female readers as passive *recipients* of advice. In his analysis of media coverage of food scares in the late 1980s, Fowler (1991: 17ff) reveals how both the problem and the solution for these scares were located with housewives. Female readers were addressed in language 'phrased in classroom fashion, with plenty of imperatives, modals of obligation ("have to", "must"), absolutes ("never", "immediately")' (ibid.: 190). The assumption that such readers were profoundly ignorant was reinforced by the ubiquity of lists of do's and don'ts which were 'spelt out' for them in a wide range of media. I will argue that this type of patronizing address is much less likely to characterize the approach to links between food, health and the environment adopted in the campaign literature of women-orientated environmental groups, such as the Women's Environmental Network (Chapter 5).

(Inter)textual traces and cues

Holmes (1995: 130) provides extensive empirical evidence from her own research and that of others which 'supports a view of women's conversational style as more interpersonal, affective and interaction-orientated compared to the impersonal and content-orientated style more typical of male interaction'. This manifests itself in textual features such as latching, cooperative sentence-building, back-channelling and a propensity to use informal discourse markers, such as 'oh', 'well' and 'right' and conjunctions, like 'so' and 'coz'. Women's greater orientation towards the interpersonal metafunction means that their increasing entry into public sphere roles is likely to have contributed towards the conversationalization of public sphere discourse types noted by Fairclough (1992, 1994, 1995b). Fairclough points out that this does not necessarily mean that a more egalitarian relationship exists between text producers and addressees. On the contrary, 'conversationalized discursive practices might be regarded not as eradicating the power of producers, professionals, bureaucrats, and so forth, but as backgrounding and disguising it, and making it more difficult to challenge' (Fairclough 1994: 264). In her provocative book on alternative medicine, Coward (1990), for instance, is sceptical about whether the more person-orientated discursive approach employed by alternative practitioners is in fact as empowering for women patients, as many analysts, including Fairclough (1992: 144ff), have claimed.

The link between the relatively intimate mode of address increasingly employed by the media and the interactional style said to be favoured by women has led some commentators to refer to this shift as the 'feminization' of the news media (see van Zoonen 1998: 41ff). The tendency for discursive strategies associated with women to be denigrated is, however, evident in the slide from 'feminization' to 'dumbing down' and, more recently, to 'bitch journalism', a term employed by the politician David Steel (cited in the *Guardian* 7 September 1999: 13). The latter appears to be alluding to media coverage of the so-called 'honey trap' technique whereby young female investigative journalists are alleged to act as 'bait' in order to trick male celebrities into revealing damning personal secrets. A comment made by one of these journalists, Dawn Alford, reveals the extent to which this coverage drew upon stereotypes of the predatory female, 'columnists used up hundreds of inches inferring I was a cross between Mata Hari and a black widow spider' (*Media Guardian* 31 May 1999: 2). This mythical narrative of *femmes fatales* and helpless male victims conveniently glosses over the fact that many of these women were accompanied by male colleagues, while the so-called 'king of the sting' is Mazher Mahmood of the *News of the World*.

The metaphors employed by text producers often serve an important relational function. Mills (1995) regards metaphor as operating at the level of discourse, and I would go further by suggesting that it should be viewed as an inherently *intertextual* phenomenon, since metaphors, by their very nature, evoke prior texts and even entire genres and/or semantic fields. For instance, in their influential study of metaphor, Lakoff and Johnson (1980) argue that metaphors do not simply serve an aesthetic function as stylistic ornament, but are fundamental to ways of thinking and structuring discursive domains. In particular, they claim that the pervasive use of the 'argument as war' metaphor presupposes that the relationship between participants in public discussions and debates is a combative one (Lakoff and Johnson 1980: 4). A similar role is performed by the widespread use of sporting metaphors. Thus in an article reporting debates in the Commons, Simon Hoggart noted that a 'thrust' at the Prime Minister, made by the Liberal Democrat MP, Jackie Ballard, failed, whereas a male MP and old pal (of Hoggart's), Mickey Fabricant, 'scored against' him and two difficult 'bouts' with William Hague tired him out (the *Guardian* 24 June 1999). Hearn argues that the conflictual model of public debate created by such metaphors is favoured by men since it affords them opportunities for competitive displays of masculinity:

> . . . standing up, strutting, performing in public, orating, arguing, saying your piece, in the competitive world of men involves a symbolic waving around of the penis, and sometimes going the whole hog, 'wanking off', as a display to others, women and men, but most importantly men.
>
> (Hearn 1992: 207)

In other words, he sees such performances not only as constitutive of their identities as men, but as helping to constitute the homosocial bonds between them and other men. Evidence from this study would suggest that women are less comfortable with the 'yah boo' style of debate that sporting and military metaphors help to normalize.

It is somewhat surprising, then, that in an empirical study of speeches made by politicians in the European Parliament, Footit (1999) found no significant difference in the overall percentage of military metaphors used by men and women (15 per cent and 13 per cent, respectively). This could be taken as evidence that women feel constrained to adopt the dominant discursive norms that prevail in male-dominated institutions and organizations. However, a more nuanced investigation undertaken by Footit into the metaphorical fields drawn upon and the types of participants involved revealed that women were more likely to use metaphors that refer to small-scale and localized engagements, rather than to the classic grand army campaigns alluded to by men. Her analysis also reveals the creative use many women made of metaphors drawn from the domestic realm, leading her to conclude that they are, in fact, imagining both politics and inter-party relationships differently. Chapter 4 of this study will provide further evidence in support of this view, especially in relation to the reverse political discourse being developed by members of the Northern Ireland Women's Coalition. Their creative use of metaphor seems calculated to challenge the tendency of the language of political debate to exclude the lifeworld of women. Yet, a note of caution needs to be sounded, since Thatcher's well-known practice of discussing economic policy in terms of domestic metaphors did not *materially* benefit women.

My research points to the fact that the news frame (Norris 1997) of gender antagonism is pervasive in media coverage of the relations between men and women in public life. With reference to the metaphorical phrase the 'battle of the sexes', Mills (1995: 137) points out that:

> in assuming at a metaphorical level that the relations between the sexes can be considered only as if they were always antagonistic, the user of this phrase will be led to consider males and females in terms of battle and warfare, rather than considering other forms of thinking.

Media texts often provide traces of women's resistance to this construction of their relationship with male colleagues. For instance, responding to a request from an interviewer to reveal stories about her unfair treatment at the hands of male colleagues, Monica McWilliams of the Northern Ireland Women's Coalition replied, 'there is a danger of tarring all men with the same brush and some of my best friends are men in politics, genuinely good people' (*Belfast Telegraph* 10 October 1998). As will become evident, media recontextualizations of women's accounts of their experiences do not always allow space for such alternative 'forms of thinking' about gender relations. A pre-scripted gendered schema of male aggressors and female victims is much more in keeping with the news value of 'negativity', and more specifically with the reporting of 'conflict between people' noted by Bell (1991: 156).

2.6.4   The ideational metafunction

As observed above, there has been a tendency in functional approaches to language to define the ideational in narrowly referential terms, ignoring its evaluative dimension. In this study, the ideational will be taken to refer to the linguistic and semiotic realization of information, facts and content, as well as the perspective text producers take in relation to these. Gee offers a corrective to the assumption that the referential function of language is more important than its evaluative role:

> It is a mistake to think that the primary function of human language is to talk about the world. Rather, any human language primarily functions to allow speakers to take various *perspectives* or *viewpoints* on the world. Each human language is rich with devices for talking about the same situation in

the world in multiple ways, depending upon the perspective one wishes to take on that situation.

(Gee 1990: 112; italics in the original)

The emphasis in what follows is precisely on questions of viewpoint and stance since the issue of how women's speech is evaluated is crucial. The question that will be answered in detail in this section is how the ideational metafunction is realized (inter)textually in ways that are relevant to the production, reproduction and transformation of normative ideologies about gender.

Lexical and collocational choices

The connotative meanings associated with lexical items are clearly an important resource which text producers can exploit in order to signal their ideological stance in relation to represented individuals. Evidence, including from this study, suggests that pejorative epithets such as 'strident' remain depressingly persistent in evaluations of the speech styles of women who occupy public sphere roles (see also Ross 1995a; Tannen 1996). Such gender specific dysphemisms provide traces of the continuing unease with which women who perform such roles are viewed. Other adjectives may not carry negative connotations in all co(n)texts, but may do so when they enter into specific collocations. One such instance is the adjective 'formidable' when it collocates with 'woman'. A straw poll among feminist friends and colleagues revealed that no one would regard the epithet as a compliment if used in relation to them, in spite of its ostensibly positive connotations. On the contrary, when asked to comment on its connotative meaning, terms like 'overbearing' and 'aggressive' recurred. Interestingly, several people mentioned that, where spoken, it is likely to be accompanied by a predictable pattern of paralinguistic behaviour, namely the rolling or widening of the speaker's eyes and/or the raising of her or his eyebrows. Although often neglected, this type of ostensive behaviour (Sperber and Wilson 1989) serves an important function in delimiting meaning. Despite the many gains made by feminists, the collocation 'formidable woman' would appear to indicate a residual surprise that women should be powerful, as well as an implicit anxiety that this should be so. In other words, it provides a textual trace of the tensions that arise when gendered identities undergo a process of adjustment and change.

While the language used to judge women's performance of public sphere roles may be both predictable and stereotypical, this study suggests that the lexical and collocational patterns employed by many women in public life are ideologically creative.[5] Many women have also sought to contest pre-existing classification schemes by which vocabulary is organized, particularly in the discourses of politics and organized religion. An obvious example is the way feminist-identified women have used their institutional status and organizational roles to promote the use of inclusive language. Another strategy has been to subvert existing idioms, since this is a powerful way of challenging folk wisdom about the nature of gendered identities and relationships. Mills (1995: 130) says of idioms, 'because of their formulaic nature, these phrases do open themselves up to the possibility of being subverted'. Other, more discourse-specific, examples of women's ideologically creative use of language will be discussed in some detail in the chapters that follow.

Pronominal choices

Given the debates surrounding gender-inclusive language, the decision by a text producer to employ the so-called generic pronoun 'he' can no longer be regarded as ideologically neutral. Such a choice presupposes a view of the world in which men are the chief actors, in this case, in public sphere roles. This study provides further evidence in support of the view, noted by a number of feminists, that such generics are, in any case, revealed as anything but, once the surrounding co(n)text is taken into account. Another noticeable pattern in my data is that pronoun slippages provide traces of text producers' affinity with, or ideological distance from, the views expressed by represented subjects. For instance, in press reports of the 1994 Labour leadership campaign, slippages between corporate and inclusive functions of the pronoun 'we' were found to signal the alignment of different newspapers with the policies of one or other of the two male candidates. The structured absence of this slippage in the case of the one woman in the race signalled their relative distance from her campaign pledges (see Chapter 3). This type of pronoun slippage acts as one of a number of evaluative framing devices available to text producers. Additional framing devices are discussed below.

Epistemic modality choices

Text producers can employ modality markers from the cautious to the categorical to signal their degree of commitment to the truth of propositions expressed. Although realized through the same formal features as markers of relational modality – namely, modal verbs, modal adverbs and aspects of tense – epistemic modality markers perform a primarily evaluative, rather than an interpersonal, function. The subjective evaluations of media producers can attain the status of fact by being cast in terms of categorical modality. Alternatively, by employing what Halliday (1994: 272) refers to as impersonal projections (e.g. 'It may be the case that . . .'), media producers can distance themselves from evaluative judgements that are in fact their own. Modality choices can, therefore, cue readers in to accepting producers' evaluations of represented individuals. Although this is true whether these individuals are male or female, I will suggest that women are likely to fare less well in an industry where a masculinist culture still prevails (van Zoonen 1998: 33).

The fact that individual linguistic items and/or semiotic modes are, to use Coates's (1987: 114) term, 'polypragmatic', can give rise to indeterminacy of meaning. Thus while a woman in a public sphere role may well intend her modal utterances to be interpreted as markers of social solidarity, empirical evidence suggests that they are often perceived as signifying a lack of authority (Holmes 1995; Tannen 1996). Lee (1992: 151) argues that 'ambiguity in the area of modality typically occurs as an exponent of the tension between interacting discourses'. This is a point that will be explored further in this study with reference to a co(n)text-sensitive analysis of modality choices. One of the claims that will be made is that some of the cautious modality choices made by women are linked to discourse type rather than gender, since such choices are in fact characteristic of certain public sphere discourse types, notably the discourse of party politics.

Transitivity choices

According to Halliday (1994: 179), 'Transitivity structures express representational meaning: what the clause is about, which is typically some process, with associated participants and circumstances.' A link between gender and preferred transitivity choices is illustrated in Chapter 5 with reference to the persuasive rhetoric employed by male- and female-orientated environmental groups. Transitivity choices in media texts are also considered on the grounds that such choices are likely to reveal a good deal about their producers' perceptions of represented subjects. It will be shown that, in spite of their institutional status and/or organizational role, women in public life are often portrayed as being acted upon by people and events outside their control. Mills' (1995: 143ff) call for a more co(n)text-sensitive approach to transitivity choices is likely to prove particularly useful for understanding the apparent investment some women appear to have in occupying subordinate roles. Halliday also points to the connection between transitivity choices and issues of voice (1994: 161ff), and it will obviously be important to consider whether agency is made clear in media reports, or whether information is attributed to unspecified sources. The *absence* of media reporting of their activities means that in many instances women in the public domain are constructed as invisible. During political leadership campaigns, this may mean that female candidates are 'written out of' influential news narratives. Interestingly, Lee (1992: 113) notes that, even where their activities are reported in news articles, women's agency is often obscured by the fact that they do not appear in the photographs that accompany these articles.

Framing devices

One way in which text producers can signal their own position *vis-à-vis* the views expressed by represented subjects is through the use of framing devices such as overtly evaluative reporting verbs (e.g. 'alleged') and glossing adverbs (e.g. 'defensively'). Caldas-Coulthard (1995) argues that, although relatively rare in her corpus comprising news reports, the use of what she terms 'stage direction verbs' revealed stereotypical assumptions about the speech of men and women: 'Men "shout" and "groan" while women (and children) "scream" and "yell"' (Caldas-Coulthard 1995: 235). In an earlier study, I noted a similarly gendered pattern of use for the verb 'giggle'. Of the 124 occurrences of this verb in the then 7.3 million word Birmingham Collection of English Text, 66 per cent were used to refer to the paralinguistic behaviour of adult females and children, while 12.5 per cent referred to that of effeminate men (Ramsey 1987: 63ff). This trivializing verb is used to frame the speech of high-profile women in all of the domains included in this study. I will suggest, however, that the *structured absence* of evaluative framing can be as ideologically significant as the *presence* of reporting verbs and inquit tags that draw on stereotypes about women's speech. Finally, in his discussion of the polyphonic nature of media texts, Fairclough (1995b: 84) makes the point that 'how voices are woven together, how they are ordered with respect to each other, becomes decisive'. Again, I will suggest that gender is often a relevant factor in determining patterns of discourse representation.

(Inter)textual traces and cues

In news genres, decisions about layout can, of course, be ideologically significant. For instance, since material in headlines and lead paragraphs is informationally foregrounded, these can slant the entire article for the reader. So, too, can accompanying photographs and other visual cues, such as cartoons. On occasions, however, it is the incongruity between linguistic and visual cues that a reader is invited to recognize. For instance, the potentially positive phrase, the 'politics of empathy', which occurs in the strapline accompanying a profile of Mary McAleese, the then newly elected President of Ireland, is wholly at odds with the image of her supplied in the accompanying photograph (the *Guardian* 14 April 1998: 4–5). In it, a frowning McAleese is pictured in a combative stance, doing verbal battle with an unseen opponent (Fig. 2.3). Both her hands are outstretched in a gesture that, far from inviting an empathetic embrace, unambiguously tells viewers to 'back off'. The tension between the strapline and the photograph prepares the reader for the gradual unmasking of her approach to politics as more in keeping with the 'politics of ego'.

As well as an ideologically creative approach to lexical classification frames, noted above, I will suggest that women also have a creative approach to the institutionally and culturally ratified genres that circulate in the public sphere. Text producers can mix elements from existing genres to produce hybrid texts, but the resulting disjunction between genre expectations and the actual text types produced may provoke a negative reaction. This is certainly true of female politicians who have sought to challenge the traditional masculinist

Fig. 2.3 Photograph of Mary McAleese that appeared in the *Guardian* (14 April 1998: 4)

genre of politics. As in the profile of McAleese referred to above, charges of insincerity and effusiveness abound. Thus both she and her predecessor, Mary Robinson, are credited with little more than a facility for 'vacuous talk' (the *Guardian* 14 April 1998: 5). In an article on Mo Mowlam's approach to her job as Secretary of State for Northern Ireland, the columnist, Charlotte Raven, claims that this approach is not even intelligible *as politics*, 'That Mowlam is good at what she does is undeniable – as long as you accept that what she does is not politics' (the *Guardian* 20 July 1999: 4). Again, it is her rhetorical style that is singled out as being incompatible with that expected of a politician:

> I cannot escape the suggestion that Mowlam might make a better marriage counsellor than Minister for Difficult Problems . . . Mowlam is a *consummate chatter* and, thus, it is as *a talker* she is judged. Since canonization following her tumour operation, people have rushed to praise her 'forthright' *way with words*, her 'no bullshit' approach to politics, her lack of 'airs and graces'.

> (the *Guardian* 20 July 1999: 4; my italics)

The implication is that her language is both inappropriately *excessive*, a common folklinguistic charge levelled against women's speech, and insufficiently formal. Related to the latter is the recurrent charge that women in public life are too 'touchy-feely', a charge which implies that they have transgressed some unwritten law of proxemics about the proper distance that should be maintained between bodies in public spaces. It is clear then that the uncritical acceptance of socially sanctioned generic norms constitutes a barrier to change in gendered identities and gendered relations in the public domain.

The power of cross-institutional fraternal networks means that women are rarely called upon as accessed voices in the media, with the result that their ideas and perspectives on events are often omitted or marginalized. Where women's public sphere activities are discussed in the media, the metaphors used to refer to them often evoke stereotypically gendered genres which afford them very limited roles. An extreme instance is the epithet 'cyborgs', widely used to refer to Labour's new female MPs, an allusion intended to signify their alleged passivity and automaton-like adherence to Party policy. Where women are assigned more proactive roles, the metaphorical fields drawn upon are often contradictory. On the one hand, they are constructed as a problem, most strikingly in the case of the recurring metaphor of 'woman as chaos' used in relation to women priests, while, on the other, they are viewed as a panacea for all institutional ills, as in the case of the frequent metaphor of 'woman as civilizer' of unruly male spaces. Such metaphors often evoke what Mills (1995: 187) refers to as gendered schemata, larger discursive frameworks which operate across the boundaries of public sphere discourse types. One such schema casts women in subordinate support roles in relation to visionary men, while another, identified by Threadgold (1997: 128), rationalizes their marginalization by assuming they are in need of care and protection. The phenomenon of role encapsulation (Powell 1993: 115) means that as long as such schemata persist, women are likely to continue to be assigned a limited number of roles within organizations and institutional structures.

2.7   Macro-level analysis: the relationship between text and social context

Whereas the micro-level of critical discourse analysis focuses on textual traces and cues, the macro-level of analysis is concerned with the way institutional and broader social constraints operate on the whole process of text production and interpretation. Fairclough (1989) refers to this as power *behind* discourse to distinguish it from what he terms power *in* discourse, which applies to the immediate context of situation in which texts are interpreted. As Fairclough (1989: 110) notes, 'in analysing texts, one's focus is constantly alternating between what is "there" in the text, and the discourse type(s) which the text is drawing upon'. In the previous chapter, a number of social-structural constraints relevant to this study were discussed in some detail. In the remainder of the study, the focus will, therefore, alternate between the critical analysis of a wide range of spoken, written and visual texts and the analysis of more global factors that contribute to the production, reproduction and transformation of normative gendered identities and gendered relations in the public sphere.

2.8   Methodology used for data collection and analysis

In the chapters that follow, I apply the critical framework set out above to the analysis of a wide range of media texts in order to establish whether any 'patterns of habituation' (Toolan 1996: 302) are discernible in the coverage of women in public sphere roles. As in the preceding sections, I also draw upon larger quantitative studies on language and gender carried out by feminist sociolinguists. Information from such studies is intended to complement the more qualitative analysis of data from interviews with women in all four of the communities of practice investigated in this study. The aim is thereby to achieve the sort of 'triangulation' effect referred to by Bergvall (1999: 288):

> Without careful attention to local practice, we cannot understand how individuals shape and interpret their gender and their social practice with the available linguistic resources. Without broad surveys and collections, we cannot know the significance of individual uses – the convergence, divergence and movement of social practices. Without the broader studies of ideologies at the textual and global levels, we cannot understand how interpretations of gender by gatekeeping elites are generated or spread.

Crawford (1995: 74) sets out a number of criteria for an 'ecologically valid' feminist methodological practice. She argues that, as far as possible, research should be conducted in naturalistic and interactive contexts which downplay the 'expert' status of the analyst. My interviewees were made fully aware of the purpose of my research and were sent a range of likely interview questions in advance. Thereafter, the interviews were conducted as informally as possible, with interviewees being encouraged to digress into areas they felt to be of particular importance. As a critical discourse analyst, my role is, of course, to go beyond the surface features of what was said to interpret the underlying assumptions that respondents brought to the interview situation.

I conducted a total of twelve interviews, resulting in approximately seven hours of taped material, as well as supplementary field notes. I chose to interview Margaret Beckett in 1995 (22 November) because her high profile campaign for the Labour Leadership the previous year coincided with the early stages of my research on women in public life. A follow-up interview on 11 June 1998 with Joan Ruddock, then Deputy Minister for Women, seemed to offer an ideal way of updating my information on possible changes to the culture of the Commons in the wake of the dramatic increase in the number of female Labour MPs as a result of the May 1997 general election. It also afforded an opportunity to find out more about the role of the newly established Women's Unit in Government. Once I decided to extend my research on women in politics to include the newly emerging devolved UK bodies, the decision to focus in detail on the Northern Ireland Women's Coalition stemmed partly from its unique status as the UK's sole women-only political party, and partly from the fact that its leader, Monica McWilliams, kindly agreed to be interviewed by me (29 January 1999). However, I was less fortunate in my request to interview the Welsh Agriculture Secretary, Christine Gwyther, with the result that I had to rely on media coverage alone.

For the purpose of my research on the Women's Environmental Network, discussed in the third chapter of the study, I decided to include an element of participant observation, by spending a day at the WEN office in London (17 September 1997). In addition to interviewing three WEN officers on this occasion, I conducted telephone interviews with WEN's founder, Bernadette Vallely (26 November 1997), and with a young anti-roads protester, Eleanor Hudson (27 August 1997), who had come to prominence in the media. For Chapter 6 on women in the Church, I contacted the Women's Officer in my local diocese of St Albans, who supplied me with a list of women priests. I tried to ensure that my interviewees practised their ministry in a range of different settings. Thus Priest A (interviewed 30 April 1996) is priest-in-charge in a relatively middle-class rural parish in Bedfordshire; Priest B (interviewed 14 May 1996) is priest-in-charge in a relatively middle-class parish in central London; while Priest C (interviewed 10 May 1996) is part of a clergy couple who minister to a largely working-class urban parish in south Bedfordshire. Since I was also interested in media representations of the campaign for women's ordination, and the subsequent media representations of women's ministry as priests, I also undertook an in-depth interview (19 July 1996) with the Public Relations Officer for the Movement for the Ordination of Women (MOW), and its successor, Women and the Church (WATCH).

2.9   Conclusions

To summarize, the theoretical approach adopted in this study is one that seeks to connect the detailed analysis of spoken, written and visual texts and intertexts to an analysis of the hegemonic ideologies that operate at the institutional and societal levels of discourse. The assumption is that such an approach is likely to yield a nuanced account of the changing nature of gendered identities and relations in the public sphere, at least with regard to the situation in contemporary Britain. While I have rejected an analytical framework that relies on a global metalanguage, I have argued that it is possible to identify recurrent patterns of use in (inter)texts that contribute to the production, maintenance and transformation of normative gender ideologies. However, I have stressed that these need to be analysed in a co(n)text-sensitive way. A corollary of viewing language as a fluid, rather than a fixed, code is that the process of (inter)textual interpretation needs to be seen as a potential site of ideological struggle and contestation. For instance, I have suggested that the ideologically creative approach many women adopt to public sphere discourse types is often evaluated negatively *because* it departs from accepted norms and conventions. This will be illustrated in the first case study in Chapter 3, on female Labour MPs at Westminster, where I seek to highlight the tensions between the choices women MPs make in discourse and the way in which these are perceived and evaluated by others, especially by the media.

Notes

1. I would agree with Cameron's (1992: 100) view that so-called 'gender-neutral' definitions of this term ignore the fact that 'sexism is a system in which women and men are not simply different, but unequal . . . and it works to the disadvantage of women, not men'.
2. For instance, the same photograph appeared in the *Daily Mirror* (8 May 1997), but in this instance the offending headline, 'Blair's babes', is accompanied by the bracketed alternative headline, 'Oh sorry . . . we mean Labour's brilliant 101 women MPs'. The 'oops' tone of this pseudo-apology appears to be calculated to let readers know that the producers know they have naughtily transgressed the rules of 'political correctness', but that this shouldn't be taken too seriously. After all, they might argue with some justification, that the overall tone of the article is positive. For instance, they claim that the newly elected women are 'determined to end the male domination of politics for ever'. The implication that this may prove to be a naive hope is reinforced, however, by the revelation that their 'innocence' of parliamentary procedures led them to clap on the arrival in the Commons of the new PM.
3. This refers to the selective transcription of my interview with Joan Ruddock (11 June 1998). Hereafter, references to transcriptions of all the interviews conducted for the purpose of this book will be numbered in this way as a convenient shorthand. Full transcriptions of these interviews, together with copies of the original tapes, can be obtained on request.

4. The term '"dossier" epithet' was first introduced by Carter and Nash (1990: 104) to describe the practice, frequently employed in both popular fiction and tabloid journalism, of compressing a great deal of information about an individual's appearance and life history into pre- and/or post-modifying phrases. The invented, but not altogether implausible, example they provide is, 'Burly, bearded Captain Andrew "Brainy" MacBraine, RN . . .' (ibid.).

5. In a paper delivered at the twentieth Poetics and Linguistics Association Conference at Goldsmiths University (2 July 2000), John Joseph argued for the logical impossibility of creative collocations, since, by definition, a collocation involves 'the association of lexical items that *regularly* co-occur' (Halliday and Hasan 1976: 284; my italics). However, a few paragraphs later, Halliday and Hasan define collocations more loosely, and I would suggest more productively, as comprising 'lexical items that stand to each other in some sort of recognizable lexicosemantic (word meaning) relation' (ibid.: 285). This definition would include the kind of 'fused formulae' alluded to by Tannen (1989: 40), whereby a fixed phrase is given a new and usually ironic inflection when one element (or more) is deliberately changed for aesthetic and/or ideologically creative ends. The resulting pattern of collocation is therefore palimpsestic since it simultaneously recalls and subverts the meaning of the more conventional collocation which it displaces. I will refer to such palimpsestic collocations as creative collocations.

3

Women in the House. A Case Study of Women Labour MPs at Westminster

This chapter, and the three chapters that follow, provide an account of my research into women's involvement in four different communities of practice within the public sphere. The definition of the 'public' sphere employed throughout the study subsumes both institutions of the state and what some social theorists have referred to as 'civil' sphere domains. Indeed, one of the central theses of this study is that women's increasing presence in public institutional spaces has helped to weaken the boundaries between what have traditionally been conceived of as public and civil sphere domains, as well as between both of these domains and the private sphere. This pattern of discursive restructuring is likely to have been overlooked had my research been confined to state institutions alone. Although the interrelationship between institutions of the state and civil society is investigated in all four communities of practice, it is explored most fully in Chapters 4 and 5, where the emphasis is on the cross-fertilization between grassroots political activity and public opinion formation. The emphasis in this chapter, by contrast, is on the central political decision-making body in Britain, namely the House of Commons.

When compared to a number of other institutions in the public sphere, women are relatively established in the House of Commons. They have been eligible for election since the Parliament (Qualification of Women) Bill was passed in 1918, although the percentage of women elected as MPs has, until recently, remained very small. For instance, Puwar (1997: 2–3) points out that 'the number of women barely altered between 1945 and 1983'. Since this averages out as less than 4 per cent of the total number of MPs, it is not surprising that the majority of women elected to the House appear to have internalized prevailing masculinist discursive norms, rather than seeking to challenge them. Thus, according to Shirley Williams, MP:

> Over the years, a few women MPs have made the betterment of women's lives their priority, fighting their corner and punching above their weight . . . Most women MPs, however, have conformed, conscientiously

done their job as a representative of their constituency and drawn very little attention to themselves.

(the *Guardian* 15 December 1997)

For most women MPs a strategy of being seen but rarely heard was, therefore, the norm.

The 1997 general election was a potential turning point, since the gender composition of the House underwent a dramatic change. This was due in no small part to the controversial quotas policy[1] adopted by the Parliamentary Labour Party (hereafter, the PLP). Overall, the number of women in the PLP almost tripled, from 37 in the 1992 Parliament, to 102 in 1997 (31 of these were selected from women-only short lists). After the general election women comprised 18 per cent of all MPs, although this is some way off the figure of 30 per cent that Dahlerup (1988) argues constitutes a 'critical mass'. Nonetheless, the widespread view, and indeed expectation, is that women are now in a position to change the masculinist discursive practices and policy agenda that prevail in the House of Commons.

Before going on to explore how these expectations and beliefs have helped to shape the gendered identities of women MPs, I will begin by outlining some of the institutional constraints that have, in the recent past, impeded the efforts of female politicians who have sought to challenge the masculinist culture of the House, and are likely to continue to do so in the future. The discussion concentrates on the PLP as a community of practice, since, as Lovenduski (1997: 709) notes, 'between 1992 and 1997, [it] was the main site of activity to increase women's representation in British politics'. However, the central argument of this chapter is that it is also necessary to examine the way political parties interrelate with the broader culture of Parliament and with the media, since the boundaries between different communities of practice in the public sphere are permeable. For this reason, I include a detailed analysis of media coverage of Margaret Beckett's campaign for the Labour leadership in 1994, since this provides an ideal opportunity to assess the relative treatment of high-profile female and male politicians who run for political office. Rather than treating women MPs as a homogeneous group, differences *between* women, as well as differences between women and men, will also be explored.

3.1   Masculinism in the institutional discourse of British parliamentary politics

It is ironic that Westminster has been called the 'mother of parliaments', since it is, in so many ways, a male-gendered institutional space. This is due partly to the historical fact that its organizational structures and procedures were invented by middle- and upper-class men of an earlier era. For instance, the hours the House sits were designed to accommodate the needs of men who combined their Parliamentary roles with managing their estates or with careers in the professions, but patently *not* with caring for children. Likewise, gruelling late-night sittings are due to the operation of an antiquated gentlemanly code of fair play which permits the Opposition to call a vote at any time.

The toll incurred by these long and erratic hours has been exacerbated by what the Labour MP, Harriet Harman, has referred to as a 'culture of presenteeism' that, in turn, results from the new managerialism that now pervades Parliament. When a number of new women MPs from the 1997 intake complained that this 'hours culture' is inefficient and tantamount to 'time-wasting', they were constructed in the media as victims of work-related stress (the *Guardian* 28 March 1998). It is not, of course, only women who are likely to find these hours antipathetic. David Hincliffe, for instance, resigned from Labour's front bench in 1995 in order to devote more time to his family. However, the tendency of members of both sexes, in all parties, to cherish the traditions of the House, no matter how arcane and out-of-date, means that such traditions are often deeply entrenched in institutional structures. How else can one account for the tediously rehearsed, but still unchanged, situation whereby the Commons has a rifle range, but no crèche? Joan Ruddock claims that women are much less likely to be 'sucked into' this culture and that the majority of Labour women MPs, in particular, are committed to changes that will render the House more women-friendly (Trans. II: 160ff).

The discursive style that predominates in debates in the chamber, as well as in a good deal of work in cross-party committees, is an adversarial one which many women say they find alienating (Sreberny-Mohammadi and Ross 1996; Puwar 1997). Ruddock recalls her sense of shock when she realized that this competitive ethos also extends to relations between peers within the same party (Trans. II: 102–6). This is exacerbated by the Whips system within individual parties which effectively means that a culture of bullying is not only tolerated, but is integral to the Parliamentary system. Brian Sedgemore, MP, points out that the physical layout of the Commons' debating chamber encourages confrontation, a view he frames using appropriately militaristic metaphors:

> Two armies face each other, separated by a thin neutral line, nerves stretched and sinews stiffened for battle on a daily basis. The job of the Opposition is to destroy the Government. The job of the Government is to ignore the Opposition. If the differences between them are small, then they must clearly be exaggerated. If there are no differences, then they must be artificially created.
>
> (Sedgemore 1995: 54)

If the overall culture of the Commons resembles a gentlemen's club, the chamber is a site of theatrical display. Debates are rarely genuine, since questions have to be put down two weeks in advance, yet, both MPs and ministers are expected to engage in a paradoxical *performance* of spontaneity. This explains the censure incurred by a number of new women MPs who elected to read questions (the *Guardian* 9 October 1997). The heckling they subsequently received is, of course, an integral part of the 'yah boo' debating style that prevails in the chamber.

However, countless women MPs from all parties have complained that, in addition to the usual political insults that are traded across the floor of the chamber, they are also subjected to sexist abuse. For example, instances of verbal sexual harassment have been recorded by women MPs in surveys carried out by Ross (1995a) and Puwar (1997). Ruddock implies that intolerance of *overt* sexism has led to an increase in more *covert* forms of abuse: 'some of the new women MPs tell me there are still you know pretty ugly remarks being made but they're not being made loudly enough to be detected' (Trans. II: 130–2). Although the Speaker and her or his deputies can request that 'unparliamentary language' is withdrawn, this only applies to language recorded in *Hansard*. This means that the undercurrent of sexist, and therefore presumably 'unparliamentary', language reported by numerous women MPs does not officially exist and is unofficially tolerated. A study by Sylvia Shaw (1999) reveals that men are more likely than female colleagues to make illegal interventions in debates, and are also more likely to engage in intense barracking. She concludes that although they belong to the same 'community of practice' (Eckert and McConnell-Ginet 1992: 95), male and female MPs do so on unequal terms, with men being the more powerful participants.

The televising of Parliament has increased the importance of the performative element in parliamentary debates, with the result that prosodic and paralinguistic features of speech have been foregrounded for a wider audience, as has accompanying body language. I would suggest that this process has had contradictory effects on the perception of women MPs and ministers. On the one hand, it has reinforced the distracting emphasis on their physical appearance, which tends to attract more comment than men's (Ross 1995a). On the other hand, the use of microphones, to ensure that output is of broadcast quality, has incidentally rendered less relevant the widespread perception that women's voices do not carry authority (Macdonald 1995: 45).

Another incidental effect, noted by Montgomery (1999: 29), is that 'television's focus on the face throws issues of sincerity into a different kind of sharp relief'. He goes on to suggest that this shift in modalities of communication is, therefore, one factor that helps to explain why sincerity appears to be assuming increasing salience as a public virtue. Again, I would argue that there is more at stake in this respect for women MPs and ministers, since there is evidence to indicate that the validity of their performance is more likely than men's to be evaluated in terms of the criterion of sincerity. For instance, the 1992 British Candidate Survey revealed that women were perceived to be more honest and more principled than their male counterparts (Norris and Lovenduski 1995: 135). In this context, women have to be particularly adept at negotiating the perilous territory involved in the 'performative paradox'.

Puwar (1997: 3) refers to a tradition of vertical segregation in parliamentary institutions whereby women tend to be concentrated in subordinate roles, while men occupy major decision-making roles. Between 1924, when Margaret Bondfield became the first woman minister, and 1997, there were only eight female Cabinet ministers, most of whom were given so-called 'soft' portfolio roles, primarily in the departments of health and education. As Wendy Webster (1990: 124) observes: 'In the male-defined world of politics these were understood as subordinate areas.' The idea that women are particularly suited to these roles is symptomatic of the tendency to define women's public sphere roles by analogy with the roles they have traditionally performed in the private sphere.

The promotion of five women to the Labour Cabinet in 1997 therefore marked a considerable advance for gender equality, especially since two of these appointments, those of Mo Mowlam as Northern Ireland Secretary, and Margaret Beckett, as President of the Board of Trade, were in non-traditional areas. However, both roles have always been perceived by aspiring Ministers as 'poisoned chalices'. The Northern Ireland Office is notorious as a graveyard for ministerial careers, while the top job at the Department of Trade and Industry is widely regarded as 'the biggest lame duck of all' (the *Guardian* 9 January 1999). And so it proved to be, since Beckett had little over a year at the DTI, before ignominiously being replaced by Peter Mandelson. Although Mowlam fared rather better, lasting for two and a half years in her role as Secretary of State for Northern Ireland – a role for which she attracted widespread praise – she was displaced, again coincidentally by Mandelson, and departed amidst rumours that she had mishandled the Peace Process (the *Guardian* 7 January 2000).

All five women who held ministerial office after the 1997 general election occupied what Diane Abbott has described as 'fixer' roles, in that they are roles which exploit what are stereotypically perceived to be women's highly developed interpersonal and organizational skills. Another Labour back-bencher is quoted as saying, 'At the top level, the girls have ended up with nannying and housekeeping jobs, while the men get the real work' (the *Guardian* 29 July 1998). According to journalist Lucy Ward, the Downing Street spin machine has not denied this, but instead, 'has sought to paint a picture of a clutch of powerful females keeping the boys under control' (ibid.). Only Clare Short, as Minister for International Development, is in charge of a spending department and this involves a very small budget, when compared to the other departments of state. When it comes to appointments to the policy group that constitutes the heart of political decision-making, informal rules still apply, with the result that only one member of the group is a woman. This supports my thesis that women continue to occupy subordinate roles within public sphere institutions, in spite of apparent gains.

3.2   Breaking through the glass ceiling: the Thatcher legacy

No discussion of the progress made by women in British parliamentary history would, of course, be complete without a consideration of the role played by Margaret Thatcher, whose long period in office as Britain's only female prime minister lasted from 1979 to 1992. The focus in this section will be on the way her performance of this role has affected women who have since pursued parliamentary careers. As noted earlier, while in Government, her record of promoting other women to positions of authority was extremely poor. She only ever included one other woman in her Cabinet, Baroness Young, briefly present as Leader of the House. In this way, she constructed an identity for herself as an *exceptional* woman, who owed her success to her difference from other women. Indeed, as Wendy Webster (1990) argues persuasively, her period in power was a reaction against feminist gains of the 1960s and 1970s and a reassertion of a regressive social morality about the proper division of labour within the family.

A key factor, of course, is that Margaret Thatcher was a woman, but not a feminist. Yet contrary to the widespread description of her as 'the best man in the Cabinet', she did not embrace exclusively androcentric discursive norms. Instead, as Fairclough (1989: 182ff) points out, she combined carefully selected features associated with white middle-class femininity and 'authoritative expressive elements' used by male politicians. This hybrid rhetorical style, which involves strategies of accommodation *and* a performative approach to gender, nonetheless made her assimilable to the dominant discourse that prevailed in parliamentary institutions, 'Paradoxically, then, what looks like a gain for women is a defeat for feminism' (Fairclough 1989: 195).

Lovenduski and Randall (1993: 53) suggest that, at the very least, Thatcher achieved a symbolic victory for women, making it easier for them to attain positions of authority within parliamentary institutions:

> Surely, the very fact of her occupation of the supreme political office and the confidence and authority with which she carried out its duties, had some effect. She must have made it seem more possible for women to be powerful, to succeed in a 'man's world'.

On the contrary, I would argue that the fact that Thatcher presented the only real role model for women who subsequently aspired to high political office in Britain has had a detrimental effect on feminist-identified women who have sought to promote an alternative way of doing politics. That this view is shared by some women politicians is evident in the comment made by Labour's Helen Liddell: 'every woman in politics has to live down the record of Mrs Thatcher' (the *Guardian* 5 June 1997). This is partly because her idiosyncratic discursive style has since become a normative touchstone against which the leadership styles of other women have been judged. Textual traces of this practice abound, especially in the media where references to her are endlessly recycled.

A striking instance of this tendency occurred when Margaret Beckett ran for the Labour leadership in 1994. Media commentators discussed Beckett's campaign using language which had unmistakable echoes of Thatcher's dogmatic and intransigent rhetorical style. Thus one interview with Beckett in the *Guardian* (18 June 1994) carried the headline, 'The lady's not for losing'. Comparisons made by others extended also to include alleged similarities in their appearance and manner, as is evident in the comment made by Sally Weale in a profile of Beckett in the *Guardian* (2 July 1994),

> political observers have detected a growing resemblance to that other Margaret. The troublesome spray-held hair seems to have an extra Thatcher-style lift, her deportment has become more regal, her manner in the Commons more icily confrontational.

These similarities were underlined in the *Daily Mail* (1 July 1994) via juxtaposed photographs. Reductive comparisons such as these obscure the very real differences in the personalities, style and, of course, politics of the two women and were therefore damaging to Beckett's campaign. This is certainly Beckett's own perception of the Thatcher legacy: 'I thought at the time that it might have been *something* of a help [but] I came more and more to the view that it was a liability' (Trans. I: 56–60).

3.3   Masculinism in the institutional discourse of the Parliamentary Labour Party

Although the Conservative Party has, on average, had fewer women MPs than Labour, prior to the last general election it was perceived as more woman-friendly, partly because of the Thatcher legacy, and partly because of a long-standing tradition of female activism at grassroots level in the Party (Short 1996: 26). This contrasts with the picture presented by Cockburn (1987: 25) of the male-dominated political culture in the Labour movement, 'that brings together the umbrella of masculine identity, of male fraternity: work, working-class allegiance, trade union membership and Labour Party affiliation'. This ideological package, she argues, creates an impression of a masculine power structure in the PLP. Likewise, Perrigo (1996: 121) refers to the bureaucratic and rule-bound discursive practices that prevailed in local Labour Party branches and constituencies and that are likely to have discouraged women from participating at grassroots level. Lovenduski and Randall (1993: 142) suggest that women who overcome these initial barriers to entry are often prevented from progressing further:

> . . . incumbency and patronage continue to be important barriers to women who seek entry to established committees . . . Many of the powerful party positions are occupied by male incumbents who are skilful at choosing their (usually male) successors. The result is that the progress of women into prized political positions is slow.

Although, as will be clear from the section below, much has changed in the Party, largely as a result of feminist challenges, there is still a perception that a masculinist culture persists.

3.4   Feminist challenges to masculinism in the Parliamentary Labour Party

It is important to stress that power struggles occur over the determination of discursive practices and that historical transformations in discourse practices are an important element in social change. Such a struggle has been taking place in the PLP since the late 1970s, when the Party's move to the left made it attractive to a number of socialist feminists who had previously been suspicious of the mainstream political process. In the early to mid-1980s the Women's Action Committee was established and made radical demands, but networking with other grassroots feminist groups led to hostile media coverage. Media-generated epithets for female Labour MPs included 'crazy Clare' for Clare Short, 'hard left harpy' for Margaret Beckett and 'harridan Harman' for Harriet Harman, thereby exploiting stereotypical assumptions about women as shrewish and/or out of control. Curran (1987: 1) notes that the collective dysphemism, 'loony left', meant that equal opportunity initiatives could be dismissed out-of-hand by opponents in a way that anticipates the current deployment of the all-purpose dysphemism of 'political correctness'. As a result, the response to feminist initiatives from an increasingly media-sensitive leadership throughout most of the 1980s was one of 'containment' (Perrigo 1996: 125–7).

The main goal of feminist activists was to challenge the discursive practices that deny women *access* to participation in the PLP. The campaign to secure quotas for women illustrates clearly the operation of a dialectic between institutional structures and feminist agency. The election defeats of 1987 and 1992 led to a crisis in the party which, in turn, offered a space for feminist intervention. The rhetorical strategy employed by socialist feminists like Clare Short, Jo Richardson and Harriet Harman, was to persuade their colleagues to recognize an ideologically creative synonymy between feminizing and modernizing the party's structures and policy. Thus, according to Perrigo (1996: 119), 'They have been able to use the modernization process, and the impetus it has generated for internal party change, to press their own agenda'. Following the example offered by the US Democratic Party, 'Emily's list' was established by the then Labour Party Public Relations Officer, Barbara Follett, in 1992. Standing for 'early money is like yeast', it was set up to provide financial support and training for prospective female parliamentary candidates, but with the proviso that only those who were pro-abortion should be so supported. It was not until 1993 that feminist activists persuaded the party to accept the controversial policy of quotas for selecting parliamentary candidates.

Inevitably, these changes have been contested both within the party, notably by the elder statesmen Neil Kinnock and Roy Hattersley, and in a sustained and vitriolic campaign in the media. A comment in the *Daily Mail* (27 July 1995) captures the tenor of this coverage, in which charges of 'political correctness' and 'tokenism' are rife and in which the term 'feminist' collocates antonymically with 'moderate'. It describes the lists as part of a 'politically correct system aimed at increasing the number of women MPs by barring men from standing in key constituencies' (ibid.). These recent and temporary overt barriers to the entry into politics of male candidates have provoked outrage, while the covert barriers which have excluded female candidates from entering the party political arena for decades have gone without comment.

Whereas tabloid coverage framed the issue by drawing on the 'battle of the sexes' news frame, the broadsheet press foregrounded differences *between* women along the axes of class and gender politics, caricaturing those who subscribed to Emily's list as metropolitan middle-class 'power feminists'. Thus one of its founders was described by a woman columnist as 'Barbara "Lipstick is Power" Follett' (the *Guardian* 29 July 1995). This type of negative media coverage is likely to have played a key role in the decision announced by the leadership in July 1995 to abandon the quotas policy after the 1997 general election.

However, for quite different reasons, the quotas policy is not without its critics among feminists. Some, like Perrigo (1996), have expressed their concern that National Executive Committee approval of the policy was 'as much to do with the instrumental rationality of the party leaders once they were convinced that increasing women's visibility would further Labour's electoral fortunes' (ibid.: 129). Nonetheless, by the time Margaret Beckett stood for the leadership of the PLP in June 1994, the structure of opportunity was particularly favourable to the promotion of women to senior positions within the party. However, whereas feminist efforts have concentrated on securing access for women, my research suggests a need for these struggles to be extended to include the crucial areas of intersection and tension between the orders of discourse of professional politics and the media.

3.5   Masculinism in mediatized political discourse

In the realm of party political discourse, the media play a central and increasingly important metadiscursive role in mediating *between* politicians and the public, yet the institutional discourses of the media are strongly masculinist. Sorlin (1994: 129) points out,

> Two thirds of the people who work in media management are men. Among the women employees, four fifths are restricted to subordinate tasks with slim promotion prospects which implies that the most profitable jobs, editorship, journalism, reportage are heavily male-dominated.

Hard news coverage, including that of political affairs, seems to be particularly subject to a male monopoly. By contrast, 'women tend to work in areas of journalism that can be considered an extension of their domestic responsibilities and their socially assigned qualities of care, nurturing and humanity' (van Zoonen 1998: 34). It is not surprising, then, that where women are employed in non-traditional areas, they tend to embrace masculinist news values and language (Macdonald 1995: 49). Margaret Beckett claims that, during her campaign for the Labour leadership, 'some of the most unpleasant and bitchy things that were written about me were written by women – mostly by women I had never met by the way' (Trans. I: 139–40). One does not have to be male to be a member of the fraternity of media workers, any more than one has to be male to be a member of the masculinist fraternity of professional politicians, as Thatcher made clear.

In his book, *Media Discourse*, Fairclough (1995a: 200) acknowledges the role of 'apparatuses which political parties have developed to train their members in using the media', but somewhat surprisingly fails to highlight the independent role of party spin doctors who seek to manipulate the mediatization of the public discourse of party politics. In an article in the *Guardian* (29 July 1995) analysing the appeal and influence with journalists of the PLP's then chief spin doctor, Peter Mandelson, Martin Wainwright points out that, 'he is almost one of us; indeed, he *was* one of us in a successful TV interlude to an otherwise relentlessly political career'. The 'us' referred to here is of course the fraternity of media men.

Alistair Campbell's defection from his job as political columnist on *Today* newspaper to take up the role of Blair's press secretary provides further evidence of the growing perception of the need to utilize 'insiders' to manage the media's reporting of political events. The Lobby system, with its rule enforcing non-attribution of news sources, is the chief mechanism by which this is achieved. Sedgemore (1995: 78) alludes to 'the rituals of secrecy and freemasonry' which govern its activities. This cross-fertilization between the media fraternity and the fraternity of professional politicians underlines the inherently masculinist nature of mediatized political discourse. It is not surprising, then, that Lobby briefings appear to have been used to damage the standing of a number of female politicians, including Clare Short (*Independent on Sunday* 31 August 1997) and, more recently, Mo Mowlam (the *Guardian* 7 January 2000).

Fairclough (1995a), among others, has noted that mediatized political discourse is undergoing a process of increasing commodification. A central thesis of this chapter is that the colonization of political discourse by the discourse of advertising has had a particularly adverse effect on *female* politicians. As Norris and Lovenduski (1995: 87) note, 'the typical candidate in all parties tends to be a well-educated, professional, white male in early middle age'. Given that she fails to match the stereotypical image of a senior politician, a female who aspires to high political office is more difficult to *sell* to the party as a credible product. Likewise, due to the apparent shift in power from producers to consumers, news media are in the competitive business of recruiting readers in a market context in which their sales or ratings are decisive for their survival. Consequently, 'producers . . . market their commodities in ways that maximize their fit with life styles and aspired to life styles of consumers' (Fairclough 1992: 110). They cultivate characteristics which are taken to be typical, in common-sense, usually stereotypical, terms, of the target audience. In this context it was perhaps inevitable that, in the 1994 Labour leadership campaign, the two male candidates in the leadership race, Tony Blair and John Prescott, would receive more favourable coverage than the one female candidate, since media producers generally address an ideal reader who is gendered as male. This is evident from the fact that both broadsheets and tabloids have female ghettos, for instance, 'The Women's Page' in the *Guardian*, the 'Femail' section in the *Daily Mail*, and those euphemized as 'lifestyle' sections, which personalize 'issues', apparently to make them more palatable to female readers.

Equally easy to sell is the male MP and his wife, of either the 'homely supporting' variety, or the 'glamorous trophy' variety, who together represent a promotional package. In the case of Margaret Beckett, a mismatch arises between this image and the reality of her career as an experienced female politician with a supporting husband. Karen Ross (1995a: 502) identifies this mismatch as part of a more general positive–negative framing of

Beckett and Blair during the leadership campaign: 'Where Blair was a youthful 40-something, Beckett was post-menopausal; . . . where Blair was happily married to the daughter of an actor, Beckett had stolen another woman's husband.' The latter comment refers to a sensational article about Beckett which appeared in the *Daily Express* on 24 June 1994 under the headline, 'I lost my husband to Margaret Beckett'. Beckett implies that this information may have been deliberately leaked to the press at this time to deflect attention away from her high-profile involvement in an international conference in Corfu (Trans. I: 227).

One feature of the so-called feminization of media discourse, noted by van Zoonen (1998), has been a tendency to focus on this type of salacious human interest angle. Again, this is likely to have different consequences for men and women, since as Macdonald (1995: 50) points out, double standards about sexual morality in the private sphere operate equally in the public sphere reproducing 'the dishonest cliché that male adulterers are "virile", while female ones are "sluts" and "whores"'. I would argue that this is symptomatic of a general tendency for women's involvement in the public sphere to be pulled back into the orbit of the private sphere, thereby undermining women's claims to be regarded as serious political actors.

Just as the visual image has become increasingly potent in advertising, so, following the American example, the image of candidates in a political leadership race has become a key factor by which media commentators gauge their electability. For a number of reasons, the media obsession with image is likely to have a disproportionate effect on evaluation of female politicians. Firstly, as Wendy Webster observes in her study of Thatcher, *Not a Man to Match Her* (1990: 75), women tend to be judged more on their physical appearance than men. She notes that: 'Surface appearance has always been more important for women than for men . . . Glamour is a notion which applies almost exclusively to women and is usually to do with the production of a particular surface – youthful, made-up and beautiful'. This view is borne out by a survey of twenty-eight female politicians which revealed that they believe their outward appearance attracts more media comment than that of their male colleagues (Ross 1995b: 16). Another key factor is that noted by King (1992: 133): 'Most images are made by men for men, creating a closed, collusive relationship between makers and prime consumers.' With the exception of Lynn Cullen at the *Independent*, all other Fleet Street picture editors are men, so it is not surprising that a four-week survey of nine national newspapers revealed that women were grossly under-represented (the *Guardian* 29 November 1999). Only 30 per cent of all photographs featured women, either on their own, or accompanied by men. Where women did appear, they were more likely to feature as celebrities or members of the public (42 per cent) than as professionals (25 per cent) or politicians (14 per cent).[2] Image making and consuming can therefore be seen as one more manifestation of fraternal networks.

Unlike Thatcher, Beckett has refused to be 'made-over' by party image-makers. That her appearance was self-evidently judged to have hindered her bid for the Labour leadership in 1994 is clear from a comment made by Edwina Currie in *Cosmopolitan*: 'Looks are important in politics – ask Margaret Beckett' (June 1995). Beckett's own frequent allusions to her untelegenic appearance throughout the campaign provide evidence of the additional surveillance-by-self which seems to be more characteristic of women in public life than of men. It is interesting to draw a comparison with the references made to the untelegenic appearance of the potential male candidate, Robin Cook. What is noticeable is that these references were offset by an emphasis on his sense of humour in a way that references to Beckett's appearance were not. Beckett claims that the widespread perception that she is humour*less* stems from her refusal to fraternize with the media, with the result that, when she makes witty remarks, they tend to be written up as 'waspish' (Trans. I: 143–6). In the case of Cook, a potential electoral disadvantage became transformed, in numerous articles, into a basis for arch collusion between male journalists and a popular male MP. As Mills (1995: 139) observes, among males, 'humour has often been portrayed as a form of bonding and solidarity display'.

In an effort to promote a newsworthy angle during the Labour leadership campaign in 1994, the media tended to focus on Beckett's gender as her most distinctive feature, ignoring her attempt to construct herself first and foremost as an experienced politician, and only secondarily as a female politician. A comment by Dave Hill in the *Guardian* (17 May 1994) is particularly telling in this respect: 'As for Margaret Beckett, the acting leader, nobody seems to be sure which set of brackets she should be slotted into except that of "woman", which at least makes her distinctive.' This reveals the difficulty that political commentators had constructing an identity for her as a political leader, in spite of the precedent established by Thatcher. The common-sense solution was to categorize her by appealing to the totalizing fiction of 'woman'. Postfeminist claims that gender is irrelevant, and poststructuralist claims that it is only one of the many and complex axes of identity, are in danger of underestimating the extent to which it continues to circulate as a salient discursive category, however much one might wish it to be otherwise.

3.6   Gender and rhetorical style

As noted above, the hybrid rhetorical style developed by Thatcher did little to challenge the adversarial discursive norms associated with political leadership. In contrast to Thatcher's imperious demeanour, the journalist, Jan Moir, reveals that on an interpersonal level Beckett immediately minimizes the status distinctions between herself and an interviewer: 'She will always insist, during the first moments of introduction, that you call her by her first name' (the *Guardian* 4 November 1992). In an interview in *The Times* (21 June 1994), she also stressed her commitment to a consensual style of politics, repeating the phrase 'coalition of support' three times, as something a politician should build on (see Fig. 3.2, ll. 47, 51 and 52–3). Whereas Thatcher was notorious for her ruthless treatment of political enemies, in the same interview Beckett deliberately eschews competitive discursive strategies, saying, 'No, I am not fighting against others. I am talking about my strengths'. She claims this was both a personal and political stance:

> in a sense if you like you could say I deliberately chose to emphasize the powers of others at my own expense at no point did I seek to say *only* I can do this I said there are eight~ten more who could do this job among whom I hope I am one I believe I am one . . . so in that sense it was a *very very* conscious decision to be consensual I hope I would have done it anyway because that is part of the way I approach things

(Trans. I: 131–6)

Indeed, throughout the campaign she scrupulously avoided any sort of personal attack on her opponents. Yet, evidence suggests that the consensual style pursued by Beckett was misunderstood and/or deliberately misrepresented by political commentators. For instance, her move from the far left to the centre right of the political spectrum paralleled the recent history of the Labour Party, as did her change of heart on Europe, but this was presented as opportunism, rather than as the outcome of her consensual approach to politics. Thanks to the Thatcher legacy, the less confrontational style favoured by many women politicians, such as Beckett, is likely to be judged as deviant and ineffective.

3.7   Encountering the glass ceiling: a case study of Margaret Beckett's bid for the Labour leadership in 1994

3.7.1   Critical analysis of media strategies during the campaign

I intend to demonstrate, with particular reference to the coverage of Margaret Beckett's campaign for the Labour leadership in the summer of 1994, the ways in which the institutional orders of masculinist political discourse and the equally masculinist discourse of the print media operate through fraternal networks to segregate and subordinate women once they have entered the arena of party politics. It needs to be acknowledged that it is not always easy to isolate the influence of gender as a separate variable on press coverage. It could be argued that the evident bias against Beckett in the majority of newspapers had more to do with hostility towards her political ideas or personality, than towards her as a female politician per se. However, the inability of leadership candidates to change established policy meant that there was little to choose between the candidates in terms of their politics. This leaves the question of personality. I would argue that the so-called personal attacks against Beckett in the press often disguised attitudes which were either explicitly or implicitly sexist. In what follows, I consider a number of key issues: the extent of media coverage which her campaign received; her treatment relative to the other candidates; overtly sexist coverage and coverage which betrayed implicitly sexist attitudes.

3.7.2   Discourse representation and gender bias

Fairclough (1995b: 54) distinguishes 'primary discourse', the representing or reporting discourse, and 'secondary discourse', the discourse represented or reported. In some styles of discourse representation there is an explicit boundary between the voice of the person being reported and the voice of the reporter(s), while in others they become merged, creating what Bakhtin terms 'double voiced' discourse. In an editorial in the *Daily Mirror* (11 June 1994), involving the common format of juxtaposed profiles of the three candidates, Beckett, Blair and Prescott, it is noticeable that the voice of the media commentators often becomes merged with the voice of the two male candidates (Fig. 3.1).[3] For instance, the profile of John Prescott blends primary and secondary discourse seamlessly, both reproducing and positively evaluating his campaign pledges. Thus we are told that: 'He was *bold enough* to put a figure on full employment . . . But *cautious enough* to stress it might take a decade' (ll. 3–5; my italics). The entire profile is dialogic in that it systematically addresses and answers criticisms made in other media, particularly the right-wing press, about his candidacy. The claim that 'Only a fool would under-rate his intellect' (l. 20) is intended to counter the widespread charge that he is an intellectual lightweight. By contrast, the praise for the fraternal *loyalty* he showed to John Smith during the One Member One Vote (OMOV) debate in 1993 (ll. 32–4) implicitly sanctions the criticism of Beckett, made in many sections of the media, for her alleged *disloyalty*, a breach of the implicit fraternal contract. The fact that at the time his 'loyalty' had been widely regarded as a betrayal of his trade union roots is suppressed, as is the fact that Beckett had been praised by the unions for her integrity. This piece of information would have conflicted with their construction of Prescott as a working-class candidate whose credentials are calculated to appeal to its assumed working-class *male* readership, in a way that frequent references to Beckett's gender are not.

Elsewhere, the assumption of a commonality of values between media men and male readers is implicit in the slippages which occur between the

TOP JOB FOR THE WINNER

JOHN PRESCOTT is presenting himself as the man to put Britain back to work.

He was bold enough to put a figure on full employment – no more than 2.5 per cent jobless. But cautious enough to stress it might take a decade.

There you have John Prescott – a brave politician tackling difficult issues head on, but careful too. He knows that Labour needs to think big, but be sensible.

By the Prescott definition, full employment means cutting the dole queues by around two million. How? That question is likely to dominate the campaign.

He said yesterday: 'The themes that will form the core of my leadership bid build on the policy initiatives John Smith had already set in train: Full employment and social justice. These are the central elements of a modern civilised society.'

Nobody should doubt Prescott's ability to answer the full employment question. 'I believe I can combine the conviction of the heart with the intellectual authority necessary to bring Labour to power', he said.

Only a fool would under-rate his intellect. He proved himself an original thinker with his plans for private finance to fund public sector projects.

He called that 'putting traditional values in a modern setting' – which sounds like a campaign catchphrase, crossing the phoney divide between traditionalists and modernisers.

John Prescott has come a long way from his beginnings as a railway worker's son who failed his 11-plus and left school at 15 to go to sea.

There would be no doubt about Premier Prescott's socialist direction. He didn't flinch from confirming his belief in progressive taxation.

Nor is there any doubt about the support and affection for John Prescott – asserts he drew on in helping John Smith deliver one-member-one-vote.

He, more than anyone, deserves the chance to test the new democracy.

'I can do this job', said Margaret Beckett, and I can do it well!. We know she can because she has led the Labour Party with dignity and distinction since John Smith died. Now she asks for the chance to do it for good – all the way to Number 10.

She said she is offering herself 'for nomination to continue to lead the Labour Party'. And she stressed the 'breadth and depth' of her experience – both in the party and in the last Labour government.

Margaret Beckett is not only the one woman in the contest – she is the only contender with government experience. She was junior Education Minister in the 1970s.

'I ask my colleagues to judge me on my ability to manage and unify our party and to communicate its ideals to the British public', she said.

Mrs Beckett is appealing to the party as its elder statesman – or woman. And she deftly recalled that there had already been a woman Leader of the Opposition, who had overcome the difficulties of 'the worst job in politics' – Margaret Thatcher.

Mrs Beckett is now the foremost woman in British politics, but she is no more a token woman than Lady Thatcher. She said she had been under great pressure to stand from women 'whose votes Labour needs to win'.

She underlined her belief in Labour as 'a broad church'; as befits a former Campaign Group member who went on to serve John Smith as a parsimonious treasury spokeswoman refusing to make spending pledges.

And she emphasised the experience gained in holding her marginal seat, Derby South, by gathering broad support – the same process Labour needs to undertake throughout the country.

TONY BLAIR has established himself by destroying the Tories as the party of Law and Order.

He has done this by presenting Labour as the party of strong community values, saying this is the modern version of traditional socialism.

He will broaden this theme to cover the full range of policy as a leadership candidate – social action providing the framework for individual fulfilment.

He is a strong believer in personal responsibility – but also in the Government's obligation to all the people. While never condoning the criminal, he takes the commonsense view that crime is more tempting to youngsters brought up amid fractured families amid high unemployment.

He believes that social division and family breakdown go hand in hand with poverty and crime. That, he says, is damaging Labour supporters in poorer areas – but also threatening to the whole community's sense of security.

Mr Blair's opening campaign speech today will say: 'I want to lead a Labour Party that is driven by change, radical in intent, underpinned by conviction, confident of its beliefs and strong enough to win the battle of ideas and sweep the Conservatives away – not just for a parliament, but for a generation'.

A close ally of Gordon Brown, he will base his economics on the policies of the Shadow Chancellor, arguing that Labour must not give the impression of promising what it can neither deliver or afford.

Labour, he feels, must offer an alternative to uncaring Conservatism as a route to economic success. Better education and training will be among his key themes – not just to create prosperity, but to give hope to those with no stake in society.

He will commit himself to full employment and the minimum wage, which he defended at the last election as Labour's employment spokesman.

Fig. 3.1 Part of the text of an article in the *Daily Mirror* (11 June 1994) comprising juxtaposed profiles of the three candidates in the 1994 Labour leadership campaign.

corporate and inclusive functions of the pronoun 'we' in media reports of the OMOV debate. For instance, an editorial in the *Sunday Mirror* (10 July 1994) seeks to implicate its readers in its condemnation of Beckett's alleged disloyalty: 'we cannot forget Mrs Beckett's failure to support Mr Smith's vital one-member-one-vote party reforms last year'. It is significant that this 'failure' is not qualified by 'alleged', despite Beckett's repeated claim that this was a misrepresentation of the facts. In an interview in the *Guardian* she is quoted as saying, 'I was very surprised in the press that I was portrayed as being disloyal. But in fairness to the press, it did become my impression that there were *people in the Labour Party* who were of that view, and who were *feeding that view*' (22 June 1994; my italics). The charge of disloyalty which was fed to the press by party spin doctors was followed by what can only be described as the 'smear' that Mrs Beckett had known that John Smith would have resigned had he lost on the OMOV vote. Fairclough (1992: 161) says of media producers:

> They systematically transform into 'facts' what can often be no more than interpretations of complex and confusing sets of events. In terms of modality this involves a predilection for categorical modalities, positive and negative assertions . . . Presupposition [is] taking categorical modality one stage further, taking factuality for granted.

Beckett's denial of any knowledge of what was a piece of unattributed information could only be read as either a lie, or as evidence of extreme political naiveté.

The profile of Blair in the *Daily Mirror* (11 June 1994) involves a similar merging of the voice of the producers with that of the candidate himself (Fig. 3.1). There is only one instance of secondary discourse in the entire piece (ll. 85–89), but Blair's views are both incorporated and favourably evaluated throughout in the primary discourse. The producers not only review his past commitment to 'strong community values' and a 'modern version of traditional socialism', but anticipate the future direction of his campaign. Thus we are told that, 'He will broaden this theme to cover the full range of policy as a leadership candidate – social action providing the framework for individual fulfilment' (ll. 73–5). The latter is recognizable as a campaign catchphrase, but the absence of quotation marks makes it clear that it is one with which the producers align themselves. The categorical modality used here occurs elsewhere, making it clear that the producers predict that Blair *will* become leader unopposed. Their positive evaluation of his policy statements is implicit on a number of occasions. He is said to be 'a *strong* believer in personal responsibility' (l. 76), while his position on crime is described as 'the common-sense view' (l. 78), indicating that it accords with the producers' own ideological position. In an obvious bid to win over potentially resistant *Mirror* readers, statements that identify him as a modernizer are carefully balanced by those that connect him to more traditional Labour values (ll. 74–80). Likewise, his 'new' Labour emphasis on education and training, as opposed to employment, is justified in 'old' Labour terms as giving 'hope to those with no stake in society' (l. 97).

Numerous studies of media discourse have highlighted the role played by reporting verbs in providing an interpretative frame for secondary discourse. Interestingly, the accompanying profile of Beckett (Fig. 3.1) has none of the illocutionary glossing verbs referred to by Caldas-Coulthard (1995: 233), and defined as verbs 'that convey the presence of the author in the text, and are highly interpretative'. Instead, the most frequently occurring reporting verb is the so-called 'neutral' glossing verb 'say'. Unlike the other two profiles, the profile of Beckett consists of a series of instances of secondary discourse, embedded in only occasional passages of primary discourse. There is no blending of the two. Thus we have the chaining of, 'She said . . . she stressed . . . she said . . . she said . . . She underlined her belief . . . she emphasized' (Fig. 3.1). Although none of these statements is evaluated, either positively or negatively, *cumulatively* they have the effect of conveying the editorial team's ideological distance from the case Beckett is making. Unlike her male colleagues, she is forced to plead her own case, with no help or hindrance from the editorial team. This underlines the need to focus on global discoursal effects, rather than on isolated linguistic items. As is clear in this instance, allowing a reported individual to speak in her or his own voice, with only minimal evaluative framing, can serve to call into question the legitimacy of what is said. In other words, the structured absence of such framing can be more ideologically loaded than framing which is either overtly positive or negative. This alerts us to the need for a more co(n)text-sensitive model to account for the ideological function of discourse representation.

A segregationist strategy is evident in the foregrounding of the fact that Beckett is the only woman in the race, relative to the information about her experience in government. The problem the editorial team have in accommodating her within the terms in which they usually discuss politics is evident in the description of her as the party's 'elder statesman – or woman' (ll. 51–2). The use of the dash here, setting the phrase 'or woman' apart syntactically from the 'normal' collocation, makes it seem like an awkward afterthought and emphasizes the oddness of her candidacy. Again, the description of her as the 'foremost woman in British politics' (l. 55) ignores her efforts to promote herself in terms of a broader agenda. Likewise, although the primary discourse apparently deflects the view of potential critics that she is 'a token woman', this is undercut by the subsequent narrow focus on the issue of gender, both in terms of her motivation for standing, or 'being stood' (l. 57), as a candidate, and in terms of her appeal to women voters. An editorial in the *Daily Mirror's* sister paper, the *Sunday Mirror* (10 July 1994) is less covert, stating that 'The argument that Mrs Beckett should be the deputy because she is a women (sic) is mere tokenism'. 'The argument' remains unattributed, but by reproducing it the editorial team afford themselves an opportunity to imply that Mrs Beckett has no other claims to aspire to a senior position in the party, thereby furthering their own agenda of promoting Prescott as the most suitable candidate for the deputy's post. In the *Daily Mirror* editorial, the producers' ideological distance from Mrs Beckett's candidacy is less explicit. It is nonetheless evident in the use of the dysphemism 'parsimonious' (l. 61) to describe her cautious performance as treasury spokeswoman, and by the fact that there is only one instance in the entire profile where their editorial voice merges with hers. Finally, in a Labour paper, such as the *Mirror*, the comparisons between Beckett and Thatcher (ll. 51–4) are more likely to have damaged her candidacy than to have aided it.

Beckett's identity was constructed as 'other', not only in terms of her gender, but also in terms of generation, in relation to Blair, and class, in relation to Prescott. Although Prescott is five years older than Beckett, his age was rarely alluded to by journalists, while the fact that Beckett was 51 at the time of the campaign was gratuitously foregrounded, as if to underline the point that she was literally and metaphorically 'old Labour'. This unequal treatment is evident also in relation to the axis of class. For instance, it was alleged that in private Prescott referred scathingly to Beckett as 'the duchess' (*The Times* 3 July 1994). This social class 'slur' was reproduced in numerous articles and no doubt helps to explain why, 'Labour men still regard her as un-forgivably horsey' (*The Sunday Times* 22 May 1994). According to Beckett, 'not only was it [the epithet "duchess"] not meant to be a compliment but it was meant to be damaging . . . [it] was meant to get to the Party members not to the public' (Trans. I: 61–3). Significantly, while Beckett's relatively middle-class background attracted negative coverage, Blair's appears to have been viewed as an electoral asset.

A detailed critical analysis of the relative treatment of the candidates in the *Daily Mirror*, here and in the subsequent more extended interviews with them on 22, 23 and 24 June 1994 respectively, is at odds with the claim expressed in the editorial on 7 July, 'We alone among the media have reported this contest without the slightest favour to any candidate'. Whether consciously or not, the all-male editorial team aligned themselves, and invited their assumed male readers to align themselves, with the two male candidates in the leadership race, segregating and subordinating Beckett as a candidate promoting herself on a narrowly gendered platform.

3.7.3   Gender and the genre of the political interview

Negrine (1989: 191) points out an inherent conflict which exists between what politicians expect of the media and the way in which media workers perceive their role: 'politicians seek, in the main, favourable publicity', while media workers 'seek to hold politicians to account'. This tension is likely to be exacerbated when male journalists have to accommodate a woman in the relatively unusual position of political power. This is evident in a number of articles written during the 1994 Labour leadership election campaign which record interviews between Beckett and journalists. Typical of many such articles is the one in *The Times* (21 June 1994), recording an interview she had with the political correspondents, Peter Riddell and Philip Webster (Fig. 3.2). I chose this article because Karen Ross (1995a: 505) regards it as one of the 'most balanced representation(s) of Beckett's views of herself and her potential to lead the party'. In particular, she points out that the article acknowledges the way party and media sexism have served to marginalize Beckett throughout the course of the campaign.

A detailed critical analysis of the article reveals an alternative reading. For instance, it is clear that Beckett wishes to emphasize her record as an experienced politician, while Riddell and Webster choose to foreground the issue of her gender, partly through their choice of metaphors (see below for a detailed discussion of these). Furthermore, a number of textual traces reveal the way in which the two journalists actively construct a subject position for her, which they claim is prevalent among parliamentary colleagues and media commentators, as merely 'competent' (l. 4). This view is reinforced by their selective depiction of the roles she has performed as bureaucratic gatekeeping ones, for example, as 'keeper of the keys' or as deputy leader 'in charge of organization' and 'coordinator of its campaigning and elections'. Her considerable political experience and expertise could have been presented in a very different light, especially given the relative inexperience of her two rivals. Instead, we are told that, 'She has suffered from being seen as an apparatchik, a manager rather than a visionary, going back to her days as a party researcher' (ll. 33–5). The use of the agentless passive here, together with the choice of the verb 'to suffer', not only serve to disguise agency, but cast her stereotypically as acted upon. That this is, in fact, the producers' own view is evident in the earlier overwording of phrases such as 'safe and competent' (l. 4) and 'highly competent' (ll. 12–13). In other words, Riddell and Webster are complicit in the very sexism they claim to be exposing.

Significantly, Beckett chooses to resignify the dysphemism 'apparatchik' as 'somebody who will do difficult jobs' (ll. 35–6). Ultimately, though, it is the producers who control the way the interview is slanted for readers. For instance, it is their prerogative to interpret the interviewee's paralanguage for readers. In this instance, Riddell and Webster attribute a range of *emotions* to Beckett, when her cool public face is said to slip (l. 8). For instance, they claim that it 'obviously hurts' (l. 2) and she was 'clearly upset' (l. 18) that she has not been taken seriously as a potential leader. They also attribute 'surprise' to Beckett that she should be seen as an apparatchik (l. 32), whereas she says 'that wouldn't surprise me in the slightest I mean erhm you know I'm very conscious of the fact that I have never been seen as a sort of visionary politician' (Trans. I: 10–12). Their assertion that she *is* surprised at

Is Margaret Beckett destined always to be the bridesmaid, ask Peter Riddell and Philip Webster

'One of my women colleagues said to me: They buried you with John'

Margaret Beckett has never been taken seriously as a possible leader of the Labour party, and it obviously hurts. Even though she has more experience than the other candidates, she has been seen as the safe and competent deputy, but never as a likely successor to John Smith. No other member of the shadow Cabinet even nominated her as leader.

During a lengthy interview in the shadow Cabinet room, the public face of the cool, composed politician at times slipped. She can be prickly and defensive, wondering whether there is a hidden point behind a straightforward question. She is like the eternal supporting actress who wants to be the leading lady, the best friend aspiring to be the heroine. For her it is not enough to be the highly competent party organiser, whether as Chief Secretary ('the keeper of the keys') before the election, or as deputy for the past two years, combining the roles as Mr Smith's frequent stand-in, shadow Leader of the Commons, in charge of reorganisation of party headquarters and co-ordinator of its campaigning and elections.

Mrs Beckett was clearly upset when, in the days after Mr Smith's death, she was virtually written out of the script. She was seen purely as the acting leader and never talked of as the next leader 'or at all', she intervened.

'One of my women colleagues said to me: "They buried you with John"'. There is no doubt that I disappeared from the frame as far as most media commentators were concerned. I cannot say I was over-surprised. I am standing because I am doing the job of leading the Labour Party, I believe I can continue to do it well'. Was she ignored because she was a woman? 'I think that is one of the reasons. It has been repeatedly said to me, so there must be something in it. A man in my circumstances would not have been assumed not to be a candidate for the leadership. It would probably have been the other way round'.

She has suffered from being seen as an apparatchik, a manager rather than a visionary, going back to her days as a party researcher. She seemed surprised at the suggestion: 'I suppose in a sense I have been seen for some time as somebody who will do

difficult jobs'. She and Mr Smith had agreed she would take on a higher public profile by going out and making more speeches. 'That was the next step'.

The only candidate to have experience in office, as a junior education minister, she draws lessons from the dark days of the last Labour Government, she would have done things differently. 'People who end up in senior posts tend to have long periods of unbroken service. The Labour Government of 1974–79 would not have taken some of the decisions it did take in the autumn of 1978 if it had had more people in the Cabinet who represented marginal rather than safe seats. In marginal seats you have to build a coalition of support and cannot take that support for granted.

'I have never had a safe seat. I stand or fall with the Labour Party. If the Labour Party wins, I win. If the Labour Party loses, I may well lose.

'That hones your political instincts. The coalition of support you have to win to hold a marginal seat is exactly the coalition of support Labour needs to win in the country'.

Mrs Beckett is determined not to be ignored. Sharp in the public debates, she has been the only one to disturb the bland surface of the campaign, and, incidentally, give ammunition to Tory researchers, by making controversial statements.

She will, however, advise her party against making specific and costed policy pledges so far away from the next election. 'We should resist the notion that we can't suggest anything unless it is in specific detail and costed down to the last tuppence. People in the Labour party are just as prone as anybody else to say "we can't say we want to improve the NHS unless we say precisely by how much". But you can't say exactly how much three years from an election.

'We thought if we had detailed policies, accurately costed and utterly defensible, that would answer the question of trust. But it didn't. They still didn't trust us. It was an emotional thing, it wasn't based on the figures.'

Referring, as she often did during the interview, to John Smith,

she said: 'That was John's great strength. John was a believable person, so when he was saying things that were maybe more specific, maybe less specific, he could carry trust with him. We've got to find a way of doing that.

'Most people most of the time are not particularly interested in the details. What they want to know: is there a different way of doing something? Is there a good chance that it will be better? And if there is a good chance that it will be better, can somebody deliver it?'

Throughout, Mrs Beckett portrayed herself as Mr Smith's heir. Despite her longstanding doubts about electoral reform, she promised to honour his pledge of a referendum.

Contentiously, she is opposed to making further changes in Labour's constitution, whether affecting the role of the trade unions or Clause Four on public ownership . . .

But surely it must have been disappointing, after all she had done, not to have received the backing of just one of her shadow Cabinet friends? 'You must ask my colleagues. It is open to each of us to make our choice as to who we think is best fitted to be leader. It may well be that when my colleagues made their choice they were being told that I was not running. But that is a matter for them'.

Was it a tactical mistake to go for both the leadership and the deputy leadership? Was she having second thoughts? Ever the professional, she was unrepentant. 'Not for a second. I have no doubt that I am capable of doing this job well and winning the election for Labour. I believe I am the best candidate fitted to do that and in those circumstances it would be wrong not to let my name go forward.

Fig. 3.2 Part of the text of a profile of Margaret Beckett by Peter Riddell and Philip Webster that appeared in *The Times* (21 June 1994).

this suggestion once again calls into question her political judgement and, more specifically, her ability to suppress her personal feelings in order to maintain a public image. Likewise, their perception that 'She can be prickly and defensive' (l. 9) is given the status of an objective 'fact', while their view of themselves as professionals, asking 'straightforward' questions (l. 10), casts her in the role of a paranoid politician. Even their praise for her is invariably double-edged. She is deemed to be stereotypically 'sharp' in public debates (ll. 54–5), while her courage in 'disturb[ing] the bland surface of the campaign' is said to have *inadvertently* given 'ammunition to Tory researchers' (ll. 56–7), again underlining their view that she lacks political judgement.

This analysis highlights the tensions and contradictions inherent in the genre of the political interview when the politician being interviewed is a woman. The account of the interview which appeared in the final article serves both to expose the overt gender bias of media coverage (ll. 22–6), while at the same time reproducing this gender bias in a covert form. This is achieved by the segregationist strategy of constructing a subject position for Beckett as someone whose main strength is her ability to occupy a practical supporting role *vis-à-vis* the activities of visionary men. The statement that 'For her it is not enough to be the highly competent party organiser' (ll. 12–13) implies that she ought to have been more realistic, as does their question as to whether she made a tactical mistake by putting herself forward for the leadership, rather than settling for the deputy's role (ll. 93–4). In the context of the article as a whole, Beckett's construction of herself as 'Mr Smith's heir' (ll. 80–1) therefore seems hopelessly naive. In this way, the article helps to contribute to the gendered division of labour within political parties, noted by Burstyn (1983: 73). The stereotypical assumptions underlying this division of political labour emerge more clearly if we place it in the context of the larger discursive framework or schema which operates across the boundaries of public sphere discourse types, casting women in subordinate support roles and men in powerful leadership roles.

Opposition to militarism and war has been an important strand in British feminism, but it introduces further dissonance into women's relationship to the role of an aspiring political leader. As Pateman (1989: 49) observes: 'Of all the male clubs and associations, it is in the military and on the battlefield that fraternity finds its most complete expression.' The military duty to defend one's country underlines the gender subtext of a politician's role. One of the objections raised to the nomination of Geraldine Ferraro for the vice-presidential role in the 1984 US presidential election was, according to Faludi (1992: 302), 'that her gender would render her incapable of defending the nation'. During the Falklands War, Thatcher had to search far back in history to find an appropriate image of a warrior woman in Boadicea. Rather than confronting the links between masculinity and war, Thatcher constructed an image of herself as a reluctant non-combatant (Webster 1990: 166).

It is in this broader context that we need to interpret Anthony Bevins's interview with Beckett during the Labour leadership campaign (the *Observer* 26 June 1994), an interview in which he deliberately chose to foreground her commitment to the Campaign for Nuclear Disarmament (CND) (Fig. 3.3). He presents his discussion with her on this subject as a sequence of questions and answers – a format which sets it apart graphically from the remainder of the article. Bell (1991: 210) cites a study by Clayman (1990) of stories drawn from the *Los Angeles Times*, which revealed that this format was used largely to signal interactional resistance, 'They show the news source as hesitating to reply, refusing to answer, giving non-answers, or admitting something under repeated questioning'. This is precisely the effect produced by the layout of this section of Bevins' interview with Beckett. It appears under the negative sub-headline, 'Never ask a CND member if she would use the bomb', alerting us to the fact that it is what Beckett refuses to say in her replies which is significant.

Bevins's contributions begin with a series of bald interrogatives, clearly designed to put Beckett on the defensive (ll. 7–8, 17–18, 32–4). Although, Beckett evades his attempts at framing the issue in a hypothetical way with 'what if?' questions, the precise detailing of her evasive replies has clearly served his purpose, which appears to have been to discredit her claim to represent a viable future prime minister. This is reinforced by Bevins's polemical comment that her position is 'preposterous' (l. 23). He then changes tack by making explicit for readers what he regards as the subtext of her refusal to answer, namely that she would not be prepared to use such weapons in any circumstances (ll. 36–40). The alleged reluctance of Beckett to countenance 'pushing the button' was recycled in a series of media accounts throughout the following week and is likely to have damaged her standing as a candidate among the modernizers in the electoral college. It is significant that this was an issue which featured only marginally in interviews with the other two candidates, despite the fact that Blair, in particular, had been a long-standing and active member of CND.

3.7.4   News narratives and gender bias

A number of media analysts have identified hard news as a subgenre of narrative discourse (see, for instance, Fairclough 1995b; Caldas-Coulthard 1995). Analysis has tended to focus almost exclusively on the narrative function, often central to hard news stories, of recounting past events. Even more ideologically implicated, however, are those hard news stories in which the narrative function of *predicting* future events is to the fore. Such predictive narratives do not structure events that have already occurred, but privilege a particular construction of events which have yet to take place. In this context, fact and forecast are apt to trade places. Although some analysts have called into question the media's influence on voting behaviour, I would

Never ask a CND member if she would use the bomb

As A member of the campaign for Nuclear
Disarmament, Mrs Beckett's views on
Britain's nuclear weaponry would be of
interest if she became Labour leader, and
5 then Prime Minister – with button-pushing
powers.
**Q: What would you want to do with our
nuclear weapons?**
A: I would want to see them, as I would
10 want to see all nuclear weapons across the
world, (as) part of a framework of
negotiations that mean, hopefully, perhaps
almost everywhere, nobody would have
nuclear weapons . . .
15 **Meanwhile, we have them.**
Meanwhile, we have them.
**And what are the circumstances in which
you could use them?**

(Pause) You know as well as I do that's not
20 a question you should ever put to a Prime
Minister or a potential Prime Minister.
**That's not a question I propose to answer.
That's preposterous.**
It's certainly not preposterous. It's like a
25 devaluation question.
**But you've got these monsters in the
cupboard.**
They go into negotiation. Other than that, I
ain't going to discuss it.
30 **There are circumstances . . .**
I'm not going to discuss it.
**Not even to say that there are
circumstances in which they could be
used?**
35 Not even.
Of course, if there are circumstances in

**which they would never be used, if there
are no circumstances in which they would
be used, there would be no point in**
40 **having them.**
You and I have known each other a long
time; don't waste your time piling hypothesis
upon hypothesis. If I say you're not going to
get an answer out of me, you're not going to
45 get an answer out of me.

Fig. 3.3 Text of part of an interview of Margaret Beckett by Anthony Bevins (*Observer*, 26 June 1994).

suggest that voter-impact analysis needs to be more context-aware. For in-stance, a particular configuration of circumstances in the 1994 Labour lead-ership election campaign created ideal conditions for the media to influence the outcome. Changes to the party's electoral college created a mass elector-ate and as Hugo Young, the *Guardian*'s chief political commentator, pointed out, 'With a mass electorate the media have much greater power to make their *story* come true than they would if the vote lay with the Parliamentary party' (19 May 1994; my italics). A second point is that the unexpectedness of John Smith's death on 12 May 1994 meant that opinions were not pre-formed, as they often are in intraparty campaigns which are foreseen. Fin-ally, the moratorium on official campaigning which prevailed between Smith's death and the European elections on 9 June created an ideal space for media speculation.

In the event, the story constructed in the media during the 1994 Labour leadership election campaign was a masculinist narrative in which the only female political actor, having initially been excluded completely, was admit-ted only as a minor character. The striking feature of the Blair bandwagon and the all-male 'dream ticket' of Blair and Prescott in the 1994 election campaign is the degree of homogeneity about them across newspapers of all shades of opinion. Five days after John Smith's death, seven national news-papers had declared their support for Blair, including the right-wing tabloids the *Sun*, *Daily Mail* and *Daily Express*, and broadsheets the *Daily Telegraph* and the *Sunday Times*. This homogeneity can be explained partly by the tendency noted by Fairclough (1995b: 198) for stories in the media to become recycled, forming intertextual chains. These intertextual networks, which operate across different media texts, make it very difficult for oppositional narratives to occupy a discursive space.

Sorlin (1994: 112) insists that coverage in the media is in itself an asset to politicians: 'if they are named, it means that they are important and deserve attention'. Conversely, in a leadership campaign, if they are not named, or are marginalized, their political ambitions are likely to be ignored or dismissed. As early as 19 May, Isabel Hinton noted that 'in the forest of comment, reporting and speculation on the forthcoming leadership contest that has filled the pages of the national press since the death of John Smith, the name of Margaret Beckett has hardly been mentioned . . . Mrs Beckett, in a remark-able piece of prestidigitation, has become invisible' (the *Independent* 19 May). The invisibility is particularly surprising given her high-profile role as acting leader and the media bias to office, noted by Seymore-Ure (1987: 14). The oddness of this situation was noted even in the right-wing press. Writing in *The Times* (21 June 1994), Riddell and Webster acknowledge that 'in the days after Mr Smith's death, she [Beckett] was virtually written out of the script'. Lakoff (1995: 29) argues that women's lack of interpretative control and, in particular, the fact that their narratives are evaluated by male author-ity, helps to explain their continued marginalization in public sphere roles. A revealing comment in this respect is that made by Hugo Young: 'With the help of Mr Paxman, each *man* will have been obliged to stake out the priorities *he* believes in' (17 May 1994; my italics).[4] This statement illustrates clearly the fraternal networks which exist between male politicians and male commentators in a variety of media, in this case the press and television. In it, one media man foregrounds the central role in the campaign of another well-known media man in literally *mediating* the political claims of implicitly *male* political contenders.

Female politicians are not only generally excluded from the masculinist narratives which pervade coverage of the public discourse of politics; if they do feature, they tend to be referred to in terms of metaphors which are drawn from low status narratives associated with girl or women readers. Riddell and Webster (*The Times* 21 June 1994) describe Beckett as 'the best friend aspiring to be the heroine' (see Fig. 3.2, line 11–12). This serves to belittle her political ambitions by linking them metaphorically to the prospects of a heroine in the genre of the girls' school story or popular romantic novel. A related discursive strategy is the tendency to refer to women who enter the public sphere in terms of metaphors drawn from the private sphere. The same article in *The Times* carried the substitute 'strapline', 'Is Margaret Beckett destined always to be the *bridesmaid*?' (Fig. 3.2). The reader is, of course, expected to supply 'and never the bride', thus being implicated in what is a trivializing metaphorical construction, given that it is used to assess the prospects of a woman aspiring to one of the highest political offices in the land.

Common collocations are less *fixed* than metaphors, yet these can also function to implicate the reader in sexism. For instance, an article in the *Sunday Mirror* (10 July 1994), carried the huge headline, in bold white-on-black, 'DESERTED', to describe the apparent defection of 'up to 12' MPs who had allegedly switched their support from Beckett to Prescott. The choice 'deserted' here invites the reader to see Beckett as a victim, by analogy with the common collocation 'a deserted wife'. In fact, the paper only names three MPs who are prepared to acknowledge this publicly, two of whom qualify their switch of allegiance. At this late stage in the campaign, when the defection of a few MPs could mean the difference between winning and losing, this is a blatant attempt by the producers to influence readers/voters to follow the paper's own stated policy of supporting Prescott for the deputy's role. It is likely, of course, that many female readers found themselves at odds with the often male-gendered reading positions established for them. Karen Ross (1995b: 507) argues that this is confirmed by the fact that, despite the media's limited and largely unfavourable coverage of her campaign, Beckett lost the deputy leadership by a narrow margin. Interestingly, her support among women MPs outnumbered Prescott's by two to one (Alderman and Carter 1995: 450).

During political campaigns, the media have a ready-made stock of masculinist military metaphors which mean that the terms of the debate are already adversarial. These were invoked by the columnist Andrew Rawnsley in his attempt to discredit claims of institutional sexism as feminist paranoia. In a characteristically glib article in the *Observer* (10 July 1994), he argues that 'There was no male conspiracy to deny the job to a woman', but the metaphors he chooses in which to frame the terms of political debate betray his own masculinist assumptions: 'I would be asking myself who I would prefer to go into the jungle with. Mr Prescott will get him [Mr Blair] into far more fights, but when the crocodiles close in, the leader could be reasonably confident that his deputy will be fighting on the same side'. The genre evoked here is the boys' adventure story. By choosing to draw his metaphors from this particular genre, Rawnsley inadvertently indicates the difficulty women experience in being taken seriously as political actors, since the inclusion of a woman in an active role would violate the norms of what Kosofsky Sedgwick (1985) terms the 'homosocial bonding' on which this genre, and by implication party politics, are premised.

When women in political life *are* referred to in terms of military metaphors, these often carry connotations of unfeminine aggressiveness which are readily caricatured, as is evident in Steve Bell's satirical cartoons of Thatcher. The caption for an inset photograph of Beckett, accompanying an interview with her in the *Daily Mirror* (22 June 1994), carries the epithet 'Battler'. The picture depicts an unsmiling Beckett in mid-debate. The term 'battler' can be interpreted in a number of ways. It appears to invite the reader to view her as a woman battling against the odds in the campaign, but it also carries connotations of an unfeminine 'battle-axe'. The latter interpretation is supported by the juxtaposed quotation which also serves to underline her contrariness, 'My origins are on the left, as John Smith's associations were on the right'. The selective use of this quotation also serves to undermine the claim, which she made the cornerstone of her campaign, that she was the continuity candidate.

3.7.5   Conclusions

The hidden power of media discourse to reinforce women's segregation and subordination in the public sphere does not depend on a single article, or even a series of articles, but on systematic tendencies in news reporting, the effect of which is cumulative. The coverage of the 1994 Labour leadership campaign needs, therefore, to be seen in this broader context of media bias against individual female politicians and, more generally, against feminist strategies aimed at challenging masculinist practices in party politics. As deputy leader, Margaret Beckett had been the most senior, as well as by far the most experienced, of the potential candidates for the leadership of the party. When she attempted to translate what was a symbolic role into a substantive one, she was punished by the loss of both. The belittling assumption, promoted by the media, that she had over-reached herself in running for the office of leader has been uncritically reproduced in post-election analyses of the campaign (see, for instance, Alderman and Carter 1995).

3.8   Media coverage of the 1997 general election: the emergence of 'Blair's babes'

The next major electoral event in the British parliamentary calendar after the Labour leadership election was the general election which took place on 1 May 1997. A Fawcett Society survey of one week's television coverage of the election makes clear that the media bias against female candidates is not confined to the print media (*Watching Women* 1997). Not a single government spokesperson interviewed was a woman, and women made only eight out of a total of one hundred and seventy-seven appearances by national politicians. It could be argued that the lack of air-time granted to female politicians does not seem to have harmed their electoral chances, since they were voted in in record numbers. However, the structured invisibility of women is likely to sustain the damaging myth that politics is primarily a 'man's game'. This is not really surprising, given that the coverage was dominated by male reporters, with four out of five election items being covered by men. This pattern was replicated on the night of the election itself. The front cover of the *Radio Times* in election week carried pictures of the BBC's four star presenters, all men, dubbed variously: the 'king of swing' (Peter Snow), the 'ruler of the airwaves' (James Naughtie), 'the grand inquisitor' (Jeremy Paxman) and 'master of ceremonies' (David Dimbleby). The impression of politics as a 'man's *game*' is reinforced further in an article inside the magazine, in which we are told, 'While Dimbleby provides all the appropriate *gravitas*, it is left to Peter Snow to supply the boyish enthusiasm' (26 April–2 May 1997). Snow himself admits, 'Oh yes, I do get a terrific schoolboy thrill from all this' (ibid.) The only woman to feature on the election-night teams of any of the terrestrial channels was ITN's Sue Lawley, whose appropriately feminine role was to interview the studio audience.

Joanna Coles of the *Guardian* provides a fascinating insider's view of the masculinist culture that prevailed among political journalists during what she describes as a 'testosterone-driven' election (the *Guardian* 28 April 1997). In one anecdote, she recalls the laddish behaviour of both male reporters and photographers on the Conservative campaign bus, where they whooped over soft-porn images downloaded onto their laptops from the internet. The fraternal bonding between male politicians and male journalists is captured in a description of one press conference at Conservative Central Office, 'John Major, Brian Mawhinney and Michael Heseltine sat facing an ocean of male hacks, with whom they started sparring' (ibid.). Her observation that only two of the females who *were* present ventured to ask questions appears to lend support to other studies that have found that women ask significantly fewer questions than men in mixed-sex public forums (Swacker 1979; Holmes 1988; Bashiruddin et al. 1990). This is generally interpreted as a sign of women's lack of assertiveness, yet Coles offers a more context-specific explanation. She insists that female journalists deliberately refrain from fielding questions at high-profile press conferences on the grounds that such questions function as showcases for the egos of male journalists and politicians, as opposed to being genuine requests for information. The sense of disaffection experienced by female journalists, such as Coles, in the male-dominated and confrontational atmosphere of political journalism makes it difficult to imagine any immediate change in the coverage of so-called 'hard news' stories, however much women may be infiltrating other areas of journalism. The tediously recycled description of Labour's record 101 female MPs as 'Blair's babes' in the post-election period certainly offers little hope of an imminent shift away from the masculinist bias of the print media.

3.9   Post-election feminist gains

In the wake of the dramatic increase in the number of women MPs in the 1997 general election, there was undoubtedly a widespread expectation that their presence would make a difference. The Labour MP, Clare Short, expresses this view with absolute conviction:

> Most institutions change significantly in their culture and style as women are promoted in significant number. We should therefore expect the culture and style of the Labour Party to change significantly. It is also likely that the presence of such a large number of women in the House of Commons will lead to major change.
>
> (Short 1996: 26–7)

Squires (1996: 77), however, points out some of the problems implicit in this view: 'This argument relies on a cohesive notion of "woman" and assumes that simply guaranteeing the number of women present can secure the values of the women present'. In particular, I would argue that Short's optimism fails to take account of the many barriers to discursive and institutional change outlined in the sections above, including the central role played by the media in shaping public perceptions of MPs' identities and of their success, or otherwise, in performing their various roles. However, one does not have to accept an essentialist notion of 'woman' to posit the existence of a good deal of common ground between the women elected, especially since a Fawcett Society survey carried out after the election discovered that four-fifths of the new intake regarded themselves as feminists (Weldon 1999). The denial of this common ground is too often used by anti-feminists to undermine feminist gains. Thus the former Conservative Chair, Brian Mawhinney, dismissed the creation of Labour's Women's Unit on the grounds that, 'Lumping women together as if they were either one homogeneous group or an oppressed minority is . . . insulting' (cited in the *Guardian* 13 July 1996).

Since the 1997 general election, the Women's Unit has been responsible for promoting women-friendly policies, despite being handicapped in a number of ways. For instance, Harriet Harman's role as Minister for Women was tagged on to an already demanding brief, while her deputy, Joan Ruddock, was forced to defend the ludicrous situation whereby her own role was unpaid. As the journalist Yvonne Roberts points out, Harman's dual roles set up a conflict of interests, 'As Social Security Secretary, her aim is to get lone mothers out to work – as women's minister, shouldn't she be arguing for a woman's right to care for her child full-time, if she so desires?' (the *Guardian* 8 May 1997). This clash of subject positions culminated in the Commons' revolt over the proposed cut to lone parents' benefits in December 1997, and to the ignominious sackings of both Harman and Ruddock in July the following year. Ruddock claims that the policy has been misrepresented. Far from compelling women to go out to work, the aim had been to afford them real choices (Trans. II: 293ff).

However, it is difficult to escape the conclusion that Harman and Ruddock allowed their feminist principles to be cynically exploited by the government to justify unpopular welfare cuts that targeted the most vulnerable group of women in society. This unfortunate episode needs to be placed within the broader context of their achievements for women. They introduced the first national strategies on childcare, and violence against women; they instigated a process of mainstreaming, designed to encourage all departments to consider the impact on women of policy-making, and they set up women-only juries to hold ministers to account for all policy areas affecting women. The latter was a key mechanism in Harman's stated commitment to improve 'the connection between people and Parliament' (the *Guardian* 3 May 1997). Both she and Ruddock should also be credited with helping to ensure that the budget announced in April 1998 was widely perceived as a 'women's budget'.

3.10   Post-election feminist losses

The revelation that Harman's replacement as Minister for Women, Baroness Jay, has eschewed the 'feminist' label makes the comparisons between herself and Thatcher rather more ominous than usual. A recent profile of Jay, carrying the headline, 'The other iron lady', states that she shares with Thatcher 'an unavoidable air of authority' (the *Guardian* 6 February 1999). Significantly, this authoritative air does not render her immune from the media's tendency to define women in public life in terms of their familial roles, 'That Jay wears the heavy mantle of power comfortably is always attributed ... to the influence of her prime minister father, Jim Callaghan, and her former husband, Peter Jay, sometime ambassador to Washington' (ibid.). The appointments of Jay, and, more recently of Fiona Reynolds, a Blairite with a strong business background, to the Women's Unit, seem calculated to foreground the perceived tension between '*New* Labour' and '*old style* seventies feminism'. For instance, the journalist, Anne Perkins, reports that Reynolds 'speaks in carefully gender-neutral terms, fearing a backlash could be provoked by too aggressive a promotion of women's interests' (the *Guardian* 1 June 1999). It could be argued that this strategy of accommodation is reflected in the Unit's new slogan in which gender equality appears to have been diluted in favour of a less radical equality-for-all agenda, hence, 'better for women, better for all'. In October 1999, the findings of the Unit's 'Listening to Women' roadshows were published in a glossy magazine format entitled 'Voices'. None of these findings came as a surprise to the many women's groups and academics who had available research on women's policy priorities, and one is left to wonder whether the Unit is becoming 'a tokenistic dumping ground' (Short 1996: 25), rather than a powerful force for promoting substantive policy changes.

The gains feminist-identified women MPs have achieved are even more qualified when it comes to overturning the dominant discursive norms and procedures that operate in the Commons. Sylvia Shaw's (1999) close analysis of patterns of illegal interruption in five Commons' debates between July 1998 and March 1999 reveals that masculinist discourse styles continue to be treated as the interactional norm. Meanwhile, when Leader of the Commons, Ann Taylor's modest attempts to reform the 'hours culture' met with considerable resistance from traditionalists. As a result, stories of burnout, especially among women MPs, were reported widely in the media after the 1997 election. In the *Guardian* alone, alarmist headlines included the following: 'Election success turns sour for stressed out MPs' (28 March 1998); 'New Labour women MPs face "super-couple" crisis' (3 August 1998); and 'Are Labour women heading for burnout?' (4 August 1998). Media attention also focused on the alleged dilemma of Yvette Cooper in having to combine her appointment as Minister for Public Health with the care of a young baby. Madeleine Bunting asks, 'Why is no one wondering how Ed Balls [Cooper's husband] can juggle his job as [Gordon's] adviser with a small baby?' (the *Guardian* 13 October 1999). The answer is, of course, that the majority of media producers continue to construct men as people who do not have to look after children, even their own children.

In her Charter 88 speech, delivered while shadow Leader of the House, Taylor had called for reforms that would 're-engage the gears of the political process in a fundamental way so that ordinary voters feel genuinely connected with the people who represent them' (*Hansard* 14 May 1996). The laudable aim would appear to have been to bridge the gap between political institutions and the public. There is a widespread suspicion, however, that some of the changes that have been introduced by Taylor to 'modernize' the practices and procedures of the House have, if anything, rendered the government less accountable to both Parliament and to 'ordinary voters'. One ostensibly positive change has been a greater reliance on consensual 'programme motions' (i.e. motions timetabled in advance), rather than the more confrontational 'guillotine motions' available to governments with a large majority. Yet these have had the effect of easing legislation through, effectively suppressing proper debate, leading Seaton and Winetrose (1999: 156) to describe them as 'guillotines by agreement'. This illustrates the way in which the type of consensual discursive practices favoured by women can be used to manufacture consent. Seaton and Winetrose (1999: 159) see a similar process at work in relation to other proposed changes:

> sending MPs away from Westminster through 'constitutional Fridays' and 'constitutional weeks'; making the Prime Minister open to questioning once rather than twice a week: all these may be seen by some as a gain for government rather than for Parliament.

There is a danger that the legitimate feminist agenda of promoting more family-friendly hours and more efficient procedures in the Commons has been appropriated by the government to further its own very different agenda of marginalizing Parliament's role in the process of policy making. This interpretation is in keeping with the fact that ministers routinely make policy announcements in the media. It is also supported by the government's replacement of Betty Boothroyd as Speaker, on the grounds of what it saw as her resistance to the process of modernization, but what she saw as the government's encroachments on the rights of Parliament (the *Guardian* 26 October 1999).

This provides one instance of Cameron's (1998: 433) claim that 'the process of interpretation is also a site where social inequalities and conflicts may have significant effects'. The potential for conflict over the interpretative assumptions participants bring to a speech event is illustrated even more clearly in the disagreements that have arisen over allegedly sexist comments and behaviour experienced by women in the House of Commons since the 1997 general election. Six months after taking up their seats, 60 per cent of female Labour MPs complained that they had experienced harassment. A comment by Labour MP, Brian Sedgemore (1995: 126), is not untypical of the rationalizations of this type of speech and behaviour by some male MPs:

'innocent touching, gallant males taking women by the arm, and innuendo are common-place in the House of Commons'. By contrast, some women MPs have perceived this type of 'innocent' and 'gallant' behaviour as both 'inappropriate' and 'disgusting' (Puwar 1997: 5). It also, of course, offers an additional source of ammunition during Commons debates. Thus Jane Kennedy, a Labour Whip, highlights what she regards as the subtext of such behaviour, 'They are trying to throw you off balance' (the *Guardian* 9 October 1997). Yet, in this instance, discursive conflict is not confined to female and male MPs; a number of Conservative women MPs deny that these complaints are justified. For instance, Gillian Shepard described them as 'absolute rubbish', while Cheryl Gillan advised Labour women not to have 'a sense of humour bypass' (ibid.). It seems that strategic misunderstanding can also be exploited by *women* to distance themselves from the charge of 'political correctness' and the related charge of lacking a sense of humour.

In addition to more traditional forms of masculinism on both sides of the House, Helen Wilkinson (1998), co-founder of the Blairite think-tank, Demos, has identified what she perceives to be a 'new lad' culture in the PLP. More specifically, she claims that 'where it really counts (lobbying, policy wonkery and spin mastery) power remains firmly in male hands' (ibid.: 9). Her article was partly a response to media revelations about the activities of the political lobbyist, Derek Draper, who had boasted that he had access to the seventeen people in the government who really 'count'. Unfortunately, Wilkinson's criticisms were undermined by the romantic metaphors in which she chose to frame them. For instance, she claimed to feel 'like a lover who has been abandoned and who fears she is about to discover a betrayal' and to find herself 'recoiling and seeking solace in the arms of the only other Labour I know' (ibid.). This led some media commentators to interpret her comments literally, as the spiteful accusations of a woman spurned by one of the very Labour lads she was criticizing (the *Guardian* 11 August 1998). However, her article prompted others to examine more critically the gender balance of the policy group at the heart of government decision-making, only to discover that men outnumber women by four to one. This led one commentator to conclude that 'New Labour's power is brokered by a closed circle of elite white males who share the same culture and values, who enjoy power and do not want to give it up' (the *Guardian* 11 May 1999).

It would seem, then, that the 'old boys' network' that held sway in Parliament for decades has been replaced by a 'new lads' network'. Whereas the criteria for entry to the former included a public school education and/or an Oxbridge degree, the criterion for membership of the new lads' network appears to be a passion for football. Thus Charlie Whelan, former adviser to the Chancellor, recalls, 'My own experience was that football was the first thing we talked about of a Monday morning just as it is for *people* across the country' (the *Guardian* 1 March 1999; my italics). Although some women are, of course, interested in football, Whelan's claim seems calculated to establish common ground between government policy-makers and the lifeworld of an implicitly *male* citizenry. This is subtly reinforced by his choice of the colloquial prepositional phrase '*of a* Monday'. However, there is none of the irony here that characterizes Nick Hornby's best-selling novel, *Fever Pitch* (1992), in which football functions as a metaphor for the alleged contemporary crisis in masculinity. Irony loses its edge somewhat when those playing the game are the most powerful men in the country.

Blair's very public association, both metaphorical and real, with football culture is analogous to his much publicized switch to Estuary vowels on the Des O'Connor show. This represents an instance of what sociolinguists have termed 'downward convergence', in which speakers alter their accent, consciously or otherwise, away from the prestige norm in order to signal solidarity with addressees. This is a phenomenon which is particularly characteristic of the speech of middle-class men who seek to appropriate the covert prestige associated with male working-class speech (Trudgill 1988: 91). Such linguistic behaviour therefore serves both an identity and a *inclusive* relational function, but when it is used by male policy-makers, it may serve discursively to *exclude* women. In the transition from the government of John Major to that of Tony Blair, the dominant sporting metaphors may have shifted from cricket to football, and the dominant accents may sound more like Estuary than modified Received Pronunciation (RP), but the norms that prevail remain distinctly masculinist. There is, however, evidence of resistance to this adversarial culture and language among women MPs in the Labour Party. For instance, Harriet Harman has criticized what she terms the 'militaristic' and 'macho' language of the laddish coterie who surround Blair, claiming that talk of 'big guns', 'big hitters' and 'big beasts' is not how women refer to one another (the *Guardian* 9 March 1999).

To invert an observation made by Cameron (1997), male bonding does not preclude rivalry. The rivalry between the Blairites (allies of the Prime Minister) and Brownites (allies of the Chancellor) is framed appropriately enough in terms of that between the rival football teams, Arsenal and Tottenham Hotspur (the *Guardian* 1 March 1999). Headlines at the time of the 1994 leadership race had talked about Blair and Brown as 'blood brothers', but Brown felt their mutual friend and colleague, Peter Mandelson, had betrayed fraternal solidarity by coordinating Blair's campaign. Labour MP, Diane Abbott, has described the jockeying for power between them since as, 'like nothing so much as Just William and competing gangs' (the *Guardian* 29 July 1998). This feud culminated in a series of three resignations in December 1998, including those of Mandelson and Whelan, Brown's spin doctor. Interestingly, the personal assistants who have been credited with keeping the relationship between them relatively amicable are both women: Anji Hunter, special adviser to Blair, and Sue Nye, who fulfils a similar role for Brown. This accords with Abbott's view that 'fixing' in the Party, including at Cabinet level, is largely regarded as the province of women (the

Guardian 29 July 1998). This is in keeping with the expectation, implicit in a good deal of media coverage after the election, that the increasing number of women in the House would help to civilize it.

The expectation that women will constitute a panacea for the widespread 'crisis of sincerity' (Fairclough 1996: 77) in British parliamentary politics may explain the media witch-hunt of the allegedly corrupt Labour MP, Fiona Jones. Her conviction in March 1999 for falling foul of the arcane rules governing election expenses was the first time in seventy-five years that a sitting MP had been found guilty of electoral malpractice. It later emerged that the charges had, in fact, been engineered by 'old Labour' dissidents within her own constituency party. However, media coverage of her conviction made clear that Jones's image as a quintessential Blair's babe was also on trial. The metonymic signifiers of this image in media reports included her hair colour, her smart clothes, her mobile phone and, most damning of all, her Millbank pager. Readers are invited to infer a connection between Jones's carefully constructed image and her fraudulent and unscrupulous behaviour, hence the description of her in the *Daily Mail* as a 'ruthless blonde' (20 March 1999).

Likewise, all the papers foreground the claim made by her campaign manager that they were going to 'spend, spend, spend'. This alludes intertextually to the title of a popular West-End show based on the exploits of another profligate blonde, Viv Nicholson, who won the Littlewoods pools in 1961. The phrase is therefore likely to have cued many readers to connect the two women as illustrative of a certain kind of brash femininity. This connection is reinforced in the *Sun*, with the revelation that Jones 'splashed out on flash cars' (the *Sun* 20 March 1999). In the account of her trial reported in the *Guardian*, her car is identified more specifically as a 'metallic red Toyota', and lest the significance of this is lost on readers, the prosecuting lawyer is quoted as saying that 'this rather smart red vehicle was all to do with image' (24 February 1999). When an appeal court later overturned Jones's conviction, enabling her to retake her seat, this event attracted far less media interest. As a result, the whole episode is likely to have undermined the standing of *all* women MPs and to have cast doubt on their claims to have brought a new integrity and sincerity into politics.

3.11   Conclusions

Given the increasing importance of mediatized discourse in politics, the media bias against female MPs is likely to undermine their ability to challenge and change the masculinist culture of the House. However, the masculinism of both Parliament and the media is increasingly coming under the scrutiny of feminist monitoring groups, including, 'the Fawcett Society, the new Women's Communication Centre, as well as organizations inside the parties and think tanks, especially Demos and Barbara Follett's "British Women" project at the IPPR'. (Lovenduski 1997: 713). Such monitoring activity did not, however, prevent the intra-party struggle for the Labour nomination as Mayor of London from being constructed in the media as a contest between the two male candidates, Ken Livingstone and Frank Dobson, while Glenda Jackson was depicted as an also-ran (the *Guardian* 22 October 1999). The media have also been complicit in the whispering campaign promoted by party spin doctors to let it be known that old style seventies' feminists, like Jackson, Short and the rehabilitated Harman, are 'off-message'. Short, for instance, has been systematically marginalized in a role far from the centre of power, while the dangerous popularity of Mowlam was contained by her appointment to the elusive role of Cabinet Enforcer. Her perception that this was, in fact, a demotion to a non-job undoubtedly contributed to her decision to leave politics at the June 2001 election.[5] It would seem then that there is still much for feminist monitoring groups to do in order to ensure that women are treated as equals within communities of practice within the public sphere. In Chapter 4, I turn my attention briefly to the gains and setbacks women have experienced in the recently established devolved political institutions in Scotland and Wales, before going on to a more detailed analysis of the contribution made by the Northern Ireland Women's Coalition to the Province's new Assembly.

Notes

1. The quotas policy meant that all-women shortlists of candidates were employed in 50 per cent of winnable seats and seats where incumbent Labour MPs were retiring in the 1997 general election. However, in terms of the proportion of women in the lower House, the UK still achieved a relatively low ranking (twenty-sixth in the world) when compared with its European partners, ahead only of countries like Italy, Ireland and Belgium. Furthermore, of the 600-plus candidates named so far for the 2001 general election, only 142 are women (the *Guardian*, 5 March 2001).

2. The survey, carried out for the monitoring group, Women in Journalism (WIJ), by Publici's trends group, also revealed that women featured in 80 per cent of the pictures that were deemed to be irrelevant to the articles they accompanied. The survey concludes that these images were employed purely to 'lift' otherwise dull stories, suggesting that women in the public eye have the wrong sort of 'media capital'.

3. This difference of treatment in terms of discourse representation is also strikingly evident in the accompanying photographs of the three candidates. Blair and Prescott are both smiling. Prescott's broad grin makes him seem approachable, while Blair's smile exudes confidence. Both men engage

the reader in direct eye-contact. By contrast, Beckett is unsmiling; if any-thing, her's is a worried expression. Her gaze is directed upwards, almost in a look of supplication. This has the effect of making her appear remote from the reader and in a weak position relative to the male candidates.

4. Although it might be claimed that both 'he' and 'man' are intended to be understood generically, their non-generic reference in this instance is made clear in the cotext in which all the potential candidates alluded to are *male*. This is particularly ironic since the article is self-reflexively critical in tone, bemoaning the media-led nature of the campaign which is said to have rendered it anti-democratic. This inadvertently betrays a view of significant political actors in the democratic process as implicitly male.

5. Shirley Williams claims that, with her characteristic frankness, Mowlam admitted to her that life as Cabinet Enforcer was 'pretty hellish' and that 'she could not see what her job was about' (the *Guardian* 30 October 2000). Whereas media coverage of other high-profile women ministers in the Labour government has been largely hostile, Mowlam's decision to resign generated a good deal of sympathetic coverage. This was especially true in the tabloid press where her popularity with ordinary voters was contrasted favourably with the perceived remoteness and arrogance of the majority of government ministers.

4

Devolving Power, Dissolving Gender Inequalities? A Case Study of the Northern Ireland Women's Coalition

There is a growing trend world-wide away from centralized nation states towards political and cultural secessionism, often based on devolved political institutions (Shiels 1984). In almost all of the situations in which devolution has occurred, women have sought to take advantage of the discursive space opened up by constitutional change in order to increase their participation in the process of political decision-making. With reference to devolution in the United Kingdom, I will attempt to assess the impact, if any, that women's efforts have made thus far on the gendered nature of the language and broader discursive practices that prevail in the new and emerging devolved bodies. According to Joan Ruddock MP, there is an expectation among women MPs at Westminster that the devolved assemblies will offer a model of what is possible when a more equitable gender balance is achieved:

> I have great hopes you know that the developments that are happening in the Welsh Assembly and in the Scottish Parliament will actually demonstrate that there can be a completely new way forward and I think when we have a model of something that looks~feels~is very different I'm hoping that will encourage people somehow to see how backward we look by comparison

> (Trans. II: 168–72)

Although the situation in both Scotland and Wales will be explored briefly, the main focus of this chapter will be on the contribution made by the Northern Ireland Women's Coalition (NIWC) towards shaping the new Northern Irish Assembly, since this offers an opportunity, unique in the UK, to examine the self-construction and representation of an all-women party political grouping. The question I will attempt to answer is whether feminist-identified women are doing, or are at least proposing to do, politics differently and, if so, how. As in Chapter 3, I will also consider the role played by the media in shaping public perceptions of the identities of the women involved, as well as considering how the media have chosen to represent measures to create institutions that are intended to be more woman-friendly than is true of Westminster.

Before turning to a detailed consideration of devolved politics in the UK, I will begin by considering in general terms some of the reasons that have led women to assume that devolved institutions offer them greater opportunities for political participation than more established and centralized parliamentary bodies. Partly this is due to a coincidence of goals between identity politics based on cultural, ethnic and/or regional autonomy, and identity politics based on gender. According to Squires (1996: 83), other types of secessionist groupings share with feminists the aim of achieving 'cultural justice without assimilation and the public recognition of different group experiences and identities'. This in turn facilitates cross-party strategic alliances among women, something that is difficult at Westminster where all other interests are expected to be subordinated to party loyalty.

The electoral system favoured in devolved institutions, including those in the UK, is often one based on some form of Proportional Representation (PR). Women candidates stand a much better chance of being fielded and selected in elections based on PR, unlike in single-member constituencies, which favour candidates of least risk, and in which factors such as incumbency and patronage tend to work against women (Ruddock Trans II: 70–6). Perhaps most important of all, however, is the fact that devolved institutions are closer to the type of grassroots political activity in which women have traditionally been very active. In addition, in practical and financial terms, such institutions are likely to be more accessible to women, especially those with family commitments, than is true of remote centralized parliaments, usually based in the national capital.[1]

4.1　The gendering of the Scottish Parliament

Following the general election in 1997, the Labour government announced plans to honour its manifesto pledge to enable Scotland, Wales and Northern Ireland to decide their own constitutional futures via referenda. Women activists in all three regions saw this as affording an opportunity for a fresh start, and in particular for ensuring a more even gender balance in the process of political decision-making. When it was established that a two-question referendum was to take place in Scotland on 11 September 1997, women formed a cross-party alliance on the basis of a minimum agenda in support of the proposed Parliament and in support of fifty–fifty representation for men and women. As in Sweden, the threat of the creation of a women's party was sufficient to encourage all parties to field women candidates (Brown 1998: 442).

According to Alice Brown, 'Women were successful in gendering much of the debate, using the language of democracy, participation and representation to stake a claim on behalf of women' (ibid.: 441). Thus in the election campaign that followed, all the major parties, with the exception of the Conservatives, supported mechanisms to maximize women's participation. For instance, the Scottish Labour Party employed a 'twinning' arrangement, whereby if a man was chosen to stand in one constituency, a woman was chosen to stand in a neighbouring constituency. In the event, 37.2 per cent of those elected to the Scottish Parliament in May 1999 were women, making it the third highest proportion of female representation in national government in the world, and exceeding the number of 30 per cent that Dahlerup (1988) claims constitutes a 'critical mass'.

This is a considerable achievement, given that prior to the 1997 general election women comprised only 9.7 per cent of Scottish MPs, increasing to 17 per cent after the election. Alice Brown (1996) attributes this tradition of under-representation to the unsocial hours in the Commons, the adversarial nature of political debate, the male-dominated nature of the Scottish Labour Party, and the remoteness of Westminster. In other words, 'the whole political culture and way in which politics is conducted is perceived as a disincentive to women's participation and a more subtle way of excluding them from the political process' (ibid.: 33). Elsewhere, Brown identifies the bitter resentment of the anti-women policies promoted by Margaret Thatcher as an important factor in encouraging Scottish feminists in the 1980s to overcome their suspicion of, and alienation from, formal electoral politics: 'She mobilized women because of the severity of the cuts she made in all our lives. Women have been forced into political discourse and realize they have to make contact with Government' (cited in the *Guardian* 23 April 1998).

Paradoxically, then, although making no efforts to promote other women while in power, Thatcher inadvertently produced a resurgence of interest in party politics among women in Scotland. What is perhaps even more paradoxical is that the assumption that women could make a real difference to the culture of politics persisted, *in spite of* the apparent counter-example offered by Thatcher herself. The growing feeling among Scottish feminists that '"voluntarism" does not produce parity' (Brown 1998: 437) led to the establishment of the lobbying and research group, Engender, in 1992. Its aim was to bridge the gap between women politicians and women community activists and, to this end, it distributed 2,000 questionnaires to women's organizations throughout Scotland in order to obtain their views on how the new Parliament should function. One of the legacies of this wide-ranging process of consultation is that all those putting forward parliamentary Bills in the Scottish Parliament have to demonstrate that they have consulted with civil sphere organizations.

Alice Brown sees women's activities across and between mainstream and grassroots politics in Scotland as symptomatic of the emergence of a more general 'third wave' of feminism: 'The third wave is pluralist. It aims to work creatively with difference while forging a common agenda' (ibid.: 443). However, I would argue that this pluralist project, also discernible in the activities of some women MPs and ministers at Westminster, is often undermined by the impact of masculinist mediatized discourse which seeks to magnify differences between women, rather than the commonalities that they themselves wish to emphasize. For instance, despite the fact that, during the referendum campaign, Scottish women transcended party political allegiances in order to pursue a feminist agenda, Brown notes that: 'Coverage has generally been reserved for the few occasions when there have been differences between women on the issue of representation' (ibid.: 442). Female MSPs have been instrumental in ensuring that the parliamentary time-table is more family-friendly than the one that operates at Westminster. Rather than sitting in the evenings, the Scottish Parliament sits during office hours, and parliamentary recesses are designed to coincide with school holidays. However, some sections of the tabloid press have chosen to construct these family-friendly measures in negative terms, by suggesting that MSPs are rewarding themselves with seventeen weeks' holiday, suppressing the fact that much of this time is used for constituency work. A telephone poll conducted by the *Daily Record*, inviting its readers to vote on whether the holiday allowance of MSPs should be reduced to six weeks, was clearly calculated to emphasize the social and occupational divisions between women, as well as between men.

An even more overt instance of negative coverage occurred when the Women's Advisory Group (WAG) was set up, to advise the new Minister for Women, since it was dubbed in the media as 'NAG' (Brown 1998: 439). It would seem that the stereotype of whingeing women persists, perhaps because women's voices are no longer muted, but instead carry institutional force. Feminist-identified women were appointed to three key ministerial posts in the first Scottish Cabinet: Susan Deacon, at the Department of Health; Sarah Boyack, at the Department of Transport; and Wendy Alexander, at the Department of Social Inclusion. Deacon, in particular, has courageously championed measures to improve the access of women and girls to sexual health education and family planning provision, in spite of, or perhaps because of, fierce criticism from some members of the Catholic hierarchy in Scotland. Alexander put the issue of domestic violence firmly at the top of her policy agenda. In practical terms, she managed to earmark an extra £8 million to provide help for survivors of domestic violence (the *Guardian* 13 December 1999).

Domestic violence was debated twice early in the life of the Scottish Parliament, and on both occasions women from across the political spectrum united in support of tougher measures to prevent violence against both women and children. Despite the best efforts of women MSPs to shepherd the press physically into the press gallery during a pause in one of these debates, the issues discussed went unreported in the mainstream media.[2] In spite of this paucity of coverage, the successful implementation of a number of feminist policy initiatives rendered rather lame the efforts of the media to dub the new women MSPs 'Donald's dollies', by analogy with their sisters at Westminster, but this time in relation to the then First Minister, Donald Dewar.

4.2 'It's not because she's a vegetarian': a critical analysis of the media treatment of the Welsh Agriculture Secretary, Christine Gwyther

The proportion of women elected to the Welsh Assembly in May 1999 was even higher than the proportion of women elected to the Scottish Parliament. This was achieved by a similar twinning system to the one that operated in Scotland, although it met with considerably more resistance in Wales. A number of female candidates received poison pen letters during their selection process, and when Anita Gayle, General Secretary of the Welsh Labour Party, attempted to persuade a reluctant constituency party in Cynon Valley to accept the twinning policy, one heckler called her a 'feminist and a trollop' (the *Guardian* 4 January 2000). According to Wilkinson (1999/2000: 54): 'The macho culture of the Labour Party in Wales – working men's clubs, rugby union, male voice choirs and the rest of it – is notorious.' This probably explains why so few women in Wales have been elected as Westminster MPs. After the 1997 general election the current number stood at four out of a total of forty, and three of these were elected on the basis of women-only shortlists in marginal seats. Huw Lewis, Welsh Assembly Member (AM) for Merthyr Tydvil, claims that positive discrimination initiatives on behalf of women have created a good deal of resentment: 'There are a lot of bitter and bruised men out there. Many simply cannot accept that a woman beat them and they won't forget that in a hurry' (quoted in the *Guardian* 4 January 2000).

Women occupied twenty-four out of a total of sixty seats in the Assembly, which meant that they comprised 40 per cent of those elected. They used their numerical strength to promote family-friendly working hours and, in marked contrast to the crèche-less Westminster, the Assembly lobby is equipped with toys and books for children (Wilkinson 1999/2000: 54). Four out of five of those appointed to Cabinet posts were women, including the beleaguered former Secretary for Agriculture and Rural Development, Christine Gwyther. Unlike the Scottish Parliament, the Welsh Assembly does not have powers of primary legislation; instead its role is to scrutinize the £7 billion pound annual budget. Partly for this reason, and partly because his is a minority administration, the first Assembly leader, Alun Michael, expressed his hope that the Assembly would work on the basis of consensus politics and an inclusive style of debate (the *Guardian* 10 May 1999). However, in its short history, the Assembly has been beset by controversy, centring mainly on Gwyther and the issue of her competence, or otherwise, to fulfil her ministerial brief. I intend to examine the controversy surrounding Gwyther's alleged lack of qualifications for her ministerial role, since it offers a salutary tale of how a critical mass of women, whether in a centralized or devolved decision-making body, is no guarantee of a woman-friendly environment.

As soon as Gwyther was appointed, there were calls for her resignation, ostensibly on the grounds that she is a vegetarian and therefore, it was claimed, unable to represent the Welsh livestock industry. The whole tenor of media coverage of the staged walk-out at a meeting between Gwyther and the Farmers' Union of Wales (FUW) is trivializing. An article in the *Guardian* (25 May 1999), carrying the strapline 'Farmers' knives out for vegetarian in charge of Welsh agriculture', was accompanied by a photograph of the leader of the FUW, Bob Parry, looking archly at the viewer, while simulating the eating of a beef burger. The visual cues in this photograph seemed calculated to make the whole issue, and indeed Gwyther herself, appear something of a joke. Likewise, a schoolboy snigger lies behind the comment attributed to an unnamed union member who is said to have 'likened the appointment to installing an atheist as Archbishop of Canterbury' (see Fig. 4.1, ll. 29–30).

Gwyther herself is reported as stressing that Alun Michael assured her she was 'the best *person* for the job', while he is reported as reassuring farmers of 'the *strength* she would bring to the job' (ibid.: ll. 38–9; and 47–8; my italics). I would suggest that the words in italics provide textual traces of an assumption, shared by Gwyther and Michael, that it is as much Gwyther's gender that is at issue as her vegetarianism. In other words, they seem to assume that the vegetarian angle is a cover for a less acceptable sexist discourse in which being a woman is perceived to be incompatible with a male-gendered portfolio such as Agriculture. The claim made by the text producer that 'Yesterday's meeting was the start of a difficult week for Ms Gwyther' (ibid.: ll. 71–2) provides an instance of an ideologically loaded predictive narrative, one that constructs Gwyther's week as 'difficult', even before it happens. In this way, the text producer implicitly aligns himself with the FUW's position that Gwyther lacks the competence to do the job assigned to her.

This negative and often trivializing media coverage of Gwyther at the outset of her ministerial career undoubtedly made her vulnerable to a second attack on her competence, this time from within the Assembly itself. This occurred in the wake of a ruling by the European Agriculture Commissioner,

Minister refuses to quit

Farmers' knives out for vegetarian in charge of Welsh agriculture

Welsh farmers angrily walked out of their first face to face meeting with the newly appointed Welsh agriculture secretary yesterday after failing to force her resignation because she is a vegetarian.

Christine Gwyther, one of four women in Labour's first assembly cabinet, said she was more than capable of representing the country's farming community, despite not having eaten meat for more than twenty years.

Leaders of the Farmer's Union of Wales, which represents about half of Wales's 25,000 farmers, walked out of the pre-arranged meeting at the Welsh Office in Cardiff after calling on the 36-year old minister her decision to accept the crucial agriculture and rural affairs portfolio.

Delegates at an emergency debate at the union's recent annual meeting unanimously voted to oppose her appointment. They argued that placing a non-meat eater in charge of an industry that is 90% dependent on the livestock industry was insensitive and would drain the remaining confidence in the already hard-hit farming sector.

One delegate likened the appointment to installing an atheist as Archbishop of Canterbury. Others threatened to disrupt this week's royal opening of the assembly if she refused to go.

Yesterday Ms Gwyther said she would do her utmost for all farmers of Wales.

She said that when the Labour leader, Alun Michael, offered her the post he had assured her that she was the best person for the job. 'Nothing since has changed my mind about that'.

She added that she had received several letters and phone calls from supportive farmers, including livestock producers.

Accompanying her at the meeting, Mr Michael, the assembly's first secretary, said he was sure farmers would see the value of the appointment and the strength she would bring to the job.

But Bob Parry, president of the FUW, said his members would not be happy until she reconsidered her position. 'Somebody who does not eat meat cannot support the agriculture industry'.

About 30 farmers, mainly from the Brecon and Glamorgan areas of south Wales, turned up to protest outside the meeting, which was also attended by landowners and leaders of the rival National Farmer's Union.

Bryan Jones, 55, a dairy and sheep farmer, said it was unfair in the industry for someone to take decisions 'when she hasn't got a clue what meat tastes like'.

However, Hugh Richards, president of the NFU of Wales, said farmers should give Ms Gwyther a chance.

He said: 'At this point in time I see no problem in working with Ms Gwyther. I was surprised at the appointment but, having said that, we will work with her'.

Yesterday's meeting was the start of a difficult week for Ms Gwyther. Today she will be called to speak on a Liberal Democrat motion calling on the assembly to revoke the ban on beef on the bone as soon as possible.

Fig. 4.1 Text of an article about the then Welsh Agriculture Secretary, Christine Gwyther, that appeared in the *Guardian* (25 May 1999).

Franz Fischler, that a compensation package for calf slaughtering, promised to farmers in Wales and Scotland, was illegal. On this occasion, the three opposition parties in the Assembly – Plaid Cymru, the Conservatives and the Liberal Democrats – united in calling for Gwyther to be censured, making it clear that they held it to be a matter of honour that she should resign, if the motion was passed. Despite the expectation of a consensual style of politics prevailing in the Assembly, the *Guardian* reported that it had become a 'battle ground' and referred to a 'confrontational mood stalking the building in Cardiff' (19 October 1999). During the censure debate, the leader of Plaid Cymru, Dafydd Wigley, asked, 'How on earth could any minister who was on top of her work be in such a situation?' and drew a patronizing analogy with sending a 'naive apprentice' to discuss a major contract with the chair of another company, even though it was in fact part of Gwyther's brief to negotiate the scheme (the *Guardian* 20 October 1999). Not surprisingly, the censure motion was carried. In reality, the decision about the scheme for slaughtering unwanted calves had been outside Gwyther's control, something that was recognized in the Scottish Parliament, where the Scottish Agriculture Minister was subject to no such censure.

In her discussion of the representation of women in politics, Norris (1997: 162) alludes to the concept of 'dequalification', a term coined by Jeane Kirkpatrick (1995) to describe the process whereby women's experiences and capabilities are undervalued in the male-dominated world of politics. This is borne out by the treatment meted out to Gwyther by both the FUW and her political opponents, in that both sought to discredit her by calling into question her qualifications for the ministerial role to which she was appointed. When Gwyther was suddenly and unceremoniously removed from her post by Alun Michael's successor, Rhodri Morgan, in July 2000, she was not replaced by someone who could bring a completely fresh approach to the job, but by her *male* deputy, Carwyn Jones. As her deputy, Jones had presumably supported, and been implicated in, her policy decisions, which leads one to wonder whether his being male was deemed sufficient to compensate for perceived policy shortcomings.

4.3 The opposite of politics? A case study of the Northern Ireland Women's Coalition

When the Northern Ireland Women's Coalition (NIWC) was established in the spring of 1996, it was widely reported that its members had mysteriously come from nowhere. In fact, all of those involved had long been active in a wide range of cross-community grassroots women's groups and other non-governmental organizations. As Rosin McDonagh (1996: 25) notes:

> Northern Ireland has a vibrant civil society, especially in territorially defined communities. This energy and dynamism has benefited, directly and indirectly, from the displacement of mainstream political activity, which rapidly became preoccupied post-1968 with constitutional concerns, to the cultural exclusion of all else.

A survey published in 1996 revealed that two-thirds of female respondents believed that politicians were not giving enough attention to issues of particular concern to women in Northern Ireland, while just under two-thirds claimed that the parties did not encourage women to participate (cited in Wilford 1996: 49). According to the NIWC's Monica McWilliams:

we were aware of what had happened in other conflicts in other countries where women have been extremely active at the informal level and grass-roots level and then when the big decision making comes to sit down at the table the men say well good on you women for making sure that you know we didn't have an all-out~all-out war but now it's the time for us to sit down and resolve it so you just go back into your communities and there was that level of patronism umm that attitude that erhm women weren't the real players on the political scene

(Trans. III: 3–10)

It was partly to remedy this situation that the Women's Coalition came into being.

4.3.1   A brief history of the NIWC

McWilliams (1995) traces the origins of women's activism in Northern Ireland to the Civil Rights Movement of the late 1960s and early 1970s. Yet, despite the high-profile role played by civil rights activist Bernadette Devlin, the primary focus of the movement on the struggle for equal rights for Catholics meant that equality for women was barely addressed. Indeed, virtually all of the grassroots women's groups identified by McWilliams were positively hostile to feminism. In an earlier article, she attempts to offer some explanation for this marked disidentification with feminist concerns among women on both sides of the religious divide: 'The traditional link between nationalists (both Orange and Green) and their respective Churches has ensured that the ultra-conservative view of women as both the property of, and inferior to, men remains strongly entrenched in Irish society' (McWilliams 1991: 84).

As the women-led Peace Movement of the 1970s came under the increasing control of church elements, its radical potential to oppose the emergence of what has been termed 'armed patriarchy' in Northern Ireland was gradually diffused. In the case of the Peace Movement, an appeal was made to women's moral *superiority*, based on a connection between pacifist and motherist ideologies. As Sara Ruddick notes, 'Peace, like mothering, is sentimentally honoured and often secretly despised. Like mothers, peacemakers are scorned as powerless' (cited in Seager 1993: 238). By acquiescing in this equation of motherhood and peacemaking, women activists in Northern Ireland throughout the 1970s and early 1980s may have inadvertently contributed to their own segregation and marginalization within mainstream politics. This may also explain why the NIWC, unlike all of the other political parties in the Province, has been careful to distance itself from essentialist claims about women.

The roots of the NIWC lie in more recent events. One such event was the appointment of Mary Robinson as President of the Republic of Ireland in 1990. She was instrumental in forging links between cross-community women's groups North and South. Likewise, the then US Ambassador to Ireland, Jean Kennedy Smith, sent Northern Irish women to the United States to network with women's groups there. Similar networking with women's groups in Europe led to the formation of the Northern Ireland Women's European Platform (NIWEP), a key player in subsequent events. This process of political networking was to culminate in an international conference in Belfast in September 1998, entitled 'Women and Democracy', attended by Hillary Clinton, Madeleine Albright and the first ever female Secretary of State for Northern Ireland, Mo Mowlam. Such cross-border and trans-national networking among women was to provide the moral, practical and financial support that enabled the NIWC to confront the powerful male homosocial networks that were deeply embedded in and between mainstream political parties and the media. This process was facilitated by the emergence of a pluralist feminist discourse which chimed well with the need to accommodate women divided from one another by class, religion and political allegiance. In particular, as Porter points out (1998: 54), the NIWC was inspired by the theory of 'transversalism' that emerged out of the concrete practices of Italian feminists and which emphasizes dialogue based on respect for different positionings.[3]

The type of support and encouragement provided by high-profile women in public life was particularly important in the Northern Irish context since its own history offered few role models for women who aspired to careers in party politics. In its 77-year history, Northern Ireland has elected only three women to Westminster as MPs, the last being the civil rights leader, Bernadette Devlin, more than thirty years ago, in 1969. Currently there are no women among MEPs from Northern Ireland. A similar pattern of gross under-representation characterized the fifty-one-year history of the Stormont Parliament in which only nine women sat, and continues to characterize local government in which only 15 per cent of councillors are female. The Northern Irish media therefore had little experience of dealing with female politicians of *any* political complexion, and absolutely none of dealing with politicians who are openly feminist in their views. For this reason, McWilliams believes that the appointment of Mowlam was particularly fortuitous:

> Mo came in like a breath of fresh air . . . took no bullshit from anybody squared up to them and it helped us to do the same and it was good to have her operating there and it's been so hard for her too but it's been good to have another very *strong* woman in the mainstream which kind of took a bit of the emphasis away from us as being you know people that were so *unbelievably radical*

(Trans. III: 346–53)

However, like Mowlam,[4] the NIWC was to find that its forthright and innovative approach to politics was dismissed by some colleagues, and, to a lesser extent, by some sections of the media, as a failure to recognize the rules of the political game, when its members were trying to rewrite those rules.

The NIWC's move from grassroots politics into the mainstream of the political process was achieved by an act of sheer political opportunism. In order to ensure that smaller Protestant paramilitary groupings were included in the All-Party Talks, the British and Irish governments devised a complicated top-up system of proportional representation which meant that the ten parties that attracted the most votes in the election in May 1996 would each be permitted two representatives at the Talks table. It is ironic that a mechanism designed to admit the 'men of violence' should also have opened the way for the entry of very different oppositional voices into the Talks process. The NIWC's determination to transcend traditional sectarian and other boundaries is evident in the fact that of the two women elected, Monica McWilliams and Pearl Sagar, one was a Catholic nationalist from a rural background, the other a Protestant loyalist from Belfast. One of the aims stated in its campaign booklet was to offer 'a comfortable space for those who have difficulty defining themselves in terms of the majority cultures' (*Common Cause*: 7). Indeed, the NIWC owes its existence to the belief that women can suppress their horizontal differences, defined along the axes of class, age and religious and political allegiances, in order to pursue common goals *as women*. The very real risks involved in this strategy were vividly illustrated when Pearl Sagar and her family were forced to move to a different neighbourhood because of systematic intimidation. The intimidation did not, however, end there.

4.3.2   Changing political structures

It is worth considering what motivated the NIWC's shift from grassroots to mainstream politics. Despite McRobbie's (1994) optimistic assessment of the potential power of new social movements, it is obvious that, like feminist activists in Scotland, the women who later formed the NIWC were frustrated by their inability to effect real political change. At best, their involvement in grassroots equality groups seemed to offer a slow track option when it came to improving the lot of women. They perceived a danger in accepting the role of second rate political actors, reliant on those stereotypical feminine qualities of patience and self-effacement. McWilliams and Kilmurray (1997: 17) say of the decision to form the NIWC:

> It was a risk, but it was felt that all the Discussion Papers in the world would not have had the same impact on the male dominated political

decision-making process in Northern Ireland as the decision by the 70 women to put their names forward for election.

However, this did not mean accommodating themselves to the type of hier-archical institutional structures that prevailed in the existing mainstream parties. They were determined to incorporate the 'organizing strategies learned from years of community networking and interest group advocacy work' (ibid.: 18) into the structures of the new party. Policy is decided in open monthly meetings, with a rotating chairperson and notetaker. Links with the wider women's movement are maintained through a series of conferences based around specific themes. The decision to share leadership, rather than appoint a formal leader, has, to some extent, been frustrated by circumstances. For instance, there was an initial requirement to identify a nominal leader for the purpose of the Electoral Order. This nominal status was accorded to Mc-Williams, but the media attention she has received subsequently has meant that she has, in fact, come to be perceived as the party leader. McWilliams is, however, careful to employ the inclusive pronoun 'we' when discussing the NIWC's achievements, supporting Tannen's observation that women in posi-tions of power are often loath to claim credit for themselves (Tannen 1996: 137). In any case, the ability to bring non-elected representatives into the negotiations means that all members of the Coalition who wish to do so have been afforded opportunities to become actively involved in shaping policy.

The NIWC's transition from grassroots activism to party politics has in itself helped to challenge the boundary between civil and public sphere political action in Northern Ireland. Fearon (1999: 78–9) says of the Talks, 'In an environment where every utterance was filtered before articulation, the NIWC tried to act as a conduit between civil society and the secretariat'. In addition, it has managed to ensure a more fundamental discursive restruc-turing of the spheres through its innovative proposals for a Civic Forum, proposals which were subsequently enshrined in the plans for the new Assembly, albeit with significant alterations. The Civic Forum was intended to bridge the gap between the public sphere of party politics and the civil sphere of community activism, from which NIWC members sprang. It is described in its campaign booklet as follows: 'a completely new body that will complement the work of elected representatives from the various sectors of civil society – community activists, trade unionists and employer bodies, youth groups and the education sector' (*Common Cause* 1998: 8). The NIWC argued that members should be nominated by the groups themselves, whereas in the final Agreement this has been diluted, since they are to be appointed by the first minister and deputy minister. Nonetheless, the creation of the Forum is likely to mitigate some of the limitations of representative demo-cracy by creating a greater sense of accountability to the community at large. The NIWC was, however, given little credit in media coverage for this important contribution to the structure and workings of the new Assembly.

4.3.3   Changing the language of political debate

The NIWC's campaign posters carried the slogan, 'Wave Goodbye to Dinosaurs', revealing the extent to which it defined itself in opposition to the monolithic and masculinist nature of traditional party politics in Northern Ireland. Its members constructed a collective identity for themselves as proactive agents of change whose aim, incorporated as the strapline in its manifesto for the Assembly elections, is no less than to 'shatter the mould of politics in Northern Ireland'. This was underscored by the key phrase that acts as a constant refrain throughout the manifesto, 'a new voice for new times'. This self-conscious focus on issues of language did not derive from essentializing ideas about how women ought to speak, or even do speak, but from a desire to forge an alternative to the aggressive, confrontational and, often militarist, discursive mode that had become 'normalized' in Northern Irish politics. As Wilford (1996: 42) points out:

> Since its inception, Northern Ireland has been a divided society within which politics has resembled a proxy war which has infused the terms of political debate with martial, thus, 'manly', virtues, epitomized in the republican camp by the 'ballot and bullet' strategy and on the loyalist side in the slogan 'not an inch, no surrender'.

In an article in the *Irish News* (19 May 1998), McWilliams eschews this militaristic language, proposing an alternative political discourse based on cooperation and interdependence, 'we either win together or we lose together'. This approach is calculated to protect the face needs of others, unlike the so-called 'zero sum game' advocated by the major parties. Rather than reproducing the conflictual 'us and them' political discourse that had held sway in Northern Ireland for decades, the NIWC employ an uncomfortably inclusive 'we', 'we're all part of the problem, and therefore we're all part of the solution' (McWilliams cited in Fearon 1999: 100). NIWC members also contest other taken-for-granted collocations, such as the equation of intransigence with strength: 'The politics of conflict is easy. You just sit there being as bigoted and obstructive as you can be. But when peace comes, people will begin asking more of their politicians' (McWilliams cited in the *Irish Times* 27 April 1998). It is obvious, then, that McWilliams and other Coalition members were forced to devote a good deal of the media space afforded to their own party in order to challenge the metalanguage in which masculinist political debate was framed. Rosemarie Bennis (*Women's News* June 1998) is one of the many journalists who has commended the 'refreshingly open and honest' language used by McWilliams herself, with its emphasis on positive terms such as 'healing', 'listening', 'embracing' and 'growing'.

The NIWC's three core principles of 'Inclusion, Equality and Human Rights' would be viewed as relatively uncontroversial in most other Western democracies, but in the conflict-ridden context of Northern Ireland, they have been perceived as radical. For instance, it appealed to the concept of inclusivity in order to justify the involvement, without preconditions, in the preliminary Talks, and subsequently in the Assembly, of parties with paramilitary connections, namely the Ulster Democratic Party (UDP), the Progressive Unionist Party (PUP) and Sinn Féin. Likewise, its promotion of an egalitarian discourse has been perceived as a direct challenge to the traditional loyalist discourse of supremacy, which stresses domination. Finally, its advocacy of human rights led it to campaign for the release of Roisin McAliskey on humanitarian grounds, since she was forced to remain in prison before and after the birth of her baby, despite the fact that she was suffering from severe depression. This afforded unionist politicians an ideal opportunity to accuse the party of being covert republicans, despite the care it took to construct itself as a broad coalition of interests, transcending the sectarian divide. The NIWC's sense of its own marginalization in the political process became a source of strength, however. For instance, it led it to champion the rights of other marginalized groups, notably those of ethnic minorities, the disabled, victims of violence and those seeking official recognition for minority languages.

Fearon argues that the single most important contribution of the NIWC has been to 'untaint the concept of compromise' (cited in the *Guardian* 17 February 1997), something that proved essential if the Good Friday Agreement was ever to come into being. It did this by facilitating debate between the opposing parties, on the grounds that no such debate was taking place. Instead, according to Fearon (1999: 79), the Coalition members were of the view that the major parties were literally talking past one another because they were operating with two distinct discursive frames: 'Nationalists were much more likely to be concerned with the big picture, with vision, and were less concerned with detail, while unionists prioritized structures and were almost obsessed with detail'. McWilliams explains the NIWC's strategy for breaking this deadlock:

> we are very process-focused and it was the process we kept addressing all of the time and told people to stop addressing the outcomes 'cos everyone was addressing their *own* outcomes and hadn't thought through if they were only going to do that they weren't ever going to achieve an agreement and whereas we address the process of how we could arrive at eh reconciliation of our differences
>
> (Trans. III: 41–5)

In other words, the NIWC's aim has been to prioritize the interpersonal function of language over its ideational content, in that it has sought to open up a discursive space for genuine dialogue *across difference*, rather than for the reaffirmation of fixed positions.

Perhaps the NIWC's most important contribution to date, however, has been to the language and substance of the Good Friday Agreement. While male politicians 'wheeled and dealed' with one another in the corridors of power, the NIWC concentrated on detailed and laborious drafting. It used the relationships it had established with everyone 'from secretaries to the Secretary of State' (Fearon 1999: 105) to ensure the insertion of clauses on the rights of women and victims of violence. Meehan (1999: 10) is among a number of commentators who have noted the fact that the Agreement bears the unmistakable imprint of the NIWC's rhetorical style. McWilliams also makes this clear: 'everything that was said at the end about creating a plural-ist society an inclusive one reaching an honourable accommodation that was all our language . . . because it wasn't seen as [tapping the table for emphasis] are you nationalist or are you unionist↑' (Trans. III: 322–37). Chris McCrudden, an anti-discrimination lawyer, is quoted in the *Guardian* (20 May 1998) as saying, 'It is one of the few documents I've read over the last 20 years that I'm completely happy with. It is unambiguous that equal treatment is a central theme of its proposals'. Despite the deeply conservative attitudes enshrined in Northern Irish law around issues of sexuality, the document even extends equality on the grounds of sexual orientation. The Agreement the NIWC helped to frame is not without its detractors, however. A number of political commentators have suggested that the language of accommoda-tion that the Coalition lobbied so hard to have adopted led to the subse-quent political deadlock in the peace negotiations. In trying to accommodate everyone, the suggestion is that it has ended up pleasing no one. Time alone will reveal whether this assessment is justified.

In addition to its contribution to the framing of the Agreement document, one of the key functions of the NIWC was to put pressure on the other parties to make clear their policies on gender equality in the pre-election debates, helping to foster healthy discussion around issues of identity politics. An article in the *Irish News* (14 April 1997), for instance, comprises juxtaposed statements from all the main parties on this issue, with the telling omission of Ian Paisley Junior's Democratic Unionist Party (DUP). The statement from the NIWC occurs first, with the implication that all the other policies need to be measured and evaluated against this. A number of these are implicitly in dialogue with the gender-specific nature of the NIWC itself and with the related policy of quotas for women which had generated con-siderable controversy within the Parliamentary Labour Party (see Chapter 3). For instance, the Social Democratic and Labour Party (SDLP) spokes-person insists that gender equality is 'not about jobs for the girls', while the statement released by the Ulster Unionist Party (UUP) rejects the quota system as 'perverse'. The NIWC is well aware of the fact that its all-women list of candidates for both the Talks and the Assembly elections could be said to offend the principle of inclusivity, but this was felt to be justified by the traditional failure of the other parties to field sufficient numbers of women candidates. For instance, in an article in the *Irish Times* (9 May 1996), Eddie McGrady of the SDLP referred to 'an appropriate gender balance' in his party, when in fact only 20 out of a total of 74 candidates who stood were female. Certainly, in its short period of existence the NIWC has done much to raise the profile of women in all of the other parties. Unfortunately, this has led some media commentators to assume that this is its only goal, thereby failing to give due recognition to its many contributions to language, structures and policy.

4.3.4 Confronting masculinism in the Talks Forum and All-Party Talks

Monica McWilliams and Pearl Sagar were the only women permitted to speak in the 'Northern Ireland Forum for Political Understanding and Dialogue', and it soon became clear that they had not been admitted on equal terms. Indeed, their experiences led them to resignify it as the 'Forum for Political Misunderstanding and Monologue'. The purpose of the Forum, which was established in May 1996, was to set the agenda for the Talks process proper. However, Sinn Féin representatives never assumed their seats, while the SDLP withdrew in the summer of 1996. McWilliams notes:

> we were a group of Catholic and Protestant women so we were the double other we were women and we were coming from different backgrounds so they had no enemies so they had to make an enemy out of us because we contested every political stand that they took on things that we felt would not stand up in both communities

> (Trans. III: 148–52)

The systematic verbal and, on occasions, physical harassment to which McWilliams and Sagar were subjected by the remaining loyalist parties was well documented in the media. The fact that the public were permitted access to the Forum discussions appears to have encouraged a number of male politicians to play to the press and the public gallery. They performed very much to an extreme misogynist script, perhaps as a defensive strategy against these feminist invaders of what had been a safe male-orientated space. One notorious example, broadcast on national television, was when the Democratic Unionist Party's (DUP's) Ian Paisley Junior told McWilliams to 'shut up and sit down, you stupid woman' (Trans. III: 111). Other epithets included, 'whingeing women', 'dogs' and 'scum', with the result that the two women posted an 'insult of the week' notice-board in the hall outside the negotiations. When McWilliams tried to address the issue of BSE, or so-called 'mad cow disease', in one Forum debate, she was greeted by 'moos' by DUP members. Cameron (1997) discusses the way ritualized insults can be used to affirm a sense of solidarity between men, but on this occasion they clearly function to position the two women as members of an out-group. McWilliams interprets their behaviour as follows:

> I think in the early days that their attempt was really to insult us so much that we wouldn't find our voice erhm that we'd lose our confidence and our self-esteem and we didn't it was very difficult and in order to counter-act it we had to become very very well prepared

(Trans. III: 160–3)

The orchestrated nature of these attacks was commented on by Sagar, 'The men from some of the parties hunted in packs' (*Irish Times* 27 April 1998).

One very effective way of exposing this abuse was the use of the media to publicly 'name and shame' politicians who engaged in sexist name-calling (McWilliams and Kilmurray 1997: 19). Fearon (1999: 55) argues that this meant that McWilliams and Sagar were thereby forced to accept a watchdog role, policing the language and discursive procedures of the Forum. Although ostensibly a constructive role, the expectation that they would set the stand-ards for polite debate in institutions that were inherently conflictual proved something of a strain on occasions. This is illustrated by an episode related by McWilliams that occurred during the All-Party Talks:

> I got very angry one day in the Assembly quite rightly because one of the members said I wouldn't go upstairs with you anytime which to me was a *horrific* sexist comment . . . and I made the erhm the presiding officer eh comment on it and he didn't rule it as un-parliamentary language he ruled it as discourteous but not un-parliamentary and I said that I wanted it put in the record and I got very very angry 'cos it seemed to me that the men were colluding in not having it in the record so it wouldn't look too bad so I said I'm going to put it in the record because I'm about to repeat what he just said and I did and I was very angry so the two journalists said after-wards one of them said God Monica you shouldn't ever let yourself get angry I said when you start saying that to the men in there and every day the men are angry then you can feel you've a right saying it to me

(Trans. III: 247–61)

This is worth quoting at some length since it provides a vivid illustration of the way in which the credibility of NIWC representatives was undermined by the sexualizing of their identities. It also provides evidence of McWilliams's rejection of the journalists' assumption that her behaviour should be judged according to different standards from those applied to the behaviour of her male colleagues.

The strategic use of humour acted as one means of deflecting attacks. According to McWilliams, when 'John Taylor described us as the WC . . . we told him, "Yes, and we'll flush away your certainties"', thereby deftly turning an intended slur into the means of exposing masculinist dogmatism. Likewise, their response to the stated mission of the DUP's William McCrea, 'to teach these two women to stand behind the loyal men of Ulster', was to burst into an ironic rendering of the Tammy Wynette song, *Stand By Your Man* (*Irish Times* 30 March 1998). In a somewhat paradoxical twist, given the total lack of respect shown for both women, members of the main loyalist parties insisted on calling the NIWC, 'the Ladies' Coalition', thereby intimating how inappropriate it was for 'ladies' to dabble in politics. This was followed by a request for them to go and 'breed for Ulster'. These epithets and exhortations were clearly calculated to remind the Coalition representatives, and by extension women throughout the North, that their proper sphere was the domestic one and that their proper roles were the subservient ones of wives and mothers. This outmoded message is likely to have alienated, rather than attracted, women voters.

The vehement sexist attacks of loyalist politicians on the NIWC can partly be explained by the religious fundamentalism that underpins loyalism and which has the effect of militating against gender equality (Porter 1998: 44). However, there was also a great deal of resentment that the top-up system had accorded the NIWC a disproportionate influence in the Forum; its candidates had jointly attracted fewer then 8,000 votes, while the DUP had attracted more than 141,000. McWilliams recalls, 'they said that we were not serious political players and we'd got in the back door and therefore we shouldn't be taken seriously therefore everything we said was nonsense' (Trans. III: 153–5). Mills (2000) argues that, 'It is possible for someone who has been allocated a fairly powerless position institutionally to accrue to themselves a great deal of interactional power.' The concept of 'interactional power' is helpful in accounting for the NIWC's ability to use 'what little influence it had to optimal effect' (Fearon 1999: 114). In particular, it pressed for consensus and reconciliation in both the Forum and the Talks. These concepts were anathema to politicians who were accustomed to believing that integrity and obduracy are synonymous. Yet, due to the influence of the NIWC, among others, this was precisely the type of language in which the Agreement document was ultimately couched. Its attempt to have non-gender specific language adopted in the Agreement was unfortunately less successful. All-too-familiar appeals to tradition and legal precedent were made to justify the ludicrous references to the then female Secretary of State as 'he' and 'him' (*Irish Times* 4 May 1998).

4.3.5 Gender and the genre of political debate

It is clear, then, that the NIWC has sought to challenge the institutionally and culturally sanctioned masculinist norms that govern the genre of political debate in Northern Ireland. Its novel approach to political campaigning was demonstrated particularly clearly in its lively and visual 'yes' campaign for the referendum on 22 May 1998. It decked its campaign bus with the suffragette colours, filled it with children, and took it on a whistle-stop tour of the Province. It distributed postcards to homes throughout Northern Ireland, inviting voters to express in writing their hopes and reservations about the Agreement. It was careful to avoid negative campaigning, 'we never ever tried to be disparaging of anyone else's views along the way' (Trans. III: 342). Not only did it try to make the campaign itself an enjoyable experience, in which everyone, young and old, was involved, but its members openly showed their joy when the campaign proved successful. The force of the image that occupied the entire front page of a supplement in the *Observer* (24 May 1998) depicting the NIWC's Jane Morrice and Ann McCann hugging one another, can be explained by the fact that it challenges both the assumption that victorious politicians should maintain a dignified air of detachment, and a more general, though implicit, rule governing the distance that should be maintained between bodies in public spaces. However, Fearon (1999: 133) makes the wry comment, 'Women were covered in the celebration of the referendum, while men had been given most coverage in the decision-making process'. This is in keeping with the media tendency, noted by Norris (1997: 149ff), to use women to provide what she describes as a 'splash of colour in the photo op', rather than treating them as serious political players. The selective coverage of the NIWC's role in the campaign would seem to lend support to Norris's claim that women often accrue the wrong kind of media capital.

On an interpersonal level, NIWC members have consciously sought to cultivate a style of address that reduces the distance between themselves and addressees. For instance, one journalist praises McWilliams for eschewing what she terms 'the politician's usual shield of jargonese' in favour of a 'plain', 'matter-of-fact and commonsense' style (see Fig. 4.2b: ll. 34–5). In the interview undertaken for the purpose of this book, McWilliams's style is characterized by a high density of affective modality markers, notably the recurrent use of the pragmatic particle 'you know', which she employs no less than 28 times in an interview lasting approximately half an hour. A context-sensitive analysis of these occurrences reveals that they are not operating as mere fillers, but in almost all instances are employed as positive politeness devices, designed to establish common ground between McWilliams and myself, as the addressee (Brown and Levinson 1987). This is evident from the following extract, where she is trying to explain some of the particular problems the NIWC faces in attempting to transcend the traditional tribal and sectarian allegiances on the basis of which most Northern Irish people define themselves:

> but it's also much more difficult for us too Clare . . . to try and say well I–I understand how it would be for anyone else erhm and that's <u>you know</u>

much harder to do . . . to bring a different angle to it which is <u>you know</u> not just my own eh background but <u>you know</u> from the Coalition's perspective and I said to the Coalition that we have to be aware and alert to the fact that we will make mistakes but <u>you know</u> not to be hard on people when they do it because em <u>you know</u> there are times when you're jumped on for a quick soundbite

(Trans. III: 305–17)

According to Holmes (1995: 91), 'you know' used in this way 'reduces power and status differences and emphasizes what participants share'.

I would argue, therefore, that an interpersonal orientation is to the fore in the extract above, despite the relative formality of the interview setting in which it was recorded. The extract also illustrates the preferred strategy of NIWC members of addressing individuals using their first names, inviting their addressees to reciprocate. In the campaign for the Assembly elections, the Coalition was unhappy with the formality implicit in the standard practice of using candidates' surnames alone on campaign posters – a convention designed to facilitate the task of marking ballot papers. It devised a novel strategy to overcome this problem by including both the first name and surname of candidates, but making the latter visibly larger and bolder. Fearon (1999: 147) notes, 'it was close to the original design, but it stretched it a little'. As in the case of Mo Mowlam, the Coalition's novel approach to the genre of political debate was not always intelligible to others, including media commentators, *as politics*. The identities its representatives constructed for themselves as political actors, and the interpersonal style they adopted, were welcomed by many, but were evaluated negatively by others. Hence, when McWilliams made a plea on BBC Northern Ireland's *Hearts and Minds* programme (March 1998) for a less adversarial and inflammatory style of political debate, her comments were dismissed as 'trite' and 'naive' by the Ulster Unionist Party's (UUP's) John Hunter.

4.3.6   Press coverage of the NIWC

Whereas feminist MSPs have complained about the lack of media coverage of their activities and Christine Gwyther is unlikely to have welcomed the largely negative coverage of hers, media coverage of the NIWC has been generally positive. This is no doubt due to the fact that its arrival on the political scene in Northern Ireland provided journalists with a novel news angle in a climate in which the battle lines between the parties are drawn in wholly predictable ways. The coverage that followed confirms Norris's finding that crude sex stereotyping is relatively rare in depictions of women in politics, but that 'gendered framing remains common' (1997: 165). According to Norris (ibid.: 2), 'news frames give "stories" a conventional "peg" to arrange the narrative, to make sense of the facts, to focus the headline, and to define events as newsworthy'. She argues that they can be positive, negative or neutral in their effects, depending on the broader political context in which they are produced. I would suggest that their effects are also likely to depend on whether individual readers/viewers take up a compliant or resistant subject position in relation to the way in which the news item is framed, something Norris largely ignores. For instance, feminist readers are likely to read *against* an item which draws on one or more stereotypically gendered news frame(s), irrespective of whether the broader political culture is reactionary or progressive in respect of gender equality issues. The analysis that follows will concentrate primarily on coverage of the NIWC in the Northern Irish press, although reference will also be made on occasion to the significant, or lack of, coverage it attracted in the national press and in the Province's broadcast media.

Masculinism in the Northern Irish media

The press in Northern Ireland is organized along sectarian lines, although readers also have access to localized editions of British and Irish newspapers. The main Protestant-owned dailies are the *Belfast Telegraph* and the *News Letter*, while the main Catholic-owned daily is the *Irish News*. There is also a Catholic-owned weekly newspaper published in West Belfast, the *Andersonstown News*. Partly because of its support for the unconditional entry of Sinn Féin into the Talks, coverage of the NIWC was most sympathetic in the latter, and least so in the loyalist *News Letter*. The largely negative coverage in the *News Letter* appears to have been calculated to appeal to traditional loyalist female readers. Thus the stand-first in one article identifies female voters/readers in terms of their familial roles as 'wives, mothers and partners' (27 May 1998). The woman journalist, Sandra Chapman, presupposes that her readers will be hostile to feminism in general, and to affirmative action in particular: 'What the Assembly doesn't need are strident females, some of whom are in the Women's Coalition, who believe they should be listened to just because they are women' (*News Letter* 27 May 1998).

In Chapter 3, I argued that informal fraternal networks operate between the masculinist institutions of party politics and the equally masculinist institutions of the media, segregating and subordinating women who enter the political arena. In Northern Ireland this situation is likely to be exacerbated by the operation of more formal networks, channelled through Orange and Masonic Lodges (*Who's Making the News?* 1996: 33). The perception of female journalists in a 1996 survey is that editors often appeal to a paternalistic discourse of care and protection in order to preclude them from covering stories where there might be a risk to their security (ibid.: 31–2). This survey vividly illustrates van Zoonen's (1994) contention that the media is infused with masculinist values and may also help to explain why the small number of female journalists employed in the Northern Irish press appear to accommodate themselves to these values, rather than seek to challenge them.

Gendered news frames

One ostensibly positive news frame identified by Norris (1997: 161) in relation to women in politics is that of women winning through against the odds. The coincidence of this news frame with world-wide secular trends explains the intense interest the NIWC attracted from the international media when it was first formed in 1996. This was in stark contrast to the initial absence of coverage in the local media. It would appear that local journalists, more accustomed to locating politicians on either side of a polarized sectarian divide, were unsure *how* to frame representatives of the Coalition. As a result, their activities went largely unreported. For example, when three of its representatives were invited to Downing Street for talks with the Prime Minister in January 1997, neither BBC Northern Ireland nor Ulster Television covered the story, while the *Belfast Telegraph* devoted only 300 words to the event. One exception to this early pattern of non-coverage is an article written by the political editor of the *Belfast Telegraph*, Mark Simpson, when the Coalition won sufficient votes to have two of its representatives appointed to both the Forum and Talks:

> The Women's Coalition had the last laugh of the polls. Critics nicknamed them the 'hen party' and called them naive, and an election distraction. But the new cross-community female group won enough votes to be at the talks table. In doing so they edged out more-established parties like the Ulster Tories, the Workers' Party and the Democratic Left. Not bad for an organization which was formed only six weeks ago.
>
> (*Belfast Telegraph* 31 May 1996)

This clearly fits into the news frame of women defying all of the predictions of political pundits by achieving an unexpected victory at the polls, but its potentially positive impact is considerably weakened by the decision of a subeditor to insert the headline, 'Hen Party Comes Home to Roost'. Whereas the article itself contests the trivializing connotations of the collocation 'Hen Party', the subeditor's decision to include this phrase in the headline, significantly *without* scare quotes, serves to give it informational prominence. This is suggestive of the way in which efforts made by individual journalists to challenge stereotypical gendered news frames can be offset by the institutional constraints that operate on the whole process of news production.

Another gendered news frame referred to by Norris (1997: 163) is one that represents women in politics as agents of change. Although this frame is discernible in media coverage of the NIWC, I would suggest that the Coalition is not given full credit for the constructive role it played in the Talks process in particular. Its major political strength in the Talks undoubtedly lay in its unaligned status, since its representatives were able to adopt the unique maverick role of moving between unionist and nationalist groups, helping to facilitate the process of negotiation. Although this facilitating role was acknowledged in press coverage, the way in which it was framed merits careful attention. Very typical was the comment made by *The Times* correspondent, Martin Fletcher: 'It discreetly facilitated, arbitrated and drafted'. This positive evaluation is immediately offset, however, by the trivializing, albeit ironic, comment that follows: 'The nearest they had been to a negotiating table before that day was to polish it' (*The Times* 15 June 1998). This is characteristic of the contradictory tendencies in media coverage of women in public sphere roles since it manages to be simultaneously positive and patronizing.

A further instance of the way in which the agency of NIWC representatives was undermined stems from the media obsession with its treatment at the hands of male colleagues. In the early days of its involvement in the Forum, such coverage was undoubtedly encouraged by the Coalition itself, as part of its deliberate strategy to name and shame persistent offenders. However, almost all the coverage it received thereafter was framed by a presupposition of gender antagonism that cast both McWilliams and Sagar in the stereotypical role of victims of male abuse. This happened despite the fact that, as McWilliams points out, both she and Sagar refused to accept such a role, 'we weren't afraid of them we weren't prepared to be bullied or silenced' (Trans. III: 159–60). In media interviews, McWilliams strove to make her resistance to this construction clear, 'there is the danger that whenever one gets asked, "How do men behave towards you?" that I end up ghettoising myself' (see Fig. 4.2b: ll. 71–3). But the majority of media texts suppressed traces of this resistance, preferring to reproduce a more familiar scenario in which women are portrayed as the inevitable losers in the age-old 'battle of the sexes'.

A related gendered news frame that accords a degree of agency to Coalition representatives is one that constructs them as civilizers of unruly male spaces. Thus the headline carried by the article in *The Times* alluded to above is, 'Women who make it hard to behave badly' (15 June 1998). This is an intertextual reference to the TV series in which the female protagonists curtail the wayward behaviour of their laddish partners. The stereotypical assumptions underlying this construction are made more explicit in the advice proffered by two male communications consultants approached by the Coalition during its campaign for the Assembly elections, 'Both suggested that the NIWC should depict its candidates as "mummies" keeping the bad boys from fighting and making everything all right' (Fearon 1999: 148). The cumulative effect of these gendered news frames is to create the impression that NIWC representatives were, at best, apolitical facilitators of the Talks process rather than key players in that process, thus obscuring the many innovative policies that the party has put forward.

Gender and the genre of the political interview

Fairclough (1995a) notes that texts often bear the intertextual traces of competing discourses and therefore serve as barometers of social change. This is strikingly true of a profile of Monica McWilliams in the *Belfast Telegraph* (10 October 1998) by Gail Walker (see Figs 4.2a and 4.2b). Walker characterizes McWilliams's rhetorical style as 'a beguiling mix of strident intellectual point-making mostly proffered in a soft country accent, making her at once authoritative and homely' (Fig. 4.2b: ll. 32–5). The collocation of 'strident' and 'intellectual' here is itself telling, since women who have intellectual pretensions or who speak out with authority in public are often viewed as 'strident'. However, it is the antonymic relationship between 'authoritative' and 'homely' which provides a trace of the competing discursive norms that women in public sphere roles often have to manage. Walker's comment is reminiscent of Fairclough's (1989: 182ff) analysis of the rhetorical style of Thatcher, which he claims was ideologically creative in that it combined features associated with white middle-class femininity and 'authoritative expressive elements' used by male politicians. I would suggest that this was not a peculiar feature of Thatcher's speech, but is the outcome of institutional

Fig. 4.2a Photograph of the Northern Ireland Women's Coalition leader, Monica McWilliams, accompanying a profile of her by Gail Walker in the *Belfast Telegraph* (10 October 1998)

Monica McWilliams, feisty blonde mother-of-two, university lecturer and founding member of the Women's Coalition, is passionate about the Stormont Agreement and the peace she believes it can bring.

But then, at 44, she has had long, tough personal experience of violence – and its bitter legacy.

She escaped serious injury several times when her childhood home, a farm nestling in the centre of Kilrea, Co Derry, was badly damaged in a series of IRA bomb attacks at the telephone exchange directly opposite.

'I remember on one occasion waking up to find a soldier standing above my bed, shouting at me to get out immediately, that there was a bomb . . .

But the worst was still to come for Monica and her chums, drawn from both sides of the community and all parts of the province.

One evening, during the tense days of the Ulster Workers Council strike in 1974, a close friend, Michael Mallon, set about hitching a lift from Toome, Co. Antrim, back to the city and university life. He never made it.

'I will never forget one of the students coming back to the house and saying Mickey – we always called him Mickey – had been murdered . . .

So many people lost their lives and I have never believed that anyone should have been killed just because someone else believed there was a cause that justified it.

'At least now there appears to be a way forward. A chance of a new beginning. A better future.'

McWilliams' style is a beguiling mix of strident intellectual point-making mostly proffered in a soft country accent making her at once authoritative and homely. She is also a very plain speaker, all matter-of-fact and commonsense, not given to hiding behind the politician's usual shield of jargonese.

For example, as leader of a party which transcends all the traditional descriptions of unionist or republican, loyalist or working class, and proudly draws support from the working class Shankill and Falls as well as the leafier suburbs, was Monica herself ever sectarian?

Of course. If you live in society that is sectarian then you must have been on the moon if you say that you were not. It's a horrible thing to admit to.

'But I was a part of this community and therefore clearly a part of what went on in it. 'But if I was part of the problem then I'm going to be part of the solution I hope, part of dealing with that problem. I believe that change comes from inside.

'I now believe that I can have my own respect without subordinating someone else's.'.

That, of course, is something of a moot point given that although the Coalition is barely three years into existence, it has been on the receiving end of some of the most vicious – and sexist jibes ever bandied in Ulster politics.

'Moo,' said the DUP's Ian Paisley jnr, 'Moo, moo, moo', when Monica was trying to speak on the BSE crisis at the Forum.

Other regularly used disparaging adjectives included 'whingeing', 'whining' and 'feckless' women.

Which male politicians have been the most vicious?

'Oh, they know who they are. But some have also been as the word suggests' gentle'men. I'm not asking people to be gentle, though, just to be co-operative and collaborative.

'But there are two risks in talking like this. First there is the danger of tarring all men with the same brush and some of my best friends are men in politics, genuinely good people.

'And secondly there is the danger that whenever one gets asked "How do men behave towards you?" that I end up ghettoising myself' . . .

[25 paragraphs follow, providing details of her childhood, familial relations, education, and lecturing experience (x 3)]

Does her burgeoning career as one of her party's two Assembly members leave much time for life at home with her husband Brian, a civil servant whom she met at a friend's wedding, and children, Gavin, 12, and nine-year-old Rowen? Is she guilty at not having enough time?

Monica is defensive. 'They are great wee fellas and they are the centre of my life. They are bored with politics, which is enormously healthy, and are more interested in watching telly, or playing computer games.

'I can put my hand on my heart and say they see as much of me as any other kids see of their mother who is in full time employment. The question is more: is anyone working not walking around with some guilt in some form as a parent and how much more does that affect a mother than a father?

'I'm there to get the sports gear ready, to make the packed lunches. And I have a fantastic childminder, one of the dearest people in my life. It's all about being organised. The basic thing is that if you are there for them and love them and care for them . . . that's where it counts.

I think my children benefit from what I do . . .

Was she always keen to have children? 'Good question. Throughout my 20s I was always saying "Not now" but yes I did want to have them. I see them as the centre of the marriage . . .

The most traumatic event that ever happened to her was the near fatal traffic accident of her much-loved sister Mary . . .

It's like so many people who have suffered through the Troubles. So many victims . . . although that's a strange word . . . most of them are survivors, tremendously good human beings.

For me, every time I think of someone in intensive care I think of the family standing around . . . it brings my own sister back to me.

'It's like the young policeman who died this week . . . he seemed like such a good man, taking the kids to football, trying to make a difference, not just in his own life but for the community.

'What a horrible way to die . . .'

Fig. 4.2b Part of the text of a profile of Monica McWilliams by Gail Walker that appeared in the *Belfast Telegraph* (10 October 1998), accompanied by the photograph reproduced on p. 127.

constraints that operate on all women in public sphere roles. The difference between Thatcher and McWilliams is that while the former saw no problem in embracing the adversarial masculinist norms that infuse political institutions, the latter has sought to challenge these and to promote alternative ways of 'doing politics'. However, McWilliams is careful to refute any assumption that this means giving up on tough political debate: 'I'm not asking people to be gentle, though, just to be cooperative and collaborative' (Fig. 4.2b: ll. 64–6).

In a large photograph accompanying the aforementioned article, McWilliams is depicted sitting on the floor, looking up at the viewer (see Fig. 4.2a). The high angle perspective from which the photograph is taken is extremely unusual in a photo-portrait of a politician: such an angle places the viewer in a position of superiority *vis-à-vis* the subject. Politicians generally go to great lengths to appear authoritative, yet the effect here seems calculated to make McWilliams appear *lacking* in authority. It could be argued that a more positive reading is cued by the strapline, where we are told that she 'gets down to earth on gritty issues'. This more positive spin is, however, in tension with the fact that she is pictured surrounded by multiple campaign posters of herself. This evokes a prescribed schema of politics as a shrewd game of self-promotion. The egotism implicit in this image is something that McWilliams herself singled out as an unwarranted instance of media misrepresentation:

> there was this big blow-up which looked~made me look like I had this enormous ego you know all of these huge posters of myself and my face which were for the flaming lamp-posts you know and I was getting them ready and it made it look like I just loved to look at myself sitting in the middle of it so I was very cross I knew instinctively when I was doing it that I didn't *want* to do it but because he told me it was not going to be seen in the country I thought well I couldn't be bothered you know fighting with him

(Trans. III: 283–9)

This provides a striking instance of the power photo-journalists have to manipulate the image of electoral candidates, even, as on this occasion, when the subject expresses a sense of unease about how the image is likely to be perceived.[5] In this instance, the visual and textual cues are already contradictory before readers approach the main body of the text.

Fairclough (1995b) argues that one of the functions of mediatized political discourse is to mediate between the public discourse of politics and the lifeworld discourse of readers. The genre of the political interview offers a very good instance of this, since the intention is to personalize politicians, providing insights into the life experiences that gave rise to their political convictions. On the surface, the account of the interview of McWilliams by

Gail Walker of the *Belfast Telegraph* appears to be positive in tone. It was for this reason that I chose to analyse this particular article in detail, since Toolan (1997: 94) urges critical linguists to move away from pointing out obvious instances of sexism, identifying instead the 'subtler and hence more insidious discriminatory and exclusionary discourses that abound'. The article begins with a rather blatant and common instance of sexism, however, by thematizing the stereotypical dossier epithet, 'feisty blonde mother-of-two', considerably undermining the force of the academic and political qualifications that follow (Fig. 4.2b: ll. 1–3). The adjective 'feisty' is, of course, a gender-specific cliché, used to describe often diminutive women who battle against the odds to make their mark. This description is followed by the information that she feels 'passionate' about the Stormont Agreement (ibid.: l. 3), reinforcing the view that women respond to political issues emotionally rather than rationally. It could be argued that McWilliams's status as a major politician is undermined by the tendency throughout the article to employ her first name only, yet this would seem to be part of a deliberate strategy to construct a subject position for her as an empathetic *person*, rather than a remote political figure. Thus much of the early part of the article provides evidence of her 'tough personal experience of violence' (ibid.: ll. 11ff).

What follows is a fairly predictable chronology of events in McWilliams's life. Such chronologies generally function in media profiles of politicians to illuminate the political stance arrived at by the person being interviewed. According to Fairclough (1995b: 189), this usually results in a hybrid text, 'an amalgam of the discourses of professional politics and ordinary life'. What is noteworthy in this instance is the structured absence of references to Mc-Williams's politics and an almost exclusive focus on her personal history per se. The only 'facts' we learn are that she is a founder member of the three-year-old Women's Coalition which has a broad constituency in terms of class, political allegiance and region (Fig. 4.2b: ll. 51–6). We are told that she was fascinated by politics as a child and has been subjected to 'vicious' and 'sexist' abuse by male colleagues (ibid.: l. 55). We learn nothing, however, about the NIWC's policies on any of the major political issues affecting Northern Ireland and nothing about its contribution to the drafting of the Agreement. By contrast, there are seven paragraphs devoted to McWilliams's views on children and her role as a mother (ibid.: ll. 83–99ff). The interviewer's questions on these issues are reproduced in reported form as follows:

Does her burgeoning career as one of her party's two Assembly members leave much time for life at home with husband Brian, a civil servant whom she met at a friend's wedding, and children, Gavin, 12, and nine-year-old Rowen? Is she guilty at not having enough time?

(Fig. 4.2b: ll. 77–82)

Hovering beneath the surface of these questions is the assumption that feminism is anti-family, but this is resisted by McWilliams. In particular, she queries why working mothers should be expected to accept a greater burden of guilt than working fathers (ibid.: ll. 89–92). Yet, Walker's subjective impression that McWilliams adopts a 'defensive' tone throughout these answers is given the status of a 'fact' as a result of the categorical modality she employs, 'Monica is defensive' (ibid.: l. 83). The obsessive focus on McWilliams's roles as wife, as mother and, elsewhere in the article, as nurturing grand-daughter and sister, as opposed to her status as a politician, is suggestive of the way in which media coverage of women in public life can paradoxically serve to eclipse their public identities, even when it appears to be drawing attention to them.

4.3.7 Managing the media

While NIWC representatives have undoubtedly been subjected to selective and distorting media coverage, they have also used the media for their own ends. McWilliams makes it clear that they were aware from the start of the need to write themselves *into* news narratives:

> we knew from day one that the press had to be on our side and that we had to get coverage because no-one would have known who we were and that therefore we needed as much coverage and we worked *extremely* hard at getting press coverage . . . the media's absolutely crucial they're a big player in all of this and you do get elected or de-selected on the back of how the media portray you

(Trans. III: 28–31, 301–3)

One such instance occurred when male politicians on both sides of the religious divide closed ranks by rejecting the NIWC's proposals for a more inclusive top-up system of proportional representation for the Assembly elections in June 1998. The system chosen, based on a single transferable vote, was calculated to exclude some of the smaller parties, including the NIWC. The Coalition responded by running a vigorous campaign in the media to foreground the fact that its representatives were in danger of being excluded from the Assembly they had helped to shape. It managed to secure coverage in the local, national and international press, with headlines such as, 'Anger as women are closed out' (*Andersonstown News* 16 May 1998), ' "It's cheerio girls and thanks for the laughs" in sexist North' (*Irish Times* 27 April 1998) and 'Irishwomen call foul as new political rules leave them out' (*The New York Times* 2 April 1998). It even attracted support from the Prime Minister, after McWilliams and Sagar were featured on BBC Radio 4's 'Woman's Hour'. Blair appeared on the programme the following day to announce his view that, 'It would be both counterproductive and wrong if we didn't find some way of involving those people' (cited in the *Irish Times* 27 April 1998). In the event, there was a certain poetic justice in the fact that the Coalition owed the two seats it won in the June 1998 Assembly elections to the cross-community transfer of votes from male-dominated parties on the two extremes of the sectarian divide. The NIWC's support for other minority parties and its courageous stand against loyalist intransigence and intimidation paid off, securing it a long-term future on the political landscape of Northern Ireland. It is unlikely that it could have achieved this, however, without a well-orchestrated and high-profile media campaign.

4.4 Conclusions

The transition made by women in Scotland, Wales and Northern Ireland from grassroots activism to mainstream politics has led to record numbers of women having their voices heard in institutions responsible for political decision-making. There is evidence that their presence is making an impact on the language and structures of these institutions. One effect has been to set in motion a process of destructuration between the civil and public spheres, a process that is likely to be of particular benefit to women. They have also raised the profile of women and issues of relevance to women among all political parties. With differing degrees of success, they have helped to promote an alternative set of discursive norms for the conduct of political debate. In the case of the NIWC, its treatment at the hands of male colleagues has helped to expose the shockingly masculinist nature of politics in the Province. More positively, it has helped to ensure that a new egalitarian language, based on inclusiveness, respect for the rights and traditions of others and political accommodation, has become enshrined in the Agreement document.

In all three contexts, the media have played a key role in shaping the perception of the intervention that feminist groups have made to secure greater gender equality in political decision-making. In Scotland, there are some signs of a media backlash against the gains women have made, as well as signs of indifference towards policy issues relevant to women. Media coverage of the Welsh Agriculture Secretary, Christine Gwyther, has been complicit with a process by which women in leadership roles experience a process of dequalification. By contrast, media coverage of the NIWC has been surprisingly positive, given the entrenched masculinism of media institutions in Northern Ireland.

I hope to have shown, however, that even *ostensibly* positive coverage has often been patronizing and, in particular, has served to reinforce women's connection with domestic sphere roles when they have sought to construct identities for themselves primarily as credible political actors. I would suggest that this is symptomatic of a more general process of discursive restructuring whereby the gendered division between private and public is being reproduced *within* the public sphere. One way in which women have sought to challenge this interpretative control is by becoming more adept at media management, as well as by utilizing their own alternative media. The NIWC has employed both strategies, in its mainstream media campaign to lobby for places at the Assembly, and in the creation of its own website, conferences and publications. Thanks to its influence, the language of the Agreement and the structures of the new Assembly are likely to be less adversarial and more gender-inclusive than would have been true had they confined themselves to lobbying activities alone. However, my study of a women-orientated lobbying group in Chapter 5 will suggest that such grassroots organizations can afford a space of political participation for women who might never contemplate more formal party-political activism.

Notes

1. This remains a problem for both men and women in remoter parts of Scotland. Thus the Highlands and Islands Alliance claimed that only a job-sharing arrangement would enable MSPs to combine family responsibilities with attendance at the Scottish Parliament in Edinburgh. One founder member, Alice Mann, said: 'The thing people are really concerned about in the Highlands and Islands is the remoteness of politicians. At the moment, as soon as they are elected they are required to leave the area. People are very frustrated by that' (the *Guardian* 22 January 1999).
2. This was reported by the Director of the Fawcett Society, Mary Ann Stephenson, at a conference in Canada House in London on 'Women's Equality and Participation in Public Life' (21–22 October 1999).
3. For a detailed discussion of the practice of 'transversal politics' in Italy, see Yuval-Davis (1996).
4. A recent biography by Julia Langdon (2000) suggests that Mowlam's widely acknowledged strength of character did not prevent her from being side-lined by Blair in the All-Party Talks, leading her, at one point, to remark bitterly to Bill Clinton that she had been reduced to making the tea.
5. McWilliams notes that NIWC members have become more practised at controlling the photographs used of them in media coverage:

    > a couple of times the media have come and wanted me to put on a kettle in the kitchen and I've said no I want to be reading the newspaper or at the computer or doing whatever so I am very very conscious now of not being stereotyped into that you know if they want photographs of children or taking them to school or doing whatever now sometimes I don't mind doing the family stuff 'cos it's very important for women to show

that they have a family and erh during the elections my children *were* coming out and canvassing with me so I didn't mind those photographs being taken but it's the kind of trivializing piece that's forced on a serious interview and then they want to take a little shot of you making the tea erh I just noticed yesterday a local group had written erhm may the women in the Assembly never have a teapot near them when a camera is close [mutual laughter] it was a kind of prayer for the women of the Assembly

(Trans. III: 290–301)

5

Consuming Politics. A Case Study of the Women's Environmental Network

Having looked at women's involvement in central and devolved political institutions in the previous two chapters, in this chapter, I intend to turn my attention to grassroots politics, and more specifically to an examination of the structure and campaigning style of the London-based Women's Environmental Network (hereafter, WEN). The decision to focus on an *environmental* pressure group was motivated largely by the fact that this enabled a comparison between a women-orientated organization and non-gender-specific groups, the aim being to establish whether gender and gender politics make a difference to organizational structures and campaign style. Habermas (1987) classifies environmental new social movements (hereafter, NSMs) as being marked by resistance and withdrawal, in contrast to the women's movement, which he regards as emancipatory. As an environmental pressure group informed by the emancipatory impulse of feminism, WEN renders this classification problematic.

More fundamentally, I will argue that the activities of feminist green consumer groups, such as WEN, by their very nature trouble the systems/lifeworld distinction[1] that underpins Habermas's theory of communicative action, since they employ strategic means in order to achieve communicative ends. For instance, by strategically exploiting the gender subtext of the consumer role, WEN manages to generate relations of solidarity between women and to create for them new spaces of political participation. Rather than passively succumbing to the intrusion of systems of money and power, it proactively seeks to use women's purchasing power to assert lifeworld control over the state-regulated economy. Fraser (1995) and Threadgold (1997) are likewise critical of Habermas's over-rigid demarcation of the discursive boundaries between systems world and lifeworld. They argue that the absolute distinction between them can only be supported in a theory that is gender-blind and ignores the fact that gender inequalities are replicated in both domains. My research lends support to this view in relation to the civil sphere, since it reveals that women are no more likely to be admitted as equal participants to mainstream NSMs than they are to the political decision-making institutions of the state, discussed in the previous two chapters.

In an influential article in *New Left Review*, McRobbie (1994: 109) explains the rise of NSMs in Britain as a response to the vacuum created by the failure of 'conviction politics' among mainstream political parties, especially the Parliamentary Labour Party, throughout the late 1980s and early 1990s. More significantly, in terms of this study, she argues that these NSMs offer 'a space of engagement which is particularly open to women' (ibid.: 115). Her analysis is supported by my discussion in Chapter 4 of the way in which the Conservative Party's monopoly of power at Westminster throughout the period referred to by McRobbie helped to mobilize grassroots women's groups in Scotland, which, in turn, ultimately influenced the gender composition of the new Scottish Parliament. Likewise, I hope to have shown that the emergence of the NIWC as a party political force could not have taken place without the existence of a vibrant civil society in Northern Ireland in which women were, and are, very active. People's disillusionment with party politicians and political institutions also meant that the environmental movement underwent something of a renaissance in Britain in the late 1980s and early 1990s. For instance, the British Green Party experienced unprecedented success in the European Elections in June 1989 when it took 14.9 per cent of the vote (Fowler 1991: 181).

According to McRobbie (1994: 114), the success of NSMs was facilitated by the increasing 'porosity' of the media throughout this period, creating spaces for opposition and contestation. This contradicts Habermas's view that the disintegration of the bourgeois public sphere has occurred in inverse proportion to the rise of a mass-mediated culture industry. Through the access they have afforded to NSMs, media institutions could be said to have contributed to the revival of a vibrant civil sphere, and one less subject to a male monopoly. Although this is true to some extent, it has not prevented media coverage of such oppositional voices from being, at the very least, contradictory, as was noted in Chapter 4, and as will also be demonstrated in relation to media coverage of WEN's campaigns. I have chosen to focus on WEN because it is the only UK group which campaigns primarily on issues that link *women*, the environment and health, although men are free to join and make up about 5 per cent of its 2,000 strong membership (Trans. IV: 153–4). Before going on to consider WEN's use of, and representation in, mainly the *print* media, I will begin by exploring how its emphasis on *women* and the environment affects its organizational structures and campaign rhetoric. In the course of this discussion, comparisons will be made between WEN and other environmental groups, notably Friends of the Earth (FoE) and, to a lesser extent, Greenpeace.

5.1 Brief background details on WEN

WEN was launched in September 1988 and is a non-profit-making organization with the stated aim of 'educating, informing and empowering women[2] who care about the environment' (Newsletter No. 1, autumn 1988). The central office is in London, and is staffed by a few paid officers and numerous volunteers, who receive basic expenses. One of the major ways in which it aims to 'empower' women is by giving them the necessary experience of, and expertise in, national campaigning on issues relevant to them, something it claims they are often denied in other environmental groups. Reflecting on the achievements of the organization over its first ten years, its founder, Bernadette Vallely, said, 'I am most proud of the hundreds of women who have come through the doors of WEN and have been personally empowered' (Newsletter No. 38, summer 1999). However, as the term 'network' implies, there has also been a strong emphasis from the outset on the importance of local groups and locally based campaigns. At the height of its popularity, there were about thirty locally active groups throughout Britain, although this number has since declined. Every effort is made to disseminate information to local groups via tape recordings of London-based meetings, seminars and so on. In terms of funding, WEN relies mainly on membership fees and donations, although individual campaigns have attracted one-off funding, including from the government and the National Lottery. In return for their membership fee, members receive a quarterly newsletter, as well as more detailed information about specific campaigns, on request.

An immediate question arises as to why an environmental group should choose to adopt a so-called 'woman's perspective'. In the case of WEN, this appears to have been motivated by both practical and theoretical considerations. Prior to setting up WEN, Vallely had been assistant to the Director of FoE, but had felt that issues of particular concern to women were either trivialized or, more often, marginalized, within FoE's overall campaign priorities. She gradually became convinced that there was a constituency for a woman-orientated environmental group. Social attitude surveys have consistently shown that women are more concerned about environmental issues than men. This continues to be true, as was evident in the much-publicized study, *What Women Want*, carried out in 1996 by the Department of the Environment. It revealed that nearly 90 per cent of women consider themselves to be 'very' or 'quite' concerned about the environment and this concern translates into action. For instance, women comprise 66 per cent of the total membership of FoE, and according to Seager (1993: 264) this proportion rises to 80 per cent or more of small grassroots groups and animal rights groups. Vallely was also keenly aware that, as primary consumers, women's purchasing power could be harnessed for ethical and political ends.

5.2   Ecofeminism and the critique of masculinism within the environmental movement

Vallely claims to have drawn her initial inspiration for setting up WEN in the UK from the newly emerging academic discourse of ecofeminism (Trans. VI: 13–16). In its 'difference' guise, ecofeminism is suffused with essentialist ideas about the 'authentic female mind' as the source of the planet's salvation (Spretnak 1990), as well as new age spirituality (Starhawk 1990). In its 'dominance' guise (Merchant 1980, 1996; Plumwood 1993, 1995) it emphasizes the link between man's exploitation of both women and nature. This more politicized approach to ecofeminism has also generated a critique of the masculinist assumptions said to be embedded in the theory of deep ecology, and in the practice of male-orientated environmental groups like Greenpeace (Kheel 1990; Seager 1993). As one instance of the latter, Seager (1993: 202ff) points to the way women were demonized in the anti-fur advertising campaign run in the UK in 1985 and 1990 by Greenpeace-Lynx and Lynx respectively. The former depicts a woman trailing a fur coat, which, in turn, leaves a trail of blood in its wake. The caption reads, 'It takes up to 40 dumb animals to make a fur coat . . . But only one to wear it'. The follow-up campaign poster in 1990 was even more misogynist since it juxtaposes a picture of a model wearing a fur coat, with the caption 'Rich bitch', and one of a dead fox, with the caption, 'Poor bitch'. Seager contrasts this sexist and woman-blaming strategy with an equally striking poster by the woman-led American group, Friends of the Animals. By depicting a series of frames in which a male trapper hunts and then stomps on the throat of the coyote to kill it, its poster locates the blame where it belongs: with a male-led industry.

When interviewed in 1997, Vallely pointed out that traces of the more implicit masculinist bias at work in FoE are evident in an officially sanctioned history of the organization by Lamb (1996). In particular, she noted that the agency of women activists is elided by their structured absence from the many photographs that occur throughout the book, recording various successful FoE campaigns (Trans. VI: 35–8). This tendency to obscure the contribution women have made to environmental politics is also evident in the second edition of an anthology of work in the field, entitled *Environmental Policy in the 1990s* (Vig and Kraft, eds, 1994). Despite claiming in the blurb to record 'the most important developments in environmental policy and politics since the 1960s', it makes no reference to WEN, its only reference to gender being in relation to population control. Paehlke (1994: 364) makes the cautious, almost grudging, claim that, on this issue, there is 'some potential for cooperation between those advancing gender equity and those seeking environmental protection'. He thereby fails to acknowledge that feminist activists are *integral* members of the environmental movement, rather than outsiders who just might, in certain narrowly defined circumstances, represent potential allies. The belief that masculinism is endemic in all mainstream environmental groups led Vallely to adopt the segregationist, though not separatist, strategy of setting up WEN.

5.3   Liberating structures?

Despite McRobbie's optimism about the woman-friendly nature of NSMs, evidence suggests that women are *no more* likely to be represented in the higher echelons of non-gender-specific environmental groups than in party political organizations. In particular, a gendered split appears to have developed over time between high-profile managerial and campaigning roles performed mainly by men, and fund-raising and administrative roles performed mainly by women. For instance, a survey of twenty-one different environmental groups, carried out by Teverson for the British Association of Nature Conservationists in 1991, revealed that, 'while almost 50 per cent of employees were women, at top management level 87 per cent were men' (the *Guardian* 19 December 1991). Seager (1993: 186) sees this gendered split as symptomatic of a more general shift taking place in the societal order of discourse around professionalization, 'a process whereby men have wrested control of activities away from women (who often conducted them as extensions of their work in the private sphere) and reconstituted them as exclusively male activities within the public sphere'.

The organizational structure of FoE, in particular, has tended towards permanent bureaucracy and an increasingly hierarchical management style. This was especially true under the high-profile leadership of old Etonian Jonathon Porritt, who had threatened to leave the Green Party unless it abandoned its 'wholly *irrational* abhorrence of political leadership' (the *Guardian* 22 March 1991; my italics). Despite the relatively high status position Vallely had held as assistant to the Director of FoE, she still felt stereotyped as a 'fixer' (Trans. VI: 39). She recalled a comment made by Porritt to explain why he thought women could not be successful campaigners: '[They] haven't the balls for it' (ibid.: 41). It is clear from this comment that, within FoE at least, women were viewed as semi-participants in the new participatory politics. This is confirmed by Iris Webb, another female FoE activist, 'For a long time it was very male-dominated and macho . . . I don't know if they were conscious of it, but there was an association between being aggressive, obsessive, not supportive, with being a good campaigner' (cited in Lamb 1996: 141). The organizational structure of WEN, with its emphasis on fluidity, networking and collaborative working practices, was conceived in direct opposition to the masculinist and bureaucratic structure of FoE (Trans. VI: 23–5). However, as in the case of Monica McWilliams in the NIWC, media pressure to identify a high-profile 'personality' led Vallely herself to assume this role, and, in her case, she also assumed the nominal title of 'Director'.

The problem with such nominal leadership roles is, of course, that they are open to abuse. Sarah Miller, editor of the WEN Newsletter in 1997, admitted that the degree to which an egalitarian ethos prevails within the organization depends on the interactional style favoured by individual directors, some of whom have been 'quite hierarchical' (Trans. IV: 248ff). It would seem, then, that even feminist-identified women who have a theoretical commitment to more egalitarian ways of working can, in practice, succumb to the lure of power. Miller tried to explain the dilemma posed by such a role:

> someone with the role of the director ... should theoretically get paid more than other people and they should have more responsibility and they should be more accountable and so if~if someone's going to be more accountable and more responsible it's difficult to address ... how much power they should have and~and you know it's a really hard balance to find and we haven't found it really

> (Trans. IV: 261–6)

This has led to a deliberate policy in WEN of allowing the role of director to lapse and, instead, of vesting collective authority in the board of directors and trustees. However, it has been deemed practically necessary to introduce an office coordinator, since, as another respondent points out, the absence of such a person has increased the administrative burden on everyone (Trans. IV: 80–2).

Ann Link, who has been involved as an active campaigner since WEN was founded, said that irrespective of structural problems, 'a lot of mutual support goes on and em except for the last few months when there's been a funding crisis *generally* I find it so positive that I want to do it' (ibid.: 379–80). Likewise, Bonnie Groves is recorded as having said, 'Though new and inexperienced, I am not made to feel like the office dogsbody' (Newsletter No. 39, autumn 1999: 3). Significantly, from its inception WEN has employed an open-plan office layout to facilitate cooperative working practices and to promote the cross-fertilization of ideas between those working on different campaigns. One of WEN's science researchers, Becky Price, tried to explain some of the benefits of working from the London office, as compared to her experience of working in other non-governmental organizations (NGOs): 'there is more freedom to actually try things out and to do things in a slightly different way erhm that would be difficult to get recognized as being important within the other NGOs ... the way we do things here has a slightly different feel' (Trans. IV: 69–74). The implication seems to be that WEN offers a safe environment in which to develop new ideas and that, unlike in other NGOs, issues of relevance to women are automatically accorded value.

It is, of course, possible to exaggerate differences, including gender differences, between environmental groups, since all my respondents acknowledged that there is a good deal of cooperation between WEN and other mainstream environmental groups, and that they have often assumed complementary roles in jointly-run campaigns. For instance, Vallely noted that 'Greenpeace provided the £10,000 for printing material in WEN's sanpro campaign. In a *quid pro quo*, WEN supported *its* campaign on chlorine in paper' (Trans. VI: 32–3). However, Link suggested that FoE's perception of itself as a major institution, and its tendency to assume an agenda-setting role, has proved a barrier to fruitful collaboration over the years. This is implicit in her comment, 'I expect to work in coalitions ... I expect some sort of positive em sharing of ideas and communication', whereas FoE is 'less open to brainstorming exciting ideas' (Trans. IV: 314–16, 332–3). It is clear from this that, unlike FoE, WEN favours the type of jointly constructed or 'collaborative floor' referred to by Edelsky (1981) in her study of academics. WEN's advocacy of egalitarian interactional strategies and structures, and its resistance to the type of bureaucratization willingly embraced by organizations like FoE, would seem to suggest that gender and gender politics *can* make a difference in environmental groups.

5.4 Image and campaign rhetoric

In terms of image and campaign style there appear to be marked differences between FoE and WEN. In the case of FoE, a discursive drift away from the communicative imperatives advocated by the movement's founder, David Brower, and towards the strategic imperatives of scientific professionalism, was evident even in the first decade of the movement's history. Brower, who drew his inspiration from the nineteenth-century nature writer and transcendentalist, Henry David Thoreau, believed that 'thinking objectively is the greatest threat to nature in America' (cited in Lamb 1996: 23) and proposed instead a more intuitive approach based on a subjective bond between people and nature. The fact that both Thoreau and Brower were men offers a timely reminder that men and male-led organizations can, and do, adopt so-called feminine interactional strategies. Sue Clifford, a British FoE board member from 1971 to 1982, expresses the deep reservations she felt at the move away from this ethos:

> What happened all through the 1970s ... was that the arguments and ways of arguing strayed ever closer to other people's frame of reference. We started outside the frame, saying: Come on, you ought to come over

here. But the arguments got to be more and more an exchange of expert opinions.

(cited in Lamb 1996: 51)

The implication is that the discursive boundaries between environmental groups like FoE and government and industry were becoming ever more permeable. As the feminist Carol Cohn famously found when she tried to talk to experts at a defence policy think-tank, it was a short step from speaking their language to sharing their point of view (in Cameron 1992: 223). Mills (1997: 12) points out that this is by no means inevitable: 'it could equally be argued that government policy is framed precisely in reaction to pressure groups such as environmental groups; therefore, each group will have its discursive parameters defined for it by the other'. Seager (1993: 193) is more pessimistic, 'Entry into the established political arenas has clearly changed the environmental movement; it is not clear that the establishment has been changed'. It is perhaps not surprising that dominant discursive norms are more likely to influence oppositional ones than vice versa.

In the mid- to late-1980s in FoE this discursive drift away from the philosophy of its founder became a conscious shift in style under the high-profile directorship of Porritt, who used the media to launch the movement's new image. The stand-first accompanying an article in the *Guardian* (7 January 1986) sums up this change, albeit in a slightly mocking tone, 'FoE are out to shed an image of cranky do-gooding. Jonathon Porritt says virtue is not enough. So he has picked up a tie and the techniques of persuasion.' It is interesting that a 'tie' is intended to function here as a metonymic signifier of the organization's decision to embrace a new bureaucratic image, since it unintentionally betrays the fact that such an image is simultaneously masculinist in its orientation. FoE's decision to distance itself from a more feminine orientation is implicit in Porritt's comment that its traditional 'appeal to the *emotions* has blunted our impact on the people who should, ultimately, be affected by our arguments – the decision-makers' (ibid.; my italics). Although he pays tribute to the 'naiveté', which he claims is funda-mental to FoE's potential success, his own emphasis is on its near-antonym, 'authority'. For instance, he stresses the '*authority* of accepted research' and expresses his determination to commit FoE only to campaigns that lend them 'an element of *authority*' (ibid.; my italics). The emphasis of FoE's campaigning since has been chiefly orientated to lobbying and corporate negotiations. This has happened despite the fact that its reputation for integrity stemmed, in large part, from its independence from the policy-making process.

Seager (1993: 190–1) suggests that 'Women are not *inherently* less suscep-tible to the "cooptation" of power – but more accustomed to being outsiders in the halls of power, [they] are in a position to be more critical of the rules of the game in ways that men on the inside can't or won't see'. Women may also experience less pressure to be taken seriously by the (usually) male representatives of government and industry. It is significant, then, that the main critics of FoE's increasing tendency to prioritize its lobbying role have been female activists within the organization, such as Val Stephens, Uta Bellion and Elaine Gilligan, who have urged a return to a local focus on real communities (Lamb 1996). They would appear to share Seager's (1993: 195) view that a reliance on bureaucratic procedures and science 'takes environmental assessment further and further away from the realm of lived experience – which is, not coincidentally, the realm in which most women are expert'. Vallely's decision to leave FoE in order to set up WEN was largely attributable to her desire to reclaim the communicative imperatives which she felt FoE had abandoned. For instance, in an article in the *Guardian* (19 December 1991), she argues for a different value system on the grounds that 'science and statistics are not enough'.

Seager (1993: 276) identifies the dominant news frame that governs media coverage of contemporary environmental issues: '[they] are often scripted as the drama of "the hysterical housewife meets the man of reason"'. Somewhat paradoxically, WEN has adopted a strategy which does not so much reject the image of 'housewife', as celebrate it (Trans. IV: 172–6). This is evident in one newsletter which recalls, with obvious delight, that 'women in pinnies and rubber gloves made an odd sight outside the Office of Fair Trading', only to be revealed as WEN activists campaigning against the duopoly on detergent by Procter & Gamble and Lever Brothers (No. 26, spring 1995). The intention here would seem to be to point up the apparent incongruity between women's private sphere identities and the reality of their roles as agents of public protest. However, the metadiscursive gap, referred to earlier, means that there is no guarantee that this is how their intentions will have been perceived and it may have led some to dismiss them as 'cranks'. Its innovative campaign on sanpro made it clear that 'housewifely' protest can be nonetheless radical, hence its iconoclastic aim of 'smash[ing] the myths around menstruation'. Its briefing sheet states that, 'Western society's concealment of menstruation has given rise to expensive, wasteful, polluting sanitary products which bring unnecessary health and period pains for women'. When Vallely told a senior FoE colleague that she was going to campaign on this issue, 'he burst out laughing and said she would get no coverage' (the *Scotsman* 6 January 1994). Yet, against the odds and expectations of male ex-colleagues, this particular campaign won the 1993 British Environment and Marketing Award, and has since led to changes in industry practice and government legislation.

Goldblatt (1996: 128) notes how such 'unconventional political protest subverts and ridicules the dominantly strategic quality of conventional political participation'. WEN's playful and creative engagement with both language, and gesture politics is designed to challenge the dominant discursive norms of both industry and government, as well as of other environmental groups, like FoE. Its critique of the advertising industry has included spoof chocolate advertisements which aim to expose the contradictions inherent in using slim models to advertise what is in reality the major binge food for women with eating disorders. Its taboo-breaking campaign to promote the binning of sanitary protection was likewise lightened by humour. One brightly coloured toilet door sticker carried the image of a bather with a beach towel and the accompanying message, 'Make sure this is the only towel you find on the beach'. Disposal bags, supplied on request by WEN, replace the euphemistic image of the crinolined woman, who poses coquettishly on more traditional bags (Mills 1995: 119), with a cartoon depiction of a bewildered family on a beach, beset by sanpro waste. A 'subvertisement' that appeared in one newsletter juxtaposed the carefree image of a windsurfing menstruating woman, familiar from TV ads, with the same windsurfer looking somewhat nonplussed as she encounters sanpro waste. According to Vallely, this subversive use of humour was calculated to refute the view, including within the environmental movement, of feminist activists as humour*less* (Trans. VI: 19–22).

Unlike FoE's strategy of addressing its campaign rhetoric to gatekeepers in government and industry, WEN primarily addresses those affected by environmental policy and industry practice. Its campaign on Toxic Shock Syndrome (TSS) was personalized by drawing on the actual experiences of women who had recovered from the rare disease. One leaflet was produced to publicize the plight of a young girl, Alice Kilvert, who died from TSS in November 1993. This uncharacteristically sensationalist leaflet, which seems to reproduce the language of tabloid journalism, was not produced by WEN, but by Kilvert's grieving parents. Given that there are relatively few reported cases, ten per year, and few deaths, the alarming headline, 'Tampons – the silent killer', hardly seems justified. However, WEN insists that women have a right to know about the risks, no matter how small, and successfully campaigned to persuade manufacturers to provide on-pack warnings offering practical advice on how to minimize these risks. In an article in the *Guardian* (19 December 1991), Vallely seeks to expose what she believes are the limitations of a purely objective approach: 'At WEN, we're often accused of being "just a load of emotional women" and recently we've begun to say, "Yes, I am emotional and I believe that's a correct response to something that might kill me".' By suggesting that it is rational to feel emotional about personal health risks, Vallely seeks to call into question the conventional wisdom, implicitly accepted by FoE, that reason and emotion are, in fact, incompatible.

One campaign that vividly illustrates WEN's characteristic tendency to prioritize the (inter)personal over the ideational is its recent breast cancer mapping project. The project, which took place between April 1997 and June 1999, was designed to collate evidence from women, including survivors of breast cancer, about their perceptions of environmental risks in their locality and possible links between these and the incidence of the disease. Through local WEN groups, trade unions and various women's organizations, those concerned about breast cancer were encouraged to come together to share their experiences and concerns. The aim was to avoid the normal practice inherent in more conventional surveys of positioning women as study subjects; instead, they were to 'be their own experts' (*Putting Breast Cancer on the Map* 1999: 11). The findings do not, therefore, claim to have the status of 'scientific facts', they simply constitute one element in a broader picture of the disease. However, WEN hopes that evidence about clustering may prompt conventional medical researchers to focus their attention on possible environmental causation[3] and positive measures to prevent cancer, rather than focusing exclusively on finding a cure. There are undoubtedly risks in this type of project. For instance, Seager cites numerous case studies in which, '"scientific facts" are thrown up in opposition to community-based and "amateur-collected" evidence against environmental agitators' (ibid.: 196). In addition, WEN's reliance on a human-needs approach has had implications for the type and extent of coverage its campaigns have received in the media (see below). Yet, the gains for the individual women involved appear to have been considerable. Although some respondents found the theory-driven concept of 'mapping' their environments alien, or even embarrassing, 41 per cent found it useful or very useful (*Putting Breast Cancer on the Map* 1999: 40). The consciousness-raising and solidarity-affirming nature of the project subsequently helped to revitalize existing local WEN groups and led to the setting up of several new groups (Newsletter No. 38, summer 1999: 12).

5.5   A detailed comparison of differently gendered rhetorical styles

It is interesting to compare the rhetorical strategies used in two information sheets produced by FoE and WEN on issues relating to paper and the environment (Figs 5.1 and 5.2). In terms of subject matter, the most striking difference is that, whereas FoE's information sheet moves from the international context of deforestation to recycling in the home via industrial processes, the equivalent sheet produced by WEN immediately locates both the problem and a range of solutions within the home by focusing on mundane items of household waste, including those of particular relevance to women. Only thereafter is the chain of causality traced via industrial waste disposal processes to the global crisis. The style of WEN's fact sheet is more inclusive of the lifeworld of readers than FoE's. For instance, the first paragraph sets the tone by ending with the rhetorical question, 'But is this the best use of fibres from trees which took a lifetime to grow?', and extensive use is

INFORMATION SHEET

RECYCLED PAPER

The production and disposal of paper impacts on the environment in a number of different ways. Friends of the Earth's research has shown that recycled paper is better for the environment than virgin paper on a number of different counts:

Forestry

In some parts of the world, for example in the United States, Canada, parts of Scandinavia and Indonesia, ancient natural forest is being cut down and cleared to make pulp for the paper industry – destroying a habitat for wildlife and plants that has taken centuries to evolve.

In some areas, such as Scandinavia and Brazil, new forests are being planted where the natural forests have already been cleared. These 'factory forests' do not provide a habitat for the same variety of wildlife that lived in the area before, and many species are disappearing as a consequence. On top of this the chemicals used to treat the trees pollute rivers and streams and can contaminate drinking water supplies. So although the paper industry claims that it 'plants more trees than it cuts down', their methods of forestry can in fact seriously damage the environment.

Energy

Some people point out that a lot of energy is used by collecting waste paper for recycling and that it would be better to burn paper to create energy. However, research has shown that considerably more energy is saved by recycling paper than is generated by incinerating it. Furthermore, paper that is not collected for recycling still has to be collected for disposal.

Pollution from Paper-Making

Paper and pulp mills discharge polluting effluent into rivers, estuaries and sewers. Some UK paper mills discharge more pollution than they are legally allowed. Comparative studies show that recycling paper causes less pollution than making virgin paper.

One of the most polluting processes in paper-making is chlorine bleaching. The paper industry is, however, now moving towards using less polluting forms of the bleach. Most recycled papers are not re-bleached and as far as we are aware none of the recycled paper in the UK has been bleached with chlorine.

Pollution from de-inking

One of the arguments used against recycling printed paper is the pollution caused by the de-inking process. Printed paper, which is to be recycled, must first be de-inked. The de-inking process uses detergents or oxygen bubbles to remove the ink from the pulp and produces a by-product which can contain heavy metals. This sludge is usually disposed of to landfill or an incinerator.

Fig. 5.1   Friends of the Earth information sheet on Paper and the Environment (updated June 1996)

However, the disposal of this sludge is no more polluting the disposal of waste printed paper which has not been recycled. The heavy metals in the ink will be released into the environment in either case.

Paper from non-wood fibres

Friends of the Earth is now calling for a major reduction in the consumption of wood products in order to take the pressure off the world's forests. This involves using less wood and paper products, re-using them, and then recycling them. Another possibility is to use alternative fibres in the production of paper. A 1995 study called 'Out of the Woods' investigates how this major reduction could be achieved in the UK and explains how straw, flax and hemp as by-products of industries such as agriculture and textiles could be used to manufacture paper thereby reducing the demand for wood.

Friends of the Earth is campaigning for

■ Industry, governments and individual consumers to reduce levels of consumption of wood products.

■ The reuse of all wood products as many times as possible before recycling.

■ Development and improvement of recycling facilities and their use.

What you can do:

■ Reduce – use less paper.

■ Reuse – envelopes can be used again and again, use scrap paper for messages.

■ Recycle – collect your old newspapers, domestic and office waste paper for recycling.

■ Buy recycled paper.

■ Join Friends of the Earth.

Further reading

For further information on these topics read:

Out of the Woods – This briefing explains and puts forward proposals on how the UK can cut its paper consumption.

Updated by G Green January 1996

Fig. 5.1 cont.

The Women's Environmental Network

Forests, Paper and the Environment

Adopt a tree!

From kitchen rolls to paper tissues, glossy magazines to mail order catalogues, newspapers to junk mail, paper is everywhere. Our lifestyles revolve around an ample supply of cheap paper products which provide us with an impression of convenience. Paper companies spend millions of pounds each year convincing consumers, especially women, that they need to buy soft yet strong high quality toilet roll with appealing images of puppies and children. But is this the best use of fibres from trees which took a lifetime to grow?

The Women's Environmental Network (WEN) is a non-profit organisation educating, informing and empowering women who care about the environment.

The WEN Information Department answer enquiries, produces briefing, papers and other information related to women and the environment.

For further details contact:

The Information Officer
WEN
Aberdeen Studios
22 Highbury Grove
London N5 2EA

Tel: 071 354 8823
Fax: 071 354 0464

Printed on recycled paper

ISBN 0-951 4297-4-4

The WEN Information Department gratefully acknowledge the support of The Joseph Rowntree Charitable Trust and the Department of the Environment.

Reusable alternatives to paper, for example terry nappies, are made from cotton which takes just one year to grow but can be used for generations. In contrast, it takes at least 100 years to grow a tree and thousands of years to grow a forest ecosystem, but we, as consumers, endorse the conversion of these ancient plants into paper products which last just a few moments and are then thrown away.

Our current level of paper consumption is ecologically unsustainable. For every paper nappy and kitchen roll we buy, there is a chain of environmental damage. The ancient forests of Canada are currently being devastated by extensive logging. In Sweden and Finland, old growth forests have been replaced by tree farms - barren systems which offer little opportunity for wildlife or stability. Toxic substances, including dioxins and other organochlorines, are released into the waterways during paper production, and pollutants are released into the air contributing to global warming and acid rain.

Much of the 13 million tonnes of paper used every year in the UK is unnecessary and is soon discarded. Over 10% of each person's annual paper consumption is disposable products which are, by design, one use and non-recyclable. They are subsequently disposed of, along with the bulk of our paper, into brimming landfill sites, fed into polluting incinerators or flushed into the sea.

Paper is an essential part of modern life as a medium for information and writing, but it is undervalued when it is thrown in the dustbin before any of its recycling potential can be realised. Now that the environmental impact of paper production has been exposed, ethical consumers are motivated to reject wasteful and non-recycled paper products in favour of durable reusables or low grade recycled alternatives.

These are relatively easy choices considering most women in the world do not have any other options. An average woman in the UK consumes 163 kilos of paper every year, compared to the average African woman, who uses less than one kilo a year.

Fig. 5.2 Women's Environmental Network information sheet on Paper and the Environment (updated May 1992)

What you can do

Whenever possible avoid disposable non-recyclable paper products. Use the right fibre for the right job. This may mean 100% low grade recycled paper for toilet rolls and it could also mean substituting paper tissues with cotton handkerchiefs or using washable crockery instead of a paper cup or plate. Switching to reusables will save the consumer money as well as saving precious resources.

- Buy only 100% recycled, unbleached toilet paper.

- Try washable nappies or a nappy washing service.

- Buy recycled stationery, cards and books.

- Support or set up local recycling initiatives.

- Recycle the paper you use.

- Switch to cotton handkerchiefs instead of paper tissues.

- Avoid overpackaging: buy in bulk or hand back excess packaging.

- Recycle your envelopes with WEN reuse labels.

- Give up your paper kitchen towels – you can live without them.

- Share your newspapers with colleagues and neighbours.

- Use returnable drink bottles instead of disposable cartons.

- Support your libraries or swap books with friends.

- Use loose tea in a pot instead of tea bags.

- Take cotton napkins to restaurants so you can reject paper ones.

- Opt for washable towels in workplace toilets.

- Try reusable sanitary towels.

- Reject free local papers if you do not read them.

- Remove your name from mail shot lists and send junk mail back.

- Reject paper bags by taking a reusable bag to the shops.

Stockists

Reusable Sanitary Towels and Nappies
Ganmill supply Ecofem reusable sanitary towels, Nappitex shaped washable nappies and reusable incontinence aids: Ganmill Ltd, 38–40, Market Street, Bridgwater, Somerset, TA6 3EP. Tel 0278 423037

For the full range of reusable nappies and sanitary towels, please refer to the WEN nappy and sanitary protection briefings.

Nappy Washing Services
A growing number of new services are listed on the WEN nappy briefing.

Reusable Coffee Filters
Lorraine's unbleached cotton filters are made in Ireland and stocked in many wholefood stores. Plastic filters are stocked in most supermarkets

Recycled Toilet Paper
Edet is 100% recycled and 85% low grade waste. Sainsbury, Safeway, Tesco, Asda and Gateway all stock own brand low grade recycled, unbleached toilet paper.

Recycled Stationery
Paperback Ltd, Bow Triangle Business Centre, Unit 2, Elenor Street, London E3 4NP. Tel 081 980 5580.

Contact the WEN information department for an extensive list of stockists in your area.

Alternative papers
Traidcraft produce a catalogue which stocks a variety of paper products made from alternatives to wood: Traidcraft Plc, Kingsway, Gateshead, Tyne and Wear, NE11 0NE.

Mailing Preference
Write and request that your name is removed from junk mail lists: Mailing Preference Service, Freepost 22, London W1E 7EZ.

Recycling Information
Contact Friends of the Earth information department: 26–28, Underwood Street, London N17JQ. Tel 071 490 1555.

The Women's Environmental Network is one of Britain's leading environmental pressure groups. WEN is a non-profit organisation funded by membership and donations. Our aim is to educate, inform and empower women who care about the environment.

Subscription rates
Supporting £30, Ordinary £13
Unwaged £7, Overseas £20
Affiliations £35
Membership entitles you to receive our quarterly newsletter and to be informed of all public meetings and events.

Acknowledgements
Researched and written by Helen O'Hara, Cat Cox and Bemadette Vallely. Desk Top Published by Helen O'Hara. Photograph page 3 supplied by The Environmental Picture Library. Cartoon by Angela Martin.
© WEN May 1992

Fig. 5.2   cont.

made thereafter of inclusive pronouns, as in 'our lifestyles' and 'we as consumers'. By contrast, the FoE fact sheet's use of agentless passive constructions, such as 'ancient natural forest is being cut down and cleared', together with its exclusive use of the pronoun 'we' in the concessionary clause, 'as far as we are aware', create the impression of a more impersonal address. Where active sentences are used, abstract processes and non-human participants almost invariably occupy the subject position. The opening sentence of FoE's fact sheet provides a representative example, 'The production and disposal of paper impacts on the environment in a number of different ways' (Fig. 5.1). The subsequent technique of listing is characteristic of technical and scientific prose, although there is a careful avoidance of alienating jargon. Also characteristic of scientific prose is the frequent reference to empirical research which is alluded to on four separate occasions to back up its claims, and to refute the counter claims of critics. The inclusion of the latter makes the style dialogic, helping to create the impression of balance, as does the acknowledgement of the improvements industry has made to date. This impression of objectivity is reinforced by the cautious deontic modality of '*as far as we are aware* none of the recycled paper in the UK has been bleached with chlorine' (Fig. 5.1.; my italics). This hedge on the maxim of quality implicitly addresses the accusation often made by opponents that environmentalists tend to employ a rhetoric that is irresponsibly alarmist, even apocalyptic.

The style of WEN's information sheet is characterized by the complete absence of many of the aforementioned analytic features (Fig. 5.2). It openly derides what it regards as the spurious claims made by industry and the misleading rhetoric it is said to employ: 'Paper companies spend millions of pounds each year convincing consumers, especially women, that they need to buy soft yet strong high quality toilet roll with appealing images of puppies and children.' The rhetoric of quantification, which Fowler (1991: 168–9) identifies as the dominant stylistic feature of media discourse on environmental crises, is used, but rather than contributing to an impression of 'huge and shifting numbers', statistics are translated into figures which reflect individual consumption of paper products. Because of the need to expose the detrimental effects of current bad practice, both fact sheets inevitably include the collocational chaining of negative vocabulary. Both presuppose an understanding of the positive benefits of recycling, but only the WEN version makes an explicit appeal to ethical arguments with the claim that paper products have an intrinsic value and are currently being 'undervalued'. This confirms Seager's (1993: 259) observation that women-orientated environmental organizations are more likely than mainstream groups to make an appeal on the basis of values and moral reasoning. The ethical dimension in WEN's fact sheet is underscored by a stark comparison between the average paper consumption of a woman in the UK and that of her counterpart in Africa.

The North/South divide is also alluded to intertextually in the accompanying cartoon with its caption 'Adopt a tree!' The image of a woman and a child hugging a tree is an implicit reference to the Chipko (literally 'hug') movement in India in the 1970s when women and children did just this to prevent the exploitation of local forests by an international conglomerate. Once again it is clear that WEN is prioritizing the interpersonal over the ideational metafunction, since its information sheet invites the reader to bridge the North/South, black/white and local/global boundaries via human empathy. This reference to the impact on indigenous peoples is also evident in the subsequent discussion of the international forestry industry, whereas the human cost is alluded to only indirectly in reference in FoE's leaflet to the possible contamination of drinking water. The link between damaging pre-birth effects in babies and the incineration of toxic waste is also stressed in WEN's leaflet. Both conclude with a list of bullet points which use verbs in the imperative mood and which exhort individuals to take action. The FoE list comprises just five verbs, 'reduce', 'reuse', 'recycle', 'buy', culminating in an injunction to 'join'. WEN's list enumerates a total of nineteen ways in which consumers can take immediate action, emphasizing the much greater emphasis it places on individual agency. Significantly, though, these include verbs with a less overtly directive illocutionary force, such as 'try', 'support', 'share' and 'opt for'.

Drawing on the Hallidayan model of field, mode and tenor choices, Martin (1986) analyses the discursive features of two texts written from opposing positions in the ecological debate. His argument is that genre choices are predictable once the ideological stance of an organization is known. However, my analysis would suggest that gender and gender politics are likely to have an influence on genre choices, even where environmental organizations are on the same side of the ecological debate. Given that it is based on a human needs approach and eschews scientific and technological paradigms, the hortatory mode employed by WEN is akin to that used by the progressive Australian Conservation Foundation (ACF) in Martin's study. The analytic style employed by FoE, with its foregrounding of non-human participants and its replication of conventional features of scientific prose, is closer to the rhetorical style favoured in the article produced by the Canadian Wildlife Federation (CWF), an organization committed to protecting the right to go seal hunting. I am not suggesting that FoE's analytic style is in itself reprehensible, but it is interesting that many former environmental purists have crossed over with apparent ease to the opposing camp and are using much the same rhetorical strategies to express what has become known as the 'contrarian' view. Exponents of this position challenge the construction of commerce and industry as 'evil empires'. Theirs is a pragmatic, rather than idealist, approach based on the view that big business alone has the spending power to solve many of the problems which 'our industrial past has visited on us' (Lamb 1996: 190). Such an approach is reminiscent of Porritt's rationale for embracing the 'executive model' for FoE, since he likewise stresses that the real agents of change are the gatekeepers in government and industry, rather than individual consumers or environmental groups.

5.6   Taking science and industry to task

Goldblatt (1996: 95) points out that 'a special feature of environment politics [is] its reliance on contestable technical information'. This opens up a discursive space for intervention by representatives of NSMs, like WEN. It is important to stress, then, that WEN does not completely eschew scientific research. Rather, as an organization informed by ecofeminist perspectives, it employs its own scientific experts to call into question the view of scientific research as invariably disinterested, suggesting instead that it is often used to justify conservative political and social values. For instance, the geneticist, Ricarda Steinbrecher, who worked for WEN for some time, used her own expertise in the field of genetics to show how scientific uncertainty almost invariably works to the advantage of those who pollute the environment. In an article on genetically engineered crops in the *Ecologist* (November/ December 1996: 279), Steinbrecher argues that, 'industry is already applying the limited and incomplete knowledge gained so far on a wide scale for commercial purposes – no matter what risks the infant technology might pose to the environment'. In this way, WEN has helped to challenge scientific paradigms from within, rather than simply rejecting them.

Indeed, WEN has been at the forefront of the debates about Genetically Modified Organisms (GMOs), and more specifically has sought to challenge the food industry's construction of women as compliant consumers, a tendency noted by Fowler (1991) in his discussion of the food scares of the late 1980s. WEN's Test Tube Harvest campaign was the first of its kind in Britain to cast doubt on the environmental credentials of international biotechnology companies, such as Monsanto. Instead, it constructs them as ruthless corporate giants who are willing to sacrifice the health of consumers in their relentless pursuit of profits: 'Wherever we live in the world, massive corporations increasingly decide over our heads what we eat and how it is produced, whilst they reap the profits' (Test Tube Harvest information sheet, December 1996: 1). The issue has attracted an unprecedented amount of media attention, partly because WEN's campaign leaflet deliberately uses emotive lexis and collocations, designed to act as bait for tabloid journalists in particular. For instance, although those who produced WEN's leaflet on GMOs are trained geneticists and biologists, and therefore capable of using a much more technical idiom, they employ the phrases 'Frankenstein foods' and 'mutant foods', as well as the compound nouns 'superweeds' and 'superpests' (ibid.: 3–4). Such language cannot simply be explained by the need to make complex information accessible, something stressed by WEN's plant scientist, Becky Price (Trans. IV: 105–10). It is symptomatic of an ideologically creative attempt to produce a hybrid rhetorical style that communicates carefully researched scientific facts in language designed to appeal to the emotions.

With the Gaia Foundation, WEN subsequently founded the Genetics Engineering Network (GEN), and in April 1997 co-organized the first Big Gene Gathering, which helped to bring the issue of GMOs to the attention of a wider public. The consumer backlash it helped to engineer, in spite of support for GMOs at the highest level of government, has led most of the major supermarket chains to remove genetically engineered ingredients from their own brand products. The media's acceptance of WEN's strategy of locating the blame unambiguously with the food industry contrasts markedly with their practice of scapegoating housewives in general, and working mothers in particular, in the moral panic over listeria and salmonella in eggs in the winter of 1988–9 (Fowler 1991: 46ff). On that occasion, ecological arguments about the benefits of freshly prepared and healthy foods, and the need for hygiene in the kitchen, became part of a backlash narrative against women who had strayed from their 'proper sphere'. By contrast, media pressure over GMOs led the normally bullish Monsanto to announce, in October 1999, that it was suspending its research into the Terminator gene and, in a dramatic *volte face*, its chairperson, Robert Shapiro, admitted, 'Our confidence in this technology and our enthusiasm for it has, I think, been widely seen – and understandably so – as condescension or indeed arrogance' (the *Guardian* 22 November 1999).

In the case of GMOs, WEN was quick to challenge the appropriation of green rhetoric by companies like Monsanto, and in particular to cast doubt on their claims that GMOs would offer an ecologically sound way of resolving the practical and ethical problem of third world hunger. It mounted a similar challenge to the Department of the Environment's acceptance in 1989 of the chemical industry's claims that toxic waste incinerators offered an environmentally friendly solution to Britain's burgeoning waste problem. In this instance, Ann Link undertook a detailed investigation into the harmful dioxins given off by the incineration process and produced an exhaustively researched report of all the available evidence, which, in turn, meant that she came to be viewed as something of an expert in the field. For instance, her evidence outweighed that of two other experts, with more mainstream academic credentials, in a waste disposal forum in Berkshire, with the result that the Council opted for recycling, rather than incineration (Trans. IV: 405ff). The fact that successive governments since have been cautious about uncritically promoting toxic waste incineration, despite protests from industry, indicates just how effective environmental NSMs can be in curbing the expansion of capitalist enterprise.

However, the battle lines in debates are not always so conveniently drawn between representatives of industry, on the one hand, and environmentalists, on the other. For instance, environmental groups have themselves been divided about the relative merits of incinerators and landfill sites as methods of waste disposal, with FoE and Greenpeace changing their respective positions on this issue, often in apparent competition with one another. When I asked Link how she manages to negotiate her way through such competing claims, she said that her response has been to move beyond the polarized arguments espoused by rival environmental groups:

> to focus on positive alternatives to wasteful products and to initiate the~the Waste Prevention Bill to make it more possible and to raise awareness as well really for~for Councils to start to prevent the waste at source . . . it really lets me out of the argument between incineration and landfills you know I think you have to move on from that and usually there is something which you can say and do which cuts through a lot of that

(Trans. IV: 295–303)

The successful passage through Parliament of the Waste Prevention Bill in 1998 was announced in WEN's newsletter under the subheadline, 'WEN gives birth to Waste Minimization Act' (No. 36, winter 1998: 1). As noted above by Link, the new Act gives local authorities the formal power to prevent waste, something they were unable to do under the existing law. This anomaly was highlighted by Link's research and the metaphor of childbirth no doubt seemed apt to describe the painstaking process that followed over three years in order to effect the necessary change in the law. The Act is particularly important because it encourages local councils to empower householders, including young mothers, the elderly, the disabled and those without cars, to become involved in practical waste prevention measures, thereby extending the base of participation in environmental activism beyond a narrow privileged elite.

5.7   The relationship between environmental NSMs and the media

In his discussion of environmental politics, Goldblatt (1996: 99) argues that, 'as with the struggle over impact identification and cost establishment, differential power and resources utterly determine the policy influence of actors'. However, this view underestimates the vital role that media intervention can play in shaping policy decisions. According to Lamb (1996: 189):

> A love-in between the mass media and environmental groups during the late 1970s and 1980s was a crucial factor in establishing a popular power

base for Friends of the Earth, Greenpeace and the rest. The media also grew to become powerful pro-environmental persuaders in their own right, especially the tv documentary genre.

McRobbie (1994) claims that this was made possible because those involved in NSMs became increasingly practised at using the media. They were/are specially trained to become 'extremely articulate and televisually skilled' (ibid.: 111). As such, they have taken their place alongside, and in some cases have even displaced, other experts who have, in the past, comprised the narrow elite of 'accessed voices' represented in the media. Traditionally these have been professional politicians from mainstream parties, academics and so-called 'moral guardians'.

As with other NSMs, WEN's success, or otherwise, has been determined to a large extent by the media's exercise of interpretative control over its campaign claims. Its tendency to prioritize the interpersonal over the idea-tional in its campaigns means that the issues raised have often been taken up by the tabloid press, rather than by the broadsheets. This, in turn, has meant that its campaign rhetoric is often susceptible to what Fairclough (1995b: 58) terms 'incorporation', whereby secondary discourse is translated into the voice of primary media discourse, through vocabulary and other changes. This can result in changes in both the interpersonal and ideational meanings of the former. Fairclough argues that incorporation often functions in media discourse to legitimize the voices of officialdom by translating them into the lifeworld discourse of readers, but I will suggest that it can equally serve to trivialize and distort the voices of unofficial representatives of NSMs, by accommodating them to pre-existing news frames. One only has to compare the matter-of-fact tone of some of WEN's campaign leaflets – especially those relating to taboo areas of women's experience – with the sensationalist coverage these issues have received in articles in the tabloid press to realize how powerful this control can be.

This is vividly illustrated by the superficially sympathetic coverage its campaign on sanpro received in the *Mail on Sunday* (12 February 1989). Because Vallely had refused to grant the paper exclusive rights to the story, which was to be covered in ITV's *World in Action* the following evening, the *Mail* ran 'a spoiler' which made unfounded allegations, deflecting attention away from the real issues and making WEN campaigners look like irrespon-sible scaremongers (Trans. VI: 50–3). For instance, the producers of the article made claims about sanitary products being made from 'recycled beer mats' and they went on to attribute to WEN spurious 'shock findings' and 'horrifying revelations', including the discovery of 'rats' droppings, needles, fish-hooks and cockroach eggs in tampons', something WEN had never alleged in relation to sanpro manufactured in the West.[4] Such irresponsible claims, guaranteed to engender revulsion in readers of both sexes, seem to reflect deep-rooted anxieties about feminine hygiene and taboos surrounding menstruation. WEN's Sarah Miller expressed the view that the media are less likely *now* to report these issues in an irresponsible way. For instance, she pointed to the noticeable absence of prurience in an article in the *Daily Express* which reported WEN's promotion of reusable sanitary protection, 'they mentioned it and it wasn't like [simulating a disgusted tone] erhh woah . . . it was kind of this is a choice you can make and . . . you know I was quite pleasantly surprised by *that*' (Trans. IV: 191–3). However, it is easy to forget how instrumental WEN's ground-breaking campaigns have been in helping to alter this climate of opinion.

In any case, negative media coverage can prove effective in raising public awareness about taboo subjects, as WEN discovered in the case of the coverage of *Blossom*, a magazine it produced in December 1994 with the aim of educating girls and young women about issues surrounding menstruation. The tenor of the coverage is captured in the *Daily Express*'s claim that the producers of the magazine were nothing short of pornographers promoting sex to nine year olds (Trans. VI: 67–9). The magazine itself both reproduces and parodies the prurient style of articles in teenage magazines, with its playfully intertextual titles such as, 'The ins and outs of advice centres', 'A womb with a view' and 'Sex ed – are you getting enough?'. The coy tone of many of the articles that appear, even in such so-called sexually explicit teenage magazines such as *More*, is parodied in another feature entitled 'Sshhh . . . masturbation. What does THAT word mean – and others?', while the advice genre, readers' true stories and the romantic photostory are each given a suitably subversive twist. Despite, or perhaps because of, the storm of sensationalist coverage in both the print and broadcast media, WEN received over ten thousand requests for copies from individuals, schools, health authorities and youth groups. These were readers who had clearly resisted the attempt by the tabloids to portray WEN as irresponsible, choosing instead to make up their own minds about the magazine's style and content. As is evident from the taboo-breaking nature of its sanpro campaign and of its advice to girls on menstruation in *Blossom*, WEN addresses women and girls as anything but passive subjects. These were campaigns about self-definition and about challenging the interpretative control that the media have over so-called 'women's issues'.

The tendency of such groups as FoE and Greenpeace to prioritize the ideational over the interpersonal has meant that their campaign rhetoric has more often been subject to a process of 'dissemination', especially in the broadsheet press, rather than incorporation into tabloidese. According to Fairclough (1995b: 58), 'dissemination' occurs when the voice of the primary media discourse borrows that of the secondary discourse. The analytic style favoured by mainstream environmental groups, like FoE in particular, chimes more with the characteristic style of news narratives in 'quality' newspapers, since, as Fairclough (ibid.: 64) notes, 'News tends to be seen as very much a conceptual and ideational business, a matter of statements, claims, beliefs, positions – rather than feelings, circumstances, qualities of social and interpersonal relationships and so forth.' He goes on (ibid.: 64) to point out that this:

> . . . seems to be characteristic of what is generally regarded as within the 'public' as opposed to the 'private' domain. There is also a system of values here: the 'public' has greater prestige than the 'private', and implicitly those aspects of discourse which merit public representation – the ideational aspects – are ascribed greater import than those which are of merely private significance.

A joint campaign run by WEN and Greenpeace into the harmful effects of emissions of dioxins in the incineration of toxic waste offers an insight into the relative media coverage received by the two groups. An article in the *Guardian* (30 August 1991) disseminates at some length the detailed scientific rhetoric of Greenpeace, through the use of both direct and free indirect discourse, which has the effect of merging Greenpeace's voice with that of the reporter. The voice of WEN, by contrast, is only reproduced in a single instance of direct discourse in which its scientific officer, Ann Link, translates a cautious scientific discourse about the inconclusive effect of dioxins on hamsters into a common-sense idiom: 'After all, we live a lot longer than hamsters.' There are, of course, dangers in such appeals to common-sense, not least of speculating beyond the available scientific evidence. However, as in the case of GMOs, WEN's justification is that the burden of proof about the unambiguous *safety* of industrial practices should lie with government and industry. Yet, the positive proof of the harmful effect of dioxins, uncovered by the independent *scientific* research carried out by Link, is more likely to have influenced government policy than WEN's promotion of healthy scepticism, however much such scepticism may have been in keeping with common-sense assumptions.

One instance in which WEN used the media to good effect was in its campaign over dioxins in milk. An obstacle to the success of NSM campaigns on such issues is a lack of access to official government information. However, as in this instance, attempts to deny pressure groups such access can sometimes prove counter-productive. Having spent a year fruitlessly trying to get the government to release an official report on the levels of dioxins in milk, WEN decided to use the media to expose this reluctance to release details as potentially sinister. The possibility of a government cover-up then became a central theme in the intertextual chaining of stories in the media. On this occasion, the Milk Marketing Board even aligned itself with WEN against government secrecy. Thus a spokesperson was reported as saying, 'We are having to get a copy of these official government results from the Women's Environmental Network because they are not being made available from the ministry. We are very concerned' (the *Guardian* 7 August

1990). When the government countered via the media in an attempt to discredit WEN's claims, WEN forced it to retract its disclaimer and again this retraction was reported in the print media. Although undoubtedly a principled commitment, WEN's focus on the potential repercussions for the health of the nation's children increased the story's news value and made the government's duplicity look all the more reprehensible.

Recently, however, the media have been instrumental in constructing a backlash narrative on environmental issues. The comment made by FoE's Tom Burke – 'Those who live by the spotlight die by it' (cited in Lamb 1996: 190) – is nowhere more vividly illustrated than in the case of media coverage of Brent Spar in 1995. Burke himself acted as chief adviser to the government, indicating the degree to which FoE activists have been accepted into the corridors of power. Interestingly, in the second in a Channel 4 series, *Against Nature* (7 December 1997), Burke claimed that the campaign over the disposal of British Petroleum's disused oil installation had never been conceived as a 'scientific' campaign and that the pressure for 'facts' came from the media. The implication is that the media, rather than FoE, were dictating the analytic style of its campaign rhetoric. In the end, FoE got its 'facts' seriously wrong and the media subsequently had a field day. The exposé of FoE's unfounded and alarmist claims over Brent Spar was only one of many doubts cast upon the claims of environmentalists in the three-part Channel 4 series. In media terms, the series fits into the long, and often distinguished, tradition of attacks on sacred cows in TV document-aries. It has become clear that the media are to some extent 'punch drunk' and that the sort of staged events favoured by WEN and Greenpeace do not so easily penetrate their defences. However, trends in media coverage are often unpredictable and contradictory. The so-called 'conversationalization' of mediatized discourse, noted by Fairclough (1995a: 9), may well make the broadcast media and the broadsheets more receptive to the interpersonally-orientated style of WEN, especially since the reliability of FoE's scientific rhetoric has been cast into doubt.

5.8   The politics of self-interest?

There are some who argue that, however laudable their aims, environmental organisations like WEN can inadvertently collude with commodity capital-ism. For instance, Mellor (1992: 192) warns that, 'Without a strong political focus, the present concern for environmental issues can easily be turned to the advantage of the market and may well increase rather than reduce consumption'. Green consumerism could also be said to reinforce women's connection with the domestic sphere, through its appeal to their roles as housewives and mothers. Perhaps more worrying is Seager's point that it can drive a wedge between women of different social classes by introducing 'a new *environmental* measure of privilege – the privilege of being safe from household environmental hazards' (Seager 1993: 262; italics in the original). In addition to these potential losses in terms of feminist politics, WEN's campaign rhetoric seems to have chimed rather conveniently with a Thatcherite discourse based on buzz words and phrases like 'individual responsibility', 'consumer choice' and so on. Thatcher herself seemed all-too-willing to embrace green issues, with her sudden declaration of concern for the ozone layer, heralded in the *Observer* (26 February 1989) under the headline, 'Thatcher hogs the green line'. I would like to suggest that the situation is, however, both more complicated and more ideologically creative than this reading would suggest.

The fact that WEN's primary focus is on issues both domestic and local undoubtedly lays it more open to charges of NIMBY-ism ('not in my back yard-ism') than groups with a primarily national and international focus. Most social theorists agree that no discussion of contemporary environmentalism can afford to ignore global constraints on nation states created by organizations like the World Bank, the International Monetary Fund and the General Agreement on Tariffs and Trade (GATT), as well as the growing body of international legislation on the environment. This supranational emphasis can be disabling for individuals who feel that the realm of political decision-making is becoming more and more remote. WEN's Bernadette Vallely, for instance, argues that the view that individuals cannot effect structural change is disempowering and leads to political ennui, especially since global forums on the environment often seem to be little more than excuses for high-profile political inaction (*Women and Environments*, winter/spring 1991: 54). In any case, WEN does not ignore the national and international context, as is evident in its own thoroughly researched publications on paper mills and deforestation; it simply approaches them in a bottom-up way, putting into practice René Dubois's famous dictum, 'Think globally, act locally'.

It is true that, unlike other mainstream environmental groups, WEN has made consumer power a central plank in its campaign rhetoric. Yet, its aim is to transform the *fiction* of consumer power into a real basis for opposing the excesses of commodity capitalism, partly by translating women's 'unpaid and usually unrecognized work – of purchasing and preparing goods and services for domestic consumption' (Fraser 1995: 34) into the power to 'vote with their purse'. In this way WEN has appropriated the rhetoric of commodity capitalism to hold commodity capitalism to account. Mellor (1992: 223) underlines the paradoxical fact that the ecological crisis has been politically productive since 'it has succeeded where socialism has failed in calling into question the mythic power of the market'. It seems particularly ironic that environmental issues, once dismissed by the political left in Britain as a retreat from politics, should be at the forefront of re-radicalizing democracy movements throughout the world. The potential power of this type of 'home-spun revolution', as the environmental activist George Monbiot terms it (the *Guardian* 6 January 2000), was dramatically illustrated by the street protests that led to the collapse of the World Trade Organization talks in Seattle in December 1999.

WEN's somewhat more modest demand that consumers should have access to information to allow them to make ethical choices has also helped to challenge the gender politics of consumer abuse, as has its exposé of attempts by such companies as Tambrands and Procter & Gamble to label products as 'eco-friendly' when they are anything but. Male-dominated industry, including the advertising industry and the media, have tradition-ally viewed women as easily manipulated consumers with little political power. As noted above, WEN is careful to avoid positioning consumers as passive. On the contrary, it seeks to offer them real and informed choices about what they buy. While it is wise to be cautious about the concept of 'empowerment', patronizing media comments in coverage of food scares of the 1980s about profoundly ignorant housewives is transformed into fighting talk in WEN's campaign rhetoric. This is recognized in a wittily intertextual headline in the *Evening Echo* (6 March 1989), alluding to one of its early campaigns: 'We'll fight on bleaches say an army of women.' This underlines the novelty of a rhetoric which addresses issues not norm-ally discussed at all in the public domain, let alone in such a politically charged way. Whereas Habermas (1987) regards the role of active citizen as being displaced by that of the passive consumer, WEN has shown that it is possible to use women's power as consumers to expand their political participation.

WEN's campaign rhetoric therefore produces a novel restructuring of traditional discursive boundaries, notably the gendered dichotomy between an apolitical private sphere and a politicized public sphere. It is a rhetoric which also challenges the traditional left/right opposition in its appeal to both the language of 'rights', associated with the political left, *and* the lan-guage of 'consumer choice', associated with the political right and, more specifically, with the political discourse of Thatcherism. Like the discourse of Thatcherism itself, it is therefore ideologically creative (cf. Fairclough 1989: 192–3). Further boundary breaking is evident in the fact that, as an actively campaigning group, WEN combines an unashamedly therapeutic function, based on the pleasure of participation, with the more overtly pol-itical function of challenging existing institutional structures. As McRobbie notes, grassroots movements generally function to 'provide support and "self-help" *as well as* feeding into the broader political culture in terms of public debate' (McRobbie 1994: 115; my italics). Organizations like WEN therefore help to challenge the prevailing orthodoxy that these two func-tions are not only incompatible, but are almost invariably at odds with one another.

John Vidal (the *Guardian* 9 August 1993) argues that far from peddling a reactionary ideology, women have been instrumental in politicizing the determinedly apolitical male-led tradition of green politics. The reluctance of the mainstream green movement in Britain to address issues about poverty and politics was, he claims, due in part to historical factors such as charity laws, as well as to 'a jealous separatism between groups which puts boxes around individual "issues"' (ibid.). He goes on to suggest that the reliance of feminist political rhetoric on arguments about equity, civil rights, social justice and so on, means that, 'Environmentalism is being driven inexorably to a new agenda which at its root owes much to feminism' (ibid.). He points out that this debt is, however, rarely acknowledged by the almost exclusively male executives of many British environmental groups.

It is worth considering whether WEN is likely to appeal to a new generation of women, or whether it is very much a movement that grew out of a particular coincidence of circumstances that no longer operate. Despite scepticism about some (eco)feminist claims, the mainly young women interviewed by me at WEN's head office in London believed that WEN offers them a unique opportunity to gain the type of relevant campaigning expertise that they are still unable to obtain in mainstream environmental groups (Trans. IV: 67ff). This experience has convinced them that WEN offers an important space for foregrounding women-orientated issues that would either be ignored, or be seen as trivial, by such groups as FoE and Greenpeace (ibid.: 158ff). Some, however, felt the need to combine their campaigning role in WEN with more radical direct action. Thus, Becky Price, then a science officer at WEN, said she liked to alternate her desk job at WEN's London office with a spate of guerrilla style action in the anti-roads protests around the country (Trans. IV: 110ff).

One female anti-roads protester who was interviewed is Eleanor 'Animal' Hudson. At 16 she became something of a media folk hero after her involvement in the Fairmile protest, confirming McRobbie's (1994) view that the media offer a space for 'folk devils' to 'fight back'. Hudson's slight physique and feminine appearance attracted a good deal of attention, especially since it was very much at odds with the expectations aroused by her media-generated alias (Trans. V). Both Price and Hudson implied that gender-crossing behaviour is common among younger environmentalists involved in direct action campaigns. For instance, Hudson said she considers herself to be 'one of the boys' (Trans. V: 27), while Price, responding to a question about her experience of the anti-roads protests, claimed that 'the macho stuff and the home-making stuff is done by *both* men *and* women' (Trans. IV: 117–18). Such gender-troubling direct action by young women seems to present a challenge to the common-sense assumptions of an earlier generation of environmental campaigners, and perhaps inadvertently reinforced by WEN, that females should confine themselves to campaigning activities that represent an extension of their roles as housewives and mothers.

5.9   Conclusions

The role of NSMs is, if anything, likely to become more important in the light of the increasing fragmentation of oppositional political discourses in Britain, as elsewhere. On the evidence of such environmental organizations as FoE, there is little likelihood that women will be admitted as equals to communities of practice in the reinvigorated civil sphere, any more than they have been admitted on an equal footing to public sphere institutions. Perhaps more promising is the politicizing of the private sphere promoted by organizations like WEN. In spite of media misrepresentation, WEN has given a voice to women who would probably never otherwise have become political activists. Perhaps even more significant than the concrete and specific gains WEN has made, such as helping to get woman-friendly legislation onto the statute book, the organization has helped women to seize interpretative control over the social meanings of their bodies, especially in relation to issues around menstruation and, more recently, breast cancer.

However, there is a danger that the feminist shibboleth that the 'personal is political' can be taken to the point where the political disappears. For instance, Vallely regards her involvement in the 'What Women Want in Bed' survey, and in the new age spirituality network called 'Angel', as a natural extension of her work in WEN (Trans. VI: 6–10). It could equally be interpreted, however, as a predictable retreat into the apolitical, confirming Elshtain's view (1993: 217) that the erosion of the distinction between the public and the private signals an end to politics. This need not be the case. For many women, organizations like WEN can provide a springboard for the kind of political activism that stopped global capitalism in its tracks at the World Trade Talks in Seattle. Significantly, on this occasion protesters mobilized and coordinated their campaign by utilizing the internet, thereby bypassing the hegemonic interpretative power of the mainstream media. In the future, women, and men, need not even stray beyond the confines of their own homes in order to participate in political and environmental networks locally, nationally and globally.

The focus in the next chapter on women's involvement in the Church of England would seem to mark a shift away from this type of subversive grassroots activity to the types of institutions of the state that formed the basis of my investigations in Chapters 3 and 4. However, I will suggest that the Church's sphere of influence is such that it cuts across the boundaries that traditionally separate the private, civil and public domains.

Notes

1. Habermas elaborates on the systems/lifeworld distinction in the second volume of *The Theory of Communicative Action* (1981, trans. 1987). He defines the lifeworld as a socially integrated domain of symbolic representation, comprising both the private sphere of family life and the 'public' or civil sphere of political participation and opinion formation. The systems world, by contrast, comprises both the official economy and the state and is, therefore, a domain dominated by what he terms the 'media' of money and power. However, he argues that the lifeworld is increasingly being colonized by strategic, rather than communicative imperatives. In his subsequent discussion of new social movements, Habermas claims that their success should, therefore, be judged in terms of the extent to which they help to decolonize the lifeworld.

2. WEN's stated aim has since been changed to read, 'working to inform and empower women *and men* who care about the environment' (my italics). In a not unrelated move, the autumn 2000 Newsletter invited members to contribute to a debate about the future identity of the organization. More specifically, it asked its members to consider how WEN can 'represent women's diverse interests and concerns without being written off as "feminist" or accused of suggesting all women are the same?' (p. 4). I hope that this chapter will act as a contribution to this debate, in that it has aimed to foreground the advantages of an organization that keeps a clear, though not exclusive, focus on environmental issues that affect women.

3. The BBC2 documentary series, *Horizon* (5 January 2000), revealed that a number of cancers, including stomach and cervical cancer, are now known to be caused by viruses, so it is not beyond the bounds of possibility that environmental factors may prove to contribute to the onset of breast cancer.

4. Such allegations *were* made in the programme about sanpro distributed by the global medical company Smith & Nephew in Malaysia, but there was no suggestion that any products in the West had ever been contaminated in this way.

6

Speaking in Different Tongues?
A Case Study of Women Priests
in the Church of England

The decision to focus on women's involvement in the Church of England in the final chapter of this book might appear rather surprising, given the more overtly political orientation of the institutions and organizations examined in the preceding chapters. What interested me about the Church is its peculiarly hybrid status as an institution which connects the state and civil society. For instance, it is the one mainstream institution that McRobbie (1994) links to new social movements, mainly on the grounds of the inner fragmentation it has undergone, and continues to undergo, as a result of the campaigns for women priests and gay rights. In other ways, however, as an official state church it is obviously associated with the vested interests of the ruling establishment. For instance, the prime minister has ultimate control over the appointment of bishops, most of whom continue to be drawn from public school and Oxbridge backgrounds, while they, in turn, are in the unique position of having an automatic right to sit in the House of Lords. The General Synod, the Church of England's governing and legislative body, has modelled itself on the practices and procedures of the House of Commons. It is not surprising, then, that the Church has often been referred to as the 'Tory Party at prayer'.

Yet, throughout the Thatcher years in particular, a number of events led the Church to earn a reputation as a 'surrogate opposition' (Medhurst 1999: 281). Its call for a spirit of repentance on all sides in the aftermath of the Falklands War produced the first signs of a cooling in the relationship between Church and state. Relations deteriorated further during the miners' strike (1984–5), when Church leaders urged the government to adopt a conciliatory policy, rather than engage in outright confrontation. The final blow came in 1985 with the publication of the *Faith in the City* report which was openly critical of the government's economic and social policies, especially as they impacted on inner city areas. According to Medhurst (1999: 281):

> The term 'marxist' was even deployed in an attempt to discredit this Church initiative – an initiative that some commentators have seen as something of

a watershed in terms of the contemporary Church's attempts to re-engage with the public arena in fresh and newly relevant terms.

For these reasons, McRobbie suggests that 'the Church might even be seen as existing alongside the pressure groups, the charities and the voluntary organizations which when taken as a whole represent a strong body of public opinion' (McRobbie 1994: 112). Unlike Medhurst (1999), who completely ignores the contribution of women priests in his 'progress report' on the Church, I intend to explore the role women's ordination to the priesthood has played in shaping the Church's view of itself as an institution relevant to the needs of society in the twenty-first century.

When the General Synod voted on 11 November 1992 to admit women to the priesthood, it was perceived as an historic victory for women. It also brought into being a new subject position for women in the Church, that of the 'woman priest'. Of course, other denominations, and even other branches of the Anglican Communion world-wide, had had women priests for many years, even decades, in some cases.[1] Nonetheless, the concept of the 'woman priest' commanded sufficient novelty value to ensure that there was a good deal of speculation, including among the largely non-church-going general populace, about what women's priestly ministry would mean. The majority of women aspiring to priesthood were acutely aware of the expectation that they would fashion a distinct identity for themselves, rather than embrace uncritically a masculinist conception of the sacerdotal role. As in the other contexts discussed in previous chapters, the media framed the story about women's ordination by portraying female aspirants to priesthood as potential agents of change. In this way, they contributed to the expectation that women priests would transform not only the nature of priesthood, but also the fundamental structures of the Church. A study of the pre- and post-ordination period affords an ideal opportunity to explore the tensions between women's construction of themselves, as both campaigning outsiders and as recently ordained insiders, and the sometimes very different ways in which they have been constructed by others, including the media. In the course of this discussion, I intend to consider the extent to which the performative view of the relationship between language use and gendered identity, set out in a collection of essays edited by Bergvall et al. (1996), can account for the complex negotiations women priests have made with the various subject positions available to them.

6.1 Background to the ordination debate

6.1.1 A brief history of women's involvement in Anglican ministry

Women have experienced a long history of segregation and subordination within the institutional structures of the Church of England. Since the early days of the nineteenth century, for instance, there have been separate spheres of ministry for men and women, with women helping to manage the welfare function of the institution in their subordinate positions as community and youth workers, parish assistants and administrators.[2] Milroy and Wismer (1994) argue that the nature of the work women performed for the Church calls into question any simple binary model of the private/public spheres. Yet, in the 'space' in between, women in the Church performed, and in many cases continue to perform, valuable roles without due recognition either in terms of status or remuneration. When the Anglican Order of Deaconesses was set up in 1862, it was widely regarded as affording official recognition to women for their contribution to the Church's pastoral work. However, in 1935 it was made subordinate to the male Order of Deacons and was deemed part of the laity, rather than part of the threefold ministry. As Aldridge (1987: 380) points out, the diminutive suffix '-ess' underlined this anomalous position, while the designation of roles as 'non-stipendiary' was, and remains, a euphemism for 'non-salaried'. Discussing the Church of England prior to women's ordination, Robson (1988) points out that two sets of contradictory discursive practices, or what she terms 'language games', appeared to be in operation and that on closer inspection these were differently gendered. Women in the Church, whether lay or ordained as deacons, appeared to have been evaluated according to a set of vocational norms, emphasizing 'service', 'self-giving', 'self-effacement', 'empowerment of others' and a *lack* of interest in worldly forms of wealth and prestige, while men were judged according to a set of middle-class professional norms, stressing 'status', 'preferment', 'stipends', 'job descriptions', etc. (Robson 1988). As will become evident, these differently gendered lexical sets have persisted into the post-ordination period.

The experiences of two of my respondents, Priests A and B, are fairly typical of those of many women who were later ordained. They both undertook training in social work, as well as in theology, and both performed a wide range of welfare roles as non-stipendiary ministers (see Trans. VII and VIII). As a result of a campaign by the Movement for the Ordination of Women (MOW) in 1985, they secured the right to be ordained to the diaconate, thereby enabling them to use the title 'Reverend' and to wear clerical collars for the first time. Priest A notes that they were easily recognizable because of their 'feminine blue cassocks' (Trans. VII: 17). Aldridge (1987) argues that a discourse of an enriched distinctive diaconate was conveniently constructed to legitimize women's continuing subordination in the clerical profession, mobilizing 'different but equal' arguments discussed below. Thus despite their admission to holy orders, female deacons continued to be denied automatic progression to priesthood. They could not consecrate the bread and wine, nor could they pronounce absolutions and blessings. Priest B said she liked to describe herself at this time as a 'common-law priest' (Trans. VIII: 24). In practice, like many female deacons, she employed subversive tactics to overcome her subordinate status. For instance, by distributing the reserved sacrament to parishioners unable to attend church, she managed, by proxy, to include herself in saying what Farrington (1994: 73) terms the 'magic words' of the eucharist.

6.1.2 Rationalizations of women's exclusion from priesthood

Cameron (1990) makes reference to women's exclusion from religious ceremonial language, 'it is not just that women do not speak: often they are explicitly *prevented* from speaking, either by social taboos and restrictions or by the more genteel tyrannies of custom and practice' (ibid.: 4; italics in the original). Dowell and Williams (1994: ix) endorse this view in relation to the debate surrounding the ordination of women in the Church of England: 'it became clear to us both that what was often really at work in this particular debate was not theology at all but prejudice and custom'. Alluding specifically to this debate, Cameron (1990: 5) sees it as symptomatic of 'an irrational dread of women taking over priestly and ritual functions, including the linguistic ones of public prayer, preaching, and saying the liturgy'. 'Irrational dread' manifested itself in metaphors of disease used by opponents to describe women supporters and their campaigning style. For instance, Furlong (1994: 23) notes that speakers in the 1984 General Synod debate spoke of women as 'a virus in the bloodstream' who were engaged in 'destroying' and 'disembowelling' the Church. The expansion of the debate into conflicts over sexuality, language and authority revealed just how endemic sexism and the subordination of women had been in the Church's traditional structures.

Arguments based on 'headship'

As long as male scholars had a monopoly on the metadiscourse of biblical commentary, they were able to promote dominant readings which selectively foregrounded certain texts, such as the infamous Pauline passages invoking women to remain silent in church. Evangelical opponents, in particular, relied on scriptural arguments about 'headship', based on the assumed God-given structure of creation in which man is the head of woman, albeit in a way which was assumed to be nurturing and benevolent. Once women were permitted to 'speak' in the field of biblical hermeneutics they were in a position to promote oppositional readings which give precedence to what they claim is the overriding fact of the inclusiveness of Jesus's call to slaves, Gentiles and women. Dowell and Williams (1994: 14) point out that in both cases appeals to scripture had to be constructed: 'One set of texts – either the ones about a new standard of relationships between Christians, or the ones about the subordination of women – has to be *chosen*, and the other minimized'. In this way the Bible became a site of ideological struggle, with a complex set of competing readings becoming polarized along gender lines.

In the event, the two extreme wings of the Church, the evangelicals and the Anglo Catholics, suppressed their theological differences in a fraternal alliance designed to block women's ordination. However, in the final debate, the persuasive power of feminist biblical scholarship was to prove decisive. MOW's public relations spokesperson Christine Rees records how its members strategically targeted evangelicals whose last-minute decision to support the motion was the key factor in shifting the balance in favour of the motion in the House of Laity (Trans. X: 57–8).

Arguments based on tradition

The strength of the fraternal networks between male clerics was most force-fully illustrated by the Anglo Catholic belief in an unbroken male line from Jesus through his apostles to their successors. This position was underscored theologically by a belief that the male priest performed an iconic function of standing in for Christ. On this reading, the maleness of the priest is not incidental, but theologically essential. Proponents countered that this view was close to heresy, given the orthodox belief that 'what He (Jesus) did not become he could not redeem'. This seemed to put women beyond the pale of salvation, as well as legitimating and maintaining the patriarchal struc-tures of the Church. It was nonetheless argued that the ordination of women would not only sever the 2,000 year old tradition of male priesthood, but would also threaten opportunities for greater unity with Rome. Robert Runcie, the then Archbishop of Canterbury, arguing against women's ordination in the November 1984 debate, did so on the grounds that such a move would be seen as an 'unfraternal disregard of very large Catholic bodies with whom we share the very fundamentals of faith' (cited in Petre 1994: 90). As Margaret Webster (1994: 145) wryly observes, 'it was easier to be concerned about the cousins in Rome than about the sister at your palace gate'. Likewise, from a Roman Catholic perspective, Schüssler Fiorenza (1993: 270) sees the femin-ist cause betrayed 'in the name of "fraternal unity"'.

The 'different but equal' argument

A third cluster of arguments against women's ordination appealed to the belief that women are not inferior to men, but different. It drew its theolog-ical justification from the cult of the Virgin Mary which emphasized a view of women as docile bodies to be acted upon by men. The construction of the debate in terms of embodied tropes underlines the Foucauldian view of the body as a site of power. McClatchey records her distaste for the same view expressed in explicitly sexual terms: 'I was deeply offended by reading an article by an American priest who saw the divine initiative in terms of the sexual initiative, a divine semen being transmitted to the believer' (cited in Petre 1994: 55). The intention was to show that priesthood is a creative, penetrative act which thereby disqualifies women whose 'natural' roles are passive and nurturing ones. Although such claims, symbolized by the image of the Church as the 'bride of Christ', were said to provide a theological justification for women's exclusion from the priestly ministry, they could just as easily have been used to argue that the priesthood was by definition the proper preserve of women. Schüssler Fiorenza (1993: 252) notes this paradox of naming: 'Although the church is called "our mother" and referred to with the pronoun "she", it is personified and governed by fathers and brothers only.'

In effect, 'different but equal' arguments were traditionally exploited by the Church to provide a theological justification for women's subordinate status. A comment which typifies this position is one made by the arch-opponent of women's ordination, Graham Leonard, then Bishop of London, who wrote, in a letter to *The Church Times* in 1971:

> Although there is equality between the sexes, a proper initiative rests with the male, even if it often has to be elicited by the female. Although normally the woman is paramount as the centre of the family, the man is normally the link between the family and society at large . . . do we want *ab*-normal women in the ministry?

(Cited in Webster 1994: 38)

This stigmatizing of women who step outside their 'proper' sphere as 'abnormal' is a powerful mechanism for maintaining their exclusion from the public sphere and for reifying the existing separate spheres model. This was a view internalized by many women in the Church. Thus one of the main strands in the arguments put forward by the exclusively female organization, Women Against the Ordination of Women (hereafter WAOW), is that women who seek to hold powerful roles are 'unwomanly'. McNay (1992) invokes the notion of 'investment' to explain the semi-conscious manner in which individuals take up different subject positions, including those which appear to be at odds with their own best interests. Women opponents invested in a theology which affirmed a sense of their 'authentic womanhood'. What was at stake in the debate, then, was no less than their sense of self. According to one of my respondents, Priest C, the view of priests as 'father' also goes some way towards explaining women's opposition to women priests (Trans. IX: 182ff). This accords with the analysis put forward by the psychiatrist, Dr Robert Hobson, who explains the opposition of some women to women's ordination on the grounds that women priests threatened the 'roundabout symbolic satisfaction of incestuous desires, which can be achieved in the relationship with a father-priest' (cited in Petre 1994: 39). Although one needs to be cautious about accepting such Freudian explanations of women's behaviour, the idea that women also invested psychologically in an exclusively male priesthood may help to explain why so many women in the Church of England felt women priests to be an anathema.

An apparently paradoxical argument against women priests is that women are not just equal, but superior, to men. This view is rooted in the Victorian romanticized myth of females as the morally superior sex. Again, the Virgin Mary was appealed to as an ideal role model for women to follow since the reward for her joyful submission to male initiation was said to be an enriched spiritual life. This view flatters women, since it emphasizes the distinctiveness of the contribution they can make to the Church. A common theme in the rhetoric of women opponents was that priesthood would mean losing this distinctive 'feminine' vocation, forcing them instead to mimic men. During the ordination debate in November 1992, WAOW member, Sara Lowe, bemoaned the 'fact' that 'the complementarity of male and female has been debased to a banal interchangeability' (*The Synod Debate* 1993: 43). Dowell and Williams (1994: 31) point to the limitations that this position imposed: 'We all take it for granted that there are more women than men in church congregations, but this spirituality becomes instantly invalid, apparently, if it moves beyond the domestic confine, or out of the convent.' An appeal to the complementarity of the sexes had the effect of rationalizing a situation in which women's spirituality was deemed unfit for the more prestigious functions that ritual language serves in the public domain.

Interestingly, 'difference' arguments were mobilized by both sides in the debate with some supporters promoting what were equally essentialist claims about the so-called 'womanly' gifts women would bring to the priestly ministry. Thus Farrington (1994: 74), a supporter of women's ordination asks, 'Where will the menstrual cycle fit in here, with its often pervasive influence on a woman's capacity for effective working?'. Such a question presupposes an extreme biological determinist view of women's nature which would not be out of place in the writings of the most misogynist opponent of women's ordination. Others referred to women's different life experiences as holding out the promise of a distinctive approach to ministry. Speaking in the ordination debate, one proponent argued that 'women, who know so much suffering love [will] carry that into the leadership' (*The Synod Debate* 1993: 27). Yet others, like Dr Christina Baxter, spoke in less essentialist terms about a coincidence between the preferred interactional style of women and 'the need for a new pattern of collaborative ministry' (ibid.: 18). Whereas opponents, like Lowe, believed that women's ordination would, regrettably, make women more like men, proponents hoped it would make men more like women.

The doctrine of 'unripe time'

A final group of opponents put forward the so-called doctrine of 'unripe time'. They stressed the danger of schism and disunity should women be ordained. According to Margaret Webster (1994), WAOW fell into this group, as did the clergy group, Cost of Conscience. As in many institutions where women have struggled to achieve equality of access and status, the argument that there were more pressing priorities acted as a convenient way of marginalizing their concerns. This is implicit in the contribution made by John Gummer MP to the ordination debate, 'I hate the fact that we have wasted all these years arguing about this instead of winning souls for Christ' (*The Synod Debate* 1993: 36). However, proponents countered with their conception of '*Kairos*', a Greek word meaning the time when action is opportune and necessary. Chopp (1989: 51) interprets this as time which calls all borders into question. The reality was, perhaps, more mundane. According to Petre (1994: 143): 'As much as anything, it was the manpower crisis within the Church of England which was forcing it to turn to women for salvation.' It is no accident that it was only when the influence and standing of the Church of England as an institution had been drastically diminished that women were finally admitted to the hallowed ranks of the priestly ministry.

6.2 Campaigning outsiders: the Movement for the Ordination of Women

The Movement for the Ordination of Women (hereafter MOW) was launched in 1979 because ordained women from abroad were refused the right to officiate at services in England. Whereas opponents hoped the decision in 1985 to ordain women to the diaconate would defuse MOW's campaign, MOW perceived this decision as an important step towards full priestly ministry for women. It would be another seven years, however, before a measure permitting women's ordination was to be passed and an additional two years before the first women priests were finally ordained. The unwieldy bureaucratic structures of synodical government seemed calculated to slow up the process of change. As a result, as Wakeman (1996: 50) notes, 'Until 1994 the priesthood was the one area of work closed to women in this country'. Many women aspiring to priestly ministry stressed the symbolic, as well as practical, significance of their exclusion. Schneider, a Roman Catholic theologian, refers to women's sense of 'sacral unworthiness' and their 'total sacramental dependence on men' (cited in Baisley 1996: 107).

6.2.1 Establishing a common identity

Not surprisingly, in the Church differences of identity are primarily constructed along the axis of Church affiliation. Aldridge (1989) identifies the four main traditions in the Church of England as evangelical, liberal, centrist and conservative catholic, and MOW members were drawn from all four. The significance of the waiting period was that it opened up a discursive space for re-thinking an affinity that did not erase or undermine these theologically-based differences. As in the case of the NIWC, such differences among MOW members were contained by the goal of pursuing benefits for women *as women*. At that time, in this particular institution, it was felt to be politic-ally necessary for women to temporarily suppress all other differences in order to unite on the basis of a sexual identity that was used by opponents as a sufficient reason to perpetuate their exclusion. By definition, then, issues of sex, sexuality, gender and gender politics were unambiguously to the fore as identity categories throughout the campaign. For instance, although not all those involved in MOW regarded themselves as feminists, the majority seemed happy to identify themselves as such in the pre-ordination period. If any-thing, being committed to feminist goals was more important than being female, hence MOW's decision, in 1991, to merge with Priests for Women's Ordination (PWO).

6.2.2   Developing alternative structures

The significance of the period of waiting is that it enabled campaigners for women's ordination to construct a coherent set of oppositional norms designed to resist, challenge, and ultimately transform hegemonic discursive practices in the Church. These included the confrontational style which prevailed in synodical government throughout the decades during which the issue had been debated (Wakeman 1996: 3). According to Margaret Webster (1994: 10), MOW developed structures that transformed the potential for conflict between its members into a 'creative and fruitful tension'. It was chaired along non-hierarchical lines by a 'moderator' whose role it was to develop new and creative ways of dealing with disagreement. Peter Selby provides an insight into the self-conscious search for alternative discursive practices:

> Whether we wanted it to or not, the group had to consider how the fact that it was a group for the ordination of women would affect its style of meeting, its way of worshipping and its exercise of concern for its members . . . The grace of mutuality seemed intrinsic to our task. So also, we found we had to find ways of combining a strength of conviction with a gentleness of execution – qualities which elsewhere seem to pull in quite opposite directions.
>
> (Cited in Furlong 1991: 128–9)

An even more radical approach was adopted by the St Hilda Community which was founded in East London in 1989, partly to worship in inclusive language and partly to experience women's ministry. For instance, when General Synod prohibited women priests from abroad from celebrating in

England, its members subverted the Church's rules by taking part in 'illegal' eucharists. One of its founder members was Monica Furlong and she explains the aims of the Community, 'We wanted a community that worked by consensus and not by hierarchy . . . and we wanted to share – gifts, leadership, vision and perhaps sometimes possessions and money' (1991: 6). Women's construction of, and participation in, communities of practice, such as MOW and the St Hilda Community, offered new visions of gender relations in the Church. Both involved women *and* men in an exploration of discursive practices which implicitly critiqued those accepted as normative in the Church, since they enacted the values of solidarity, and cooperation, while respecting difference (Webster 1994: 169).

6.2.3   Developing gender inclusive language

Like many campaigners for women's ordination, Furlong (1991: 72) sees the campaign to have gender inclusive language, such as the use of 's/he' rather than so-called generic 'he', and 'people' rather than 'man', accepted as central to the feminist project of securing equality for men and women in the Church. She argues that 'a change in language indicates whether the change in church attitudes to women goes "all the way through" or is merely cosmetic'. She points out, however, that on this issue, as on many others in the Church, men have the power to legislate on behalf of women. A Commission set up in 1988 to investigate the issues surrounding gender inclusive language comprised two women and fourteen men. One of the two women notes the contradictory responses evoked by the issue, 'A feature of the response to pressure for inclusive language is the paradoxical insistence that, on the one hand, the issue is too trivial to be discussed and, on the other, that to raise it is positively satanic' (Morley 1984: 60). Objections include claims that it leads to a 'lack of dignity', a 'weakening of sense' and 'a diluting of richness' (Thomas 1996: 168). Interestingly, research shows that it is older women who are most offended by its use, 'It is as if having accepted the *status quo* all their lives, they have come to see that after all they are not included' (Baisley 1996: 113). Yet, as long as public prayer and liturgy implicitly gender readers/listeners as male, the majority of women are likely to feel discursively excluded from their address. This point was made by one of my respondents: 'it jars with me every *time* I hear something that is non-inclusive' (Trans. IX: 16). Her reaction challenges the oft-quoted claim that it is inclusive language which constitutes a needless distraction in Church services.

Rather than awaiting inclusive material officially sanctioned by the Church, the St Hilda Community produced a non-sexist prayer book that was used by the networks of women's liturgy groups which met up and down the country throughout the pre-ordination period. It was, however, disowned by Lambeth Palace and condemned by some as blasphemous. Petre (1994: 113) scathingly describes the liturgies the Community devised as 'New Age-style feminist' because they referred to God as 'mother' and 'her'. Yet, this ignores the fact that *both* maternal and paternal address forms were used. For instance, the revised version of the Lord's prayer began, 'Beloved our Father and Mother, in whom is heaven'. Clack (1996: 149) is among many feminists who argue that '"God the Father" is an image which . . . supports patriarchal claims to male supremacy'. This recalls Mary Daly's (1973) famous dictum, 'Since God is male, the male is God'. The feminist counter strategy to conceptualize God as mother, or father and mother, as in the case of the St Hilda prayer book, is dismissed by Bishop Graham Leonard in the book *Let God Be God*, on the grounds that it distorts 'the whole fine balance of the content of revelation. It is to introduce sexuality where none was intended' (Leonard et al. 1989: 55–6). As Furlong (1991) observes, Leonard's position betrays the erroneous assumption that the image of 'God the father' is somehow neutral in respect of sexuality.

6.2.4   Encounters with feminist theology

Women's relatively recent role as theologians has been a crucial means of seizing interpretative control within the Church. According to Dowell and Williams (1994: 50), 'Women's exclusion from the means and sources of theological reflection has proved as dispiriting as our exclusion from the Church's ministerial structures'. In order to disseminate the rich body of work that has been produced by Christian feminists in both Britain and the US, Women in Theology (WIT) was founded in 1983 and operated thereafter via a network of cell groups throughout the country. Some, inspired by the American feminist theologian Rosemary Radford Ruether's (1983) conception of 'womanchurch' as an exodus church, decided to leave what they came to see as an intrinsically patriarchal institution in order to seek an 'authentically woman-centred' spirituality (Dowell and Williams 1994: 58). For others, the encounter with feminist theology seems to have influenced their sense of the 'proper' exercise of their sacerdotal role. The existence of a link between feminist theology and sacerdotal practice is borne out by Lehman's (1993) survey of women in ministry in the US. He found that younger women, trained in seminaries with courses in feminist theology, manifested more 'feminine' ministry styles.[3] He concludes that the 'preference' for such styles among younger women owes more to their encounter with feminist theology than it does to their life experiences as women (ibid.: 198).

A central theme of feminist theology is an attack on what is seen as the pervasive heresy of dualism in the Church, whereby body and spirit are seen as incompatible. Furlong (1994: 21) points out that this denigration of the body goes back to the early Church and is tantamount to a denigration of women, 'to despise the body is to despise women's unique ability – that of giving birth – and to despise sexuality is to despise the one who inspires sexual desire'. The very word 'pregnant', as used by Janet Morley in the phrase 'pregnant with power' in a draft edition of the Church commissioned report, *Making Women Visible* (1988), was felt to be too loaded and was removed without her permission (in Furlong 1991: 81). The view of women as culpable inspirers of lust is illustrated by a comment made in a radio interview by Graham Leonard, then Bishop of London, to the effect that, 'if he saw a woman in the sanctuary, he would be unbearably tempted to embrace her' (in Dowell and Williams 1994: 33). This comment betrays a view of women's bodies as saturated with sexuality, whereas, as noted above, men are perceived as sexually neutral. The Old Testament's ritualized taboo about blood, and the tradition of churching which it produced, have likewise contributed to a view of women as 'unclean'. Feminist theologians argue that these taboos, though rarely acknowledged, help to explain the irrational dread some opponents felt about women as embodied subjects performing priestly functions. Many feminist theologians believe that the sight of women ministering the sacraments in itself constitutes a powerful challenge to these taboos.

6.3 Marginalization and subordination in the post-ordination period

The idea that the passing of the November 1992 legislation introduced equality for male and female priests is, according to Maltby (1998: 44), 'a deeply inaccurate perception'. Despite fears expressed by opponents in the debate that they would subsequently be marginalized and denied preferment, the opposite has proved to be the case. In fact, the second and third most senior appointments in the Church are currently held by men who do not ordain women as priests and do not have a record of appointing women to positions of responsibility.[4] This means that their views are at a variance with the majority view of the Church which is supportive of women's ministry. In the sections that follow I will outline a number of ways in which women priests have effectively exchanged exclusion for subordination and marginalization within the Church's institutional structures.

6.3.1 Legislating for inequality and the 'doctrine of taint'

Even opponents acknowledge that institutional subordination was built into the November 1992 legislation, since Clause 1(2) states that, 'Nothing in this Measure shall make it lawful for a woman to be consecrated to the office of bishop'. It is difficult to imagine any other public institution which would explicitly legislate to exclude women from its most senior positions. This was a point strategically mobilized during the ordination debate by the main speaker for the Opposition, David Silk, Archdeacon of Leicester, who claimed that the legislation 'discriminates against women, confuses the theology of order by driving a wedge between the episcopate and the presbyterate, and invites the Synod to vote for legislation barring women from the episcopate' (*The Synod Debate* 1993: 14). Other clauses ensured that, 'No parish was obliged to receive women priests, no male priest was obliged to work with them, no bishop was obliged to ordain them' (Mayland 1998: 71). In this way, legislation designed to ensure equality for women within the Church simultaneously denied that equality. Under this legislation it is clear that some priests are more equal than others.

The subsequent Act of Synod (1993) enshrined further concessions to opponents in perpetuity, unless rescinded. The Act was intended to enable bishops to preserve their fraternal collegiality at all costs, as is evident from a comment made by the Archbishop of Canterbury, George Carey: 'It was the sense that we had been drawn together in a brotherhood, which was historic and deeply moving' (cited in Petre 1994: 169). This fraternal unity was only achieved, however, by further institutionalizing the subordinate status of women priests. Particularly detrimental to the force of the original legislation was the concept of the 'two integrities', a piece of casuistry which states that there are two *equally legitimate*, albeit opposing, views on women's ordination. Christina Rees, who has come to regret bitterly her support for the Act and who feels MOW's charitable inclinations were cynically exploited, points out the incoherence of this concept:

> if you feel that that God is calling women to be priests you can't really accept that God is *not* calling women to be priests that is not a valid option either he is or he isn't and if you believe that God is *not* calling women to be priests you can't really go along with people who say oh yes he is . . . you cannot *have* two integrities 'cos one is always counteracting the other

(Trans. X: 121–35)

The Act also ensured that the pastoral needs of opponents were catered for by making provision for the appointment of three Provincial Episcopal Visitors (PEVs), the so-called 'flying bishops', whose activities, despite denials, are implicated in the 'doctrine of taint'. The PEVs act as a 'safe pair of hands' for those who perceive their own bishop as having been compromised by his involvement in the ordination of women. For instance, one opponent in the diocese of Durham said of his bishop, who ordains women, 'I find it very difficult to even contemplate receiving communion at his hands' (cited in Mayland 1998: 74). This is mirrored by the behaviour of parishioners within individual parishes. For instance, my respondent who is priest-in-charge of a parish in London explained that a male priest comes in on the first Sunday of every month to administer the eucharist to those who refuse to accept it from her hands (Trans. VIII: 42–3). Jane Shaw (1998: 21) concludes that the Act thereby gives legitimacy to a view of women and their sacramental ministry as 'polluting'. Fraternal conflict among bishops was avoided, but only at the cost of reviving and legitimizing deep-seated fears about women and women's sexuality. In turn, this has made it difficult for some priests to employ the premodifier 'woman' as a mark of pride, despite the obvious joy they experienced in finally being ordained as '*women* priests'.

6.3.2 Tainting the concept of sexual harassment

Textual traces of deep-seated prejudices about women and women's sexuality can be found in a report on sexual harassment produced since women's ordination to priesthood, in the diocese of Oxford. The report, entitled *The Greatness of Trust: The Report of the Working Party on Sexual Abuse by Pastors* (1996), implicitly genders its readers as male, even though women also occupy professional roles as priests and lay pastoral workers in the Church. Appendix III of the report contains much special pleading on behalf of male perpetrators of abuse whom it constructs as misguided individuals who are unwittingly led into sin by their 'high moral standards'. At one point we are told, without any supporting evidence, that 'men in particular are more vulnerable to affairs when they pass through critical stages of their life' (ibid.: 43). This is reinforced by a whole section, attributed to the 'expert' psychologist, Dr Archibald Hart, which reproduces the kind of outdated stereotypes of the symptoms of the female hysteric one would expect to encounter in popular usage, rather than in the academic discourse of psychology:

> One particular personality type is particularly risky for the male minister: the female hysterical personality. This person is typically shallow, overly reactive, even vivacious, uninhibited in displaying sexuality, given to flirtations, coquetry, and romantic fantasy – such a person is also impressionable and craves excitement but is naive and frigid. She is, in essence, a caricature of femininity, drawing attention to herself to obtain admiration . . . the pastor who falls prey to her seduction is bound to be destroyed.
>
> (*The Greatness of Trust* 1996: 43–4)

This passage manages to reproduce an entire set of stereotypical assumptions about destructive and predatory women who lack sexual restraint, but who ultimately prove (disappointingly?) frigid. Given that the implicit addressee is a male priest, it is also likely to evoke a theological schema of woman as the wicked temptress of man and instigator of his spiritual downfall, which has its origins in the biblical story of Eve and is reinforced by the terms of the Act of Synod. The implication, however, of the psychological turn given to this theological narrative is that it is now the vulnerable priest, rather than the brazen woman who seduced him, who is likely to be 'destroyed' by their mutual contact. This conveniently glosses over the asymmetrical power relationship which exists between a male pastor and a woman who is the subject of his pastoral care.

Elsewhere, it is presupposed that the addressee has a wife whose unsupportive behaviour and attitude once the adultery has been discovered is deemed reprehensible, 'What she doesn't know is that her pastor/husband desperately wants to confide his struggle to her. He wants to channel his arousal back to her, where it belongs. But sometimes her veil of silence and condemnation only increases the emotional distance' (ibid.: 46). It is he who is desperate and who struggles, whereas she is cold and unforgiving. The analyst's 'voice', in this case that of another psychologist, Paul Tournier, who is cited here by Hart, merges with that of the male adulterer in a way that makes it very clear where his sympathies lie. Indeed, we are told that the adulterer's view of his wife as 'the incarnation of moral law' is the 'driving force of much adultery' (ibid.). This suggests that women who are 'over virtuous' are just as likely to incite sexual waywardness in their husbands as female hysterics. In what is a remarkable piece of prestidigitation, the victim of the abuse is not only turned into the abuser, but the perpetrator's wife is made to bear a considerable portion of the blame for his failure to renounce his adulterous relationship. The credibility of these views is underscored by the long list of qualifications and 'numerous journal and magazine articles' attributed to Professor Hart. In addition, the reader is told at the outset that, 'It [the Appendix] sets out with great clarity the issues involved, and it should be read by everyone engaged in pastoral work' (ibid.: 18). The 'everyone' referred to, however, takes no account of female addressees who will find nothing here to guide their conduct when dealing with those in their pastoral care and everything to reinforce their sense of alienation from a Church which is deeply imbued with masculinist assumptions.

6.3.3 Covert and overt discrimination against women priests

Women priests are still very much in a minority in a male-dominated institution, with projected figures for 2001 of 11 per cent (*Numbers in Ministry* 1996: 2–3). All the evidence suggests that a two-tier clerical system is likely to persist for decades, with women priests disproportionately clustering in assistant roles, almost half of which are unpaid. Purchas (1996: 123) makes the observation that, 'It is hard to imagine, for instance, women solicitors, accountants or doctors accepting a situation where nearly half their profession were expected to work unpaid because they are women'. Particularly adversely affected are women priests in clergy couples: 'Some couples found that they were only offered one and a third stipends for two full-time jobs;

others had been told that the Church would never pay the woman in a joint clergy couple team although they would be happy to give her a job for no remuneration!' (the *Guardian* 10 March 1999). This may be due in part to the Church's tradition of relying on women in ministry to respond to the language of service.

In addition, as Aldridge (1989: 55) points out, a woman's access to career routes is often blocked by the operation of an informal fraternal network, whereas for the male priest:

> There are frequent meetings with brother clergy for him to attend and there are many clerical societies for him to join. If he aligns himself to one of the 'churchmanship' groups, he gains access to a nationwide network of debate, information exchange, sponsorship, sociability and friendship.

The *Windsor Consultation Document* (September 1995) also notes the way job advertisements reveal implicit masculinist assumptions about the limitations of women priests, including their alleged inability to carry out church maintenance and their greater vulnerability in relation to security issues. It reproduces the following from a parish profile:

> After deep and prayerful discussion, we feel that although we seek the best person for the post, in view of:
> a. the extremely large parish.
> b. the combination of church and parish problems.
> c. the security problems we are facing at the moment.
> d. the feelings of a minority of the congregation which must be respected.
> e. the loneliness of the situation of the Rectory . . .
>
> the position would not be suitable for a woman incumbent at the moment although we are open to the ministry of women.
>
> *(The Windsor Consultation Document* 1995: 5)

This is reminiscent of the doctrine of the 'unripe time' used to rationalize women's exclusion from ordination, and is consonant with a general climate in which the views of a minority of opponents hold sway. Potential candidates have no grounds for appeal against these strategies of exclusion, since the clergy's conditions of employment are not covered by equal opportunities legislation. Indeed, it is perfectly acceptable within ecclesiastical law to discriminate against women where Parochial Church Councils pass the relevant motions to this effect. This means that hundreds of parishes remain no-go areas for women priests. A recent Manufacturing, Science and Finance Union survey (1998) of women priests already in post revealed that 75 per cent of respondents had been subject to bullying and harassment by both parishioners and male clergy. The most common strategy used to marginalize them was verbal abuse, including pejorative naming, sexual innuendo and patronizing comments.

6.3.4   The exclusion of women priests from decision-making

Although they have finally achieved the right to be ordained, women in the Church of England do not participate as full members of decision-making bodies. This means that they are not entirely free of what Herbert (1994: 36) terms their 'long adolescence' in the structures of the Church. For example, the Turnbull Committee, set up to review the central policy-making and financial structures of the Church of England, comprised eleven men and one woman. The theological consultant was also a man, as were all three assessors, but two women were represented in secretarial roles. The report employs the exclusive term 'chairman/men' (1995: 47ff), sporadically acknowledging in brackets that some of the posts referred to could be filled by a female (ibid.: 47). The pattern of pronoun use throughout the report is also very uneven, as if the inclusion of women ministers were an after-thought. Although it is the most wide-ranging review of the Church's struc-tures ever undertaken, it makes no reference to the recently implemented ruling on the ordination of women as a substantive issue. In the introductory chapter entitled, 'The Organization of the Church in the light of the gifts of God', no reference is made to the potential contribution women might make to priestly ministry. Despite the Chairperson's opening remarks about the Church's need to face 'cultural change', the report fails to address the most dramatic cultural change that has occurred in its recent history. Its most important recommendation is the establishment of a National Council. How-ever, no women, clerical or lay, are automatically included on the Council. One conservative lay woman, Rachel Stowe, was initially appointed as the sole female voice among twenty men. A second lay woman has since been co-opted after protests, but no women priests have been included.

In order to challenge the continuing mechanisms for subordinating and segregating women priests, MOW was relaunched under the new name of Women and the Church (WATCH) on 9 November 1996. Its aim is to keep statistical information on the deployment of women priests and to press for positive discrimination to encourage more black women to seek to enter the priesthood. Its biggest challenge, however, is to secure women's access to episcopal appointments. Rees describes it as 'a logical step and it's a step of justice you can't have women priests without having women bishops because there is nothing qualitatively different between the two' (Trans. X: 152–4). Darling (1994: 223) records the effect this had on the US Episcopal Church in 1989, twelve years after the first female ordinations: 'The actual admis-sion of women to the brotherhood of bishops shattered a powerful symbol of male control over women that the episcopate had represented.' However, according to WATCH's newsletter, *Outlook*, this is unlikely to occur in the

Church of England until at least 2009 (1999, No. 7: 15). Yet, *
women are excluded from becoming bishops in the Church of En*
will remain second-class priests.

6.4 Clerical self-fashioning: from woman deacon to woman priest

Poststructuralist theorists, such as Butler (1990), stress the instability of identity categories and the potential individuals have to 'perform' different sexual and gendered identities, in particular. Such identities are, she argues, constituted through a variety of different discursive routes or acts (ibid.: 145). To some extent, this performative thesis is supported by my research into women priests in the Church of England, since what is interesting is the range of different, sometimes contradictory, subject positions they occupy. In particular, their behaviour since ordination, linguistic and otherwise, cannot be accommodated within a polarized gendered framework. Nonetheless, it is possible to identify a set of competing expectations and norms with which they have had to negotiate and which constrain the subject positions available to them. On the one hand, they are aware of the expectation that they will promote discursive norms that challenge the dominant masculinist ones that prevail in the Church, but, on the other, they have had to confront an institution that is not only male-dominated, but in which they occupy officially sanctioned subordinate roles. This involves them in an entirely different set of negotiations from those they engaged in as campaigning outsiders, often connected to women-oriented communities of practice.

I will suggest that, by underestimating the type of material constraints that operate on speaking subjects, linguists who draw on Butler's (1990) work tend to overstate the constitutive nature of discourse (see Bergvall et al. 1996). I will illustrate this by outlining some of the constraints that influence both the subject positions adopted by women priests, and the ways in which these are evaluated by colleagues and parishioners. The latter are particularly important, since, as I argue elsewhere, advocates of a performative approach to language and gender also tend to neglect the metadiscursive control exercised by those who evaluate the appropriacy of the language used by women in public sphere roles. Following Dorothy Smith (1990: 86), I will suggest that women priests 'actively work out their subject positions and roles in the process of negotiating discursive [and, I would add, material] constraints'.

6.4.1 The role of mediatized discourse

A particularly potent source of the widespread expectation that women will be priests in a completely new way is the mainstream media. The ordination debate attracted the sort of attention in the mainstream media that is usually reserved for important parliamentary occasions and political party conferences, despite the fact that fewer than 5 per cent of the population are regular church-goers. A trial vote in July 1992 was narrowly defeated and the uncertainty this generated created an ideal space for media intervention. The fact that the coverage which followed was wholly at odds with the cultural importance of the event for a largely secular society, suggests that its cultural significance lay elsewhere. It can be explained partly by the Church's status as one of the last bastions of male exclusivity in British society and partly by the symbolic investment people have in an institution inextricably tied up with English history. Opponents saw a media conspiracy at work, designed to promote a liberal secular agenda. Yet the conspiracy theory ignores the trivializing coverage of women's aspirations to be priests and the disproportionate focus on the opposing minority following the passing of the legislation.

Nonetheless, coverage prior to, and including, the November vote was largely sympathetic to women aspiring to priesthood, with every newspaper except the *Daily Telegraph* coming out in favour. This is in marked contrast to the largely hostile coverage campaigners for ordination received throughout the 1970s and 1980s. This apparently dramatic *volte face* was mainly due to a shift in attitudes towards issues of gender equality in society as a whole. Hence, the tenor of media coverage reflected the fact that 80 per cent of the general public supported women's ordination, as did two-thirds of all church-goers (Petre 1994: 88). Another factor, however, was MOW's decision early in 1992 to appoint Christina Rees as its PR officer in charge of coordinating the media campaign. Recognizing the crucial role the media would play in influencing public opinion, like the NIWC and WEN, MOW decided to ensure that it maintained a degree of control over how its campaign was represented. Rees relates how she set out to cultivate close working relationships with the religious affairs correspondents on all the major national dailies, as well as with those who worked for the church press (Trans. X: 80ff). She would phone them and say what she wanted them to report and, in general, she feels they responded responsibly. It got to the stage where they contacted her for verification and/or comments. However, she admits, 'it was not a smooth ride because the media was not entirely in favour and could also trivialize it as well' (ibid.: ll. 57–8). One-third of traditionalist church-goers were adamantly against and this seems to have been the constituency addressed by the *Daily Telegraph*, whose Editor, and religious affairs correspondent, Damian Thompson, remained steadfastly opposed. The following discussion is designed to give some indication of the contradictions inherent in the media coverage, as well as the central role it played in *mediating* between women priests' construction of themselves, and the image of them that circulates in the public domain.

Women priests as problem insiders

In the aftermath of the debate, almost all newspaper headlines reproduced the apocalyptic rhetoric of opponents. The headline in *The Times*, 'Joy, Dismay and Warnings Greet Synod Vote', gives a relatively accurate impression of the 'balance' of the coverage. Perhaps not surprisingly, given its oppositional stance, the *Daily Telegraph's* headline is marked by the structured absence of any mention of joy, but instead focuses selectively on the alleged, 'Turmoil Over Synod Vote'. Its address is to traditionalists for whom women's ordination opened up 'a Pandora's box, after the lid had been opened, out would pop women bishops, practising gays and lesbian clergy and feminist, pagan liturgies which referred to God as her' (Petre 1994: 12). The metaphor of 'woman as chaos' is pervasive, even in the majority of newspapers that had openly come out in support. For instance, George Austin, an outspoken opponent, was quoted in the *Guardian* (12 November 1992) as saying that women priests would bring something 'wild' into Christianity. While some of the more extreme views of opponents were negatively evaluated by media producers, there was a *general* acceptance of opponents' construction of women priests as even more of a problem as insiders than they had been as campaigning outsiders, clamouring to be let in.

This can, of course, be explained by the fact that 'negativity' and, more specifically, 'conflict between people' are perhaps *the* key factors that renders an event newsworthy (Bell 1991: 156). In this context, the possibility of schism afforded more opportunities for sensational revelations than accounts of the hopes and fears of women priests. This is especially true since the majority of women priests were anonymous individuals, whereas a number of defectors to Rome were elite people, including the high-profile Conservative MPs, John Gummer, Emma Nicholson and Ann Widdecombe. The *Church Times* wryly observes, 'more column inches were devoted to John Gummer's departure than to the event which precipitated it' (4 March 1994). By August 1993, three hundred clergy and lay people had defected to Rome, but it was not the high-profile exodus that had been threatened and anticipated, and which had fuelled claims that the Church would suffer financial ruin. The latter fear was due to the fact that each priest who left was to receive compensation of £30,000, leading the *Daily Mail* to produce the alarmist headline, '£100m Church threat over women priests' (23 February 1994). Petre acknowledges that 'the departures have constituted a trickle rather than a flood' (1994: 183).

Margaret Webster suggests that the disproportionate focus on the opposing minority in the media led to a distorted view of the mood in the aftermath of the debate:

> The conviction of two-thirds of church-going Anglicans was being set aside while all eyes were fixed on a vociferous minority. The women, who

over so many years had been told that they must not speak about their pain and frustration, were now faced with the spectacle of the pain of the opponents being publicized with considerable effect.

(Webster 1994: 190)

The burden of guilt fell upon the very women who should have been celebrating a hard-won victory. It is likely that media coverage, together with episcopal warnings about the dangers of triumphalism, helped to create a climate which was conducive to the relatively unopposed passage a year later of the retrograde Act of Synod. This in turn is likely to have had a negative impact on the conditions in which the first generation of women priests have practised their ministry. For example, some women priests who were formerly deacons claim to have experienced a rise in hostility among those previously unconcerned.

Women priests as agents of change

Almost all media coverage, whether sympathetic or hostile, presupposed that women's ministry *would* be distinctive and the question then became *how* this would manifest itself. This suggests the extent to which the 'difference' arguments advanced by feminist sociolinguists, psychologists and so on, have come to infuse everyday discourse and have attained the status of 'common-sense' (Mills 1998; Coward 1999). The presuppositions cued in the majority of media texts served to construct women priests as stereotypically gendered subjects. Fairclough (1989: 154) argues that 'presuppositions can . . . have *ideological* functions, when what they assume has the character of "common sense in the service of power"'. Intertextual traces of the process of ideological framing and of resistance to it are implicit in the following account of an interview between the journalist, Christian Tyler, and a London curate, Rev. Dilly Baker (see Fig. 6.1). Baker, having made the modest prediction that 'Women will bring a breath of fresh air, a little more imagination and creativity' (ibid.: ll. 65–7), is pressed further by Tyler. He reports, 'I asked her how women priests would differ from men. *Once more*, she was reluctant to employ "stereotypes". She *finally* agreed that women *might* find it easier to extend sympathy, especially to other women' (ibid.: ll. 70–5; my italics). The sentence adverb, 'finally', implies a degree of resignation by Baker to the journalist's pre-scripted schema of gender difference. However, the cautious modality she employs reveals her obvious efforts to resist the compliant subject position established for her by the interviewer's repeated cues. Elsewhere in the article, Baker is equally resistant to Tyler's attempts to construct her as a militant career feminist, intent on asserting her God-given 'right' to be ordained (ibid.: ll. 27, 38, 77).

An article by Neal Ascherson, in the *Independent on Sunday* (11 December 1994), is suggestive of the way in which even those journalists who seek to

A mother in waiting to be a priest

DILLY BAKER is expecting to become a mother in two weeks' time and an Anglican priest within two years...

Dilly Baker's tomboy haircut and progressive views could suggest a militant feminist, a woman subconsciously trying to be a man. But there is nothing mannish about her big eyes, wide mouth and giggly laugh – she is younger than her 30 years – and nothing strident about the way she talks. I asked her to describe her vocation ...

Have you a vocation or do you really mean you want a career?

It depends how you want to define vocation. I feel that I have. I can pinpoint the time when I felt very, very strongly that this was something that I had to do: it was during a pilgrimage week at Iona.'

How do you know your vocation is for the priesthood?

'I feel my ministry is incomplete without the priestly part. When you've been involved in people's lives, birth and death and everything in between, and then the shutter comes down on Sunday morning that feels very, very wrong'.

And if ordination were denied you?

'I would find it very difficult to continue in the church in my present position.

Do you see it as a woman's right to be ordained priest?

'It's a very loaded term, that'.

Yes, I said; it was deliberate.

The curate sighed, 'I don't think I want to talk in terms of rights because that just turns people off. I might want to talk in terms of justice. Men and women are created together in the image of God and to deny women the ability to represent Christ is, I think, a fundamental break with justice. But I'm not the sort of person to go around talking about women's rights too earnestly'.

Is what you're doing part of the feminist movement?

'I'm reluctant to say Yes because feminism is such a dirty word for a lot of people. But feminism has helped us to see more clearly what has been going on in the church, the way women have been treated and understood' ...

Dilly Baker (her real name is Hilary) acknowledged a theological connection. 'It's not simply a matter of who says the Eucharistic prayer. We're dealing with something very important: how we understand God, how we understand sexuality and relations between women and men. So long as the church says that women cannot adequately represent Christ at the altar then our theology is open to question.

Is the gender of God separate from the issue of whether women should be priests or not?

She hesitated, 'I personally don't think it's separate. But let's be honest. There's no sex to God. It's a convenient metaphor. We're talking metaphors all the time here and I think we ought to enlarge our vision of God all the time. But "women priests equals female God" is not what I want to say at all' ...

She agreed that the Church of England could be seen as the last male bastion. 'Men have been heading this show for so long. Women will bring a breath of fresh air, a little more imagination and creativity, and will open the whole thing up. Maybe that is why some men are so very threatened by the whole issue'.

I asked her how women priests would differ from men.

Once more, she was reluctant to employ 'stereotypes'. She finally agreed that women might find it easier to extend sympathy, especially to other women. The family of a parishioner whose funeral she recently conducted had said as much.

Finally I asked her: do you think it's God's will that women should be priests?

'Yes', she said, very quietly, 'I certainly do'.

Do you kneel down and pray to be told this is the right thing for you?

'Yes. That would be quite an apt way of putting it' ...

Fig. 6.1 Part of the text of an article recording an interview of Rev. Dilly Baker by Christian Tyler that appeared in the *Financial Times* (22 February 1992).

...e, rather than reinforce, stereotypical assumptions about women's ministry as priests, nonetheless create unrealistic expectations about their power to transform the Church as an institution. Ascherson begins by rejecting the idea that women will merely become, 'vicars plus feminine intuition', but then goes on to assert his belief that, instead, they will 'bring a different sense of the sacred that in the end will be implacable towards the compromises on which this particular church is founded' (ibid.). By inverting the traditional prejudice against women as biologically tainted, he seems to imply that their spiritual integrity is superior to that of their compromising and compromised male colleagues. He does not offer any details of what their 'different sense of the sacred' might be, but he takes for granted that it has the power to challenge, and ultimately transform, the whole cultural and spiritual ethos of the Church of England. This is something of a tall order, given that women's continuing subordination within the Church's institutional structures was built into the November legislation.

Familial relationships and bodily tropes

One way in which the subordinate status of women priests was reinforced by media coverage is that they tended to be represented as embodied sexual beings attached to families. The emphasis on their role as mothers amounted to a positive obsession. For instance, Christian Tyler's profile of the London curate, Dilly Baker, carries the headline 'A mother in waiting to be a priest' (see Fig. 6.1), while all the major newspapers featured photographs of the Rev. Susan Mayoss-Hurd, the first woman priest to give birth, holding her baby in a madonna-like pose. This preoccupation also manifested itself in the widespread use of bodily tropes, notably in punning headlines about pregnancy such as, 'Women expectant: from deacons to priests' (*Tablet* 19 February 1994) and 'Pregnant pause for ordinand' (the *Guardian* 21 February 1994). Such coverage was not only calculated to magnify the difference between female and male clergy, but in the process reinforced women priests' connection with nurturing roles in the home at a time when they were trying to escape the assumption that was their 'proper' sphere. This assumption has been cleverly and humorously subverted in the MOW slogan, 'A woman's place is in the house of bishops' – a slogan that has, somewhat paradoxically perhaps, since appeared on aprons, mugs and tea-towels in its campaign to secure women's access to episcopal roles.

Femmes or frumps

Another way in which media commentators can undermine the efforts of women who aim to achieve a public voice is by exhibiting an inappropriate interest in their appearance at the expense of what they are actually trying to say. This trivializing tendency is evident in media coverage of women priests, most notoriously in the headline in the *Sun* the day after the successful passage of the legislation: 'Church say yes to their vicars in knickers' (12 November 1992). In his profile of Dilly Baker, journalist Christian Tyler notes that her 'tomboy haircut' might suggest a 'militant feminism', but reassures *Financial Times* readers that 'there is nothing mannish about her big eyes, wide mouth and giggly laugh' (Fig. 6.1: ll. 6–8). Numerous articles since have focused on the implications of women's ordination for clerical dress (the *Guardian* 25 November 1993; the *Sunday Times* 25 June 1995).

The anomaly that was felt to exist between the priestly role and feminine appearance is strikingly evident in an article by Mary Kenny in the *Daily Express* (17 February 1997: 11). Referring to the Rev. Lucy Winkett, she begins by posing the rhetorical question, 'How could one see such a pretty little thing as a priest?', thereby ostensibly establishing a dialogic relationship with her reader. Like many commentators, she views earrings as particularly jarring metonymic signifiers of an inappropriate femininity in women priests. She concludes her article with a lame bid for tolerance which is undermined by the terms in which she frames it, 'If pretty girls in earrings can perform a holy and priestly function for some worshippers, then so be it'. The collocational chaining of the trivializing lexical items 'pretty' (twice), 'little' and 'girl' are designed to make it difficult for readers to resist the conclusion that women and the priestly role are wholly incompatible.

Tannen's (1996) claim that women's appearance is marked, no matter what choices they make, is confirmed by the fact that those women priests who strategically distanced themselves from traditional signifiers of gendered identity were, and continue to be, found wanting for this very reason. For instance, an article in *The Times* (25 June 1995) reports that 'Newly ordained Anglican women priests have already gained a reputation for frumpiness'. Both responses have signalled unequivocally to women priests that they are women in a male environment. The cumulative effect of representing women priests in terms of familial relations, bodily tropes and aspects of their dress and appearance is to undermine their claims to professional status. Such practices of representation contribute to a more general discursive restructuring, discussed throughout this study, whereby the gendered nature of the private–public dichotomy is reproduced *within* the public sphere.

Patterns of naming

The increasing priority of newspapers to sell in a competitive market probably accounts for their tendency to report some of the worst rhetorical excesses of those opposed to women's ordination. For instance, the term 'priestess', used as a dysphemism by those who view women priests as an anathema, became a peg on which to hang numerous sensational stories bearing headlines such as, 'Call for women priests to be burnt at the stake' (*The Times* 9 March 1994: 4) and 'Cathedral circle dancers accused of witchcraft' (*The Daily Telegraph* 29 June 1994: 4). The implicit charge that women's ordination as priests has led the Church beyond the theological pale into the dangerous territory of neo-paganism was invariably discredited by the liberal press. Nonetheless, such coverage may have contributed to a discursive context which has made it more difficult for women priests to be taken seriously when they raise theological objections to exclusive language, including the tendency to gender God as male. This is evident in the hesitant reply offered by Dilly Baker to the question as to whether 'the gender of God [is] separate from the issue of whether women should be priests' (Fig. 6.1: ll. 55–6ff). She is obviously aware that any attempt to question the gendering of God as male tends to be interpreted reductively as an assertion that God is, in fact, female (ibid.: l. 62).

Fictional representations of women priests

Women priests are generally positive about the effect fictional representations have had on the way their ministry has been received. Radio 4's long-running soap, *The Archers*, made a well-intentioned attempt to expose some of the problems confronted by the new woman vicar, the Rev. Janet Fisher, and included conversion stories of hardline opponents, such as Tom Forest. This may have helped to assuage the fears of some of the more conservative members of the Church who, like Forest, were wary about change per se. By far the most well-known fictional representation of a woman priest, however, is the eponymous heroine of the BBC sitcom, *The Vicar of Dibley*, a role played by the popular comedian Dawn French. It is based loosely on the ministry of a London priest, Joy Carroll, although the idyllic rural setting for the series could not be more remote from Carroll's experience of working with people on the margins of society in inner city London. Wakeman (1996) feels that the series has been very effective at countering stereotypes through humour: 'The caricature of a forceful and aggressive woman minister seems to be fading. Possibly the sting was drawn by *The Vicar of Dibley*, television's series about a lovely but terrible woman vicar who must have been an amalgam of everyone's worst fears' (Wakeman 1996: 15). The *Windsor Consultation Document* (September 1995) likewise records the unanimous opinion expressed by all those present that the series brought humour and humanity to the new role of women priests. So positive is the perceived impact of the series that one Synod member referred to it as the 'Vicar of Dibley spread of tolerance' (the *Guardian* 15 March 1999).

The response from one of my respondents was, however, more qualified. She noted that the media have a long-standing record of trivializing the Church and cited the role played by Derek Nimmo in the popular 1960s sitcom, *All Gas and Gaiters*, as establishing a precedent for subsequent depictions of priests as effeminate and ineffectual buffoons (Trans. VII: 50–4). This is a tradition which has been reproduced more recently in the Channel 4 sitcom, *Father Ted*. In this context, she felt that the character played by

French is likely to perpetuate, rather than challenge, the popular image of vicars, and in this case women vicars, as figures of fun at a time when they are striving to be taken seriously. Yet, the writer of the series, Richard Curtis, claims he deliberately set out to subvert the traditional image of the 'wet male buffoon' by making Geraldine 'compassionate and intelligent' (*The Times* 5 November 1994). More suspect is another of his comments on the series, quoted in the same article:

> Many recent comedies, including *Blackadder, Fawlty Towers, One Foot in the Grave*, etcetera, are about people who are rude, dismissive, angry. I thought it would be fun to write about someone who was keen, enthusiastic and, in moments of conflict, has to be the soul of sweetness.

While male characters in comedies are permitted to get angry, Geraldine is, as Curtis notes, invariably the 'soul of sweetness'. Such saintly restraint may be possible for Geraldine in the face of the comic antics of the inhabitants of Dibley, but it may be much less so for the many women priests who have had to confront hostility and abuse from their parishioners. Likewise, while Geraldine is both a strong and attractive character, much of her humour is self-denigrating, and a number of storylines have centred on her frustrated attempts at romance. A particularly poignant episode was the 1998 Christmas special in which she mistakenly assumes that a handsome BBC producer is attracted to her. Although the series has undoubtedly countered some stereotypical assumptions about women priests, it may have reinforced others, particularly the assumption that single women turn to priesthood because of their failure to find fulfilment in heterosexual relationships. It may also have contributed to the demanding expectation that women priests will invariably be models of good-humoured restraint, whatever provocation they encounter.

6.4.2 Strategies of subversion or accommodation: priests or *women* priests?

Some women priests have chosen to distance themselves from the identity criteria of sex, sexuality and gender that were necessarily to the fore in the pre-ordination campaign. Instead, they emphasize the institutional force of their ordination as priests and insist that gender is largely irrelevant to the exercise of many aspects of their sacerdotal role. For instance, one of my interviewees feels that the use of the premodifier 'woman' is self-marginalizing: 'I think it's time we stopped referring to ourselves as women priests we're priests that's all . . . I'm a little worried that we shall hive off into our little ghetto' (Trans. IX: 108–16). The implication is that the gender-marking of what should be a gender-neutral occupational role is an unnecessary distraction, 'whether you're a woman or a man shouldn't make any difference at all your gender should~*I feel* your gender should disappear in a service' (ibid.: 147–9). Hence, her rejection of the 'feely' and 'personal' aspects of some women's approach to ministry, and of their propensity to 'go on endlessly about birth' (ibid.: 94). She also admits to minimizing aspects of her appearance and dress that would draw unwarranted attention to her femininity:

> I will do all sorts of things when I'm in mufti erhm I like bright colours when I'm off duty it's an antidote to the sort of quietness and so on of clergy dress I like earrings I~I very quickly decided that it wasn't appropriate to wear fun earrings when taking a service because it's a distraction you do not want people looking at your earrings instead of listening to what you're saying so I tone every-thing down then and big rings and so on I don't wear those during services

> (Trans. IX: ll. 151–6)

These de-gendering strategies may have been influenced by the media's trivializing focus on the appearance of women priests. However, they are also likely to be connected to Priest C's conviction, stated later in the interview, that men in the Church have a 'deep' and 'unacknowledged' fear of women's sexuality (ibid.: ll. 197ff). This is a fear that many women priests feel has been reinforced, rather than challenged, in the post-ordination period because of the revival of the 'doctrine of taint' (see Furlong 1998).

While both Priests A (Trans. VII: 58–61) and C embrace occupational norms as gender-neutral, such norms have been perceived by others as male-identified, because of their connection with a traditionally male-dominated institution. Maggie Ross (1994, p. 116), for instance, is critical of what she sees as the failure of women priests to challenge the male-oriented bureaucratization of the Episcopal Church in the US: 'the women seem more and more to be adopting the "executive" model, and they dress like upper-level management cum dog collars'. This is reminiscent of Daly's (1978) dysphemistic neologism, 'fembots', to designate women careerists who, in her view, inevitably collude with masculinist institutional norms. Such negative evaluations of women priests are not confined to feminist critics, but have been appropriated by those who oppose women's ministry on quite different grounds. This is evident in an article recording the reaction of traditionalists to the ministry of Miriam Byrne, Provost of St Paul's Cathedral in Dundee and the first woman priest in Britain to take control of an Anglican cathedral (Fig. 6.2). She has been dubbed 'Atilla the Nun' (ibid.: l. 12), because, in the words of one parishioner, 'She is a woman doing a man's job and is over compensating because of that. She is dictatorial and does not care what other people think' (ibid.: ll. 24–6). The implication is that hers is an exaggerated performance of a certain kind of authoritarian masculinity, yet, when journalist Gerard Seenan attempted to find evidence to substantiate claims of her

Knives out for first woman provost

From the beginning it was going to be a difficult job. But for a twice-married former Roman Catholic nun, the mantle of being arguably Britain's most senior Anglican woman priest is proving to be more arduous than she could ever have imagined.

Only months after her appointment, Miriam Byrne, aged 52, is facing calls for her resignation from the church committee that presided over her installation.

Some parishioners at St Paul's Cathedral, Dundee, have dubbed her Atilla the Nun, accusing her of over-compensating in her role as a 'woman in a man's job'.

Worse still, a petition was yesterday circulating among her flock for the reinstatement of her predecessor, Michael Bunce, who was forced to resign after embezzling £44,000 from a company he set up to help the unemployed.

Despite this disgrace, to some sections of the highly conservative congregation at St Paul's, Dr Bunce retains one advantage over Ms Byrne: he is a man.

'She is a woman doing a man's job and over-compensating because of that. She is dictatorial and does not care what other people think.

'She is throwing her weight about in a way no man would dream of', said one member of the congregation . . .

When news of Ms Byrne's appointment broke, George Greig, the cathedral's honorary chaplain for 13 years, resigned, He took with him around a dozen members of the congregation.

Another faction who continue to attend St Paul's refuse to take communion when Ms Byrne is conducting the service . . .

Although precise accounts of how Ms Byrne has earned her Atilla the Nun moniker and her reputation for 'Thatcher-like decision-making' are not readily forthcoming, there is a dedicated corps in the congregation who are intent on seeing her leave before Christmas.

It is also claimed that the Bishop of Brechin, Neville Chamberlain, has asked her to consider leaving the church.

But there are some members of the church who say Ms Byrne is merely the victim of traditionalist intolerance.

She came to St Paul's on a convoluted route. She began her religious life as a nun with the Vocation Sisters – but although she spent seven years with the order, she never took her final vows and eventually she left the convent to get married to a former monk.

They divorced 18 years later, and Ms Byrne married again to a university librarian. She later returned to the religious life working her way up to her present position . . .

For the traditionalists, the provost of St Paul's was always going to be a difficult job for a woman to fill. But for a woman with a past and strident views to boot, it may simply be beyond the pastoral pale.

Fig. 6.2 Part of the text of an article about the Right Rev. Miriam Byrne that appeared in the *Guardian* (16 November 1998).

'Thatcher-like decision-making', it was not 'readily forthcoming' (ibid.: l. 40). Instead there are some in the church who see her as a *victim* of traditionalist intolerance' (ll. 47–8; my italics). Seenan discovered that for Byrne's opponents even a professionally corrupt man (the previous incumbent had embezzled £44,000 from a company he set up to help the unemployed) is preferable to a 'strident' female who is merely playing at being a man.[5] This illustrates the 'performative paradox' (Montgomery 1999), whereby women who seek to construct themselves as competent professionals are, nonetheless, vulnerable to the charge of mimicking men.

This is particularly paradoxical, since priestly ministry is, in many ways, a feminine occupation. Indeed, priesthood can be seen as an instance of socially and institutionally sanctioned gender-crossing behaviour by men. Thus the Roman Catholic theologian, Schüssler Fiorenza (1993: 100), says of the sacraments, 'as rituals of birthing and nurturing, [they] appear to imitate female powers of giving birth and nurturing the growth of life'. The psychiatrist, Robert Hobson, believes men who are drawn to the priesthood are motivated by an envy of women's reproductive powers, finding 'refuge in the "motherly aspects" of priesthood and such "feminine" expression as ceremonial or ritual dress' (cited in Petre 1994: 39). Indeed, Wakeman (1996: 6) implies that a large measure of the hegemonic power which has historically been vested in the priesthood appears to come precisely from the fact that men have been performing women's private sphere roles in a public institution, 'He [the male priest] does not become female, but by adding female functions to his own masculinity becomes culturally hermaphrodite or complete'. This may help to explain the bitterness experienced by many male clergy who recognized that women's entry into the priesthood would unmask their masquerade, rendering their feminized rituals a parodic imitation of the 'real thing'. This has led some opponents to engage in exaggerated and reactionary performances of masculinity.[6] Whereas Bing and Bergvall (1996: 6–7) suggest that both sexes are equally penalized for transgressing normative gender roles, in the Church at least, men and women are clearly not equal players in the game of gender-crossing.

Interestingly, all three of my respondents refer to empirical studies that indicate that male priests have traditionally taken up gendered subject positions at variance with their sexual identity (see also Francis 1991; Lehman 1993). They appear to regard this 'fact' as offering them a way out of defining themselves in narrowly gendered terms. Referring to the Myers Briggs personality test, a test widely used in the Church's training institutions, Priest B alludes to her own masculine character trait of being 'guided by the head, rather than by the heart' (Trans. VIII: 40). Her comment is suggestive of the way in which so-called gender-crossing behaviour can reify stereotypical assumptions about gender, even as it appears to trouble them. Her identification with a masculine subject position does not, however, preclude a radical stance on gender politics. For instance, she regards the Act of Synod as an 'act of apartheid' (ibid.: 45), and, in her own ministry, actively promotes inclusive language via an inclusive style of address (ibid.: 33).

The strategic appropriation of a range of discursive subject positions is especially likely to occur in liminal periods in an institution's history, such as that which currently exists in the Church of England, where newly ordained women priests are in an ideal position to negotiate the boundaries of gendered identity. For instance, Priests A and C both claim that their gender affiliation is contingent on the gendered nature of the domain in which they find themselves. They strategically exploit connections between women and qualities such as empathy and sensitivity in situations where this seems appropriate, like funerals, but elsewhere, for instance in mixed-sex meetings working to male agendas, they suppress these. In other words, women priests construct themselves as 'like men' in some respects, in order to assert their equality in relation to, for instance, the criterion of competence, and 'like women' in other respects where the aim is to point up male 'lack' of qualities such as empathy. According to Priest C, 'at moments of emotional stress and so on women are quite welcomed because . . . men disappear into the back room and get on with the job or something they're afraid to show their emotions or something' (Trans. IX: 54–7). This is in marked contrast to her claim, noted above, that gender is irrelevant to the exercise of the priestly role.

The apparently contradictory, and often highly qualified, claims Priest C makes about gender and occupational role can be explained by the fact that she stresses the importance of gender in informal interactional settings where it is likely to be perceived as advantageous to women, and she minimizes its importance in more formal interactional settings where it might be perceived to disadvantage women. Yet, both Priests A and C are aware that their gender-crossing behaviour may be negatively evaluated by others. Priest A, for instance, notes that male Church Wardens in her parish regard her leadership style as 'bossy' (Trans. VII: 45–6), while Priest C says of herself:

I have to be conscious very much that I don't come over too powerfully . . . I haven't experienced {negative evaluations} because I am very careful not to fall into that trap I can be sharp-tongued and I know I'm powerful . . . I have found that I can sway a meeting but I have to be careful when I use it [laughs]

(Trans. IX: 136–43)

This offers an insight into the type of pragmatically motivated form of self-surveillance that women in professional roles have to engage in order to overcome the perennial double bind.

6.4.3   The strategic disidentification with feminism

There is a good degree of unanimity when it comes to how women priests choose to situate themselves in relation to gender politics in the period since ordination. Time and again my interviewees, and numerous other women priests who have written about their experiences, seek to distance themselves from the 'feminist' label, even though they admit that they were happy to employ it in the pre-ordination campaign. It could be argued that this is symptomatic of the recent and widespread post-feminist backlash, but this does not explain the reluctance with which women priests give up the label. It becomes clear from their responses that this is a strategic decision designed to enable them to promote an implicitly feminist agenda more readily in an institutional environment that is particularly hostile to feminism. For instance, one of my interviewees said she wouldn't admit *publicly* to being a feminist because in the Church it is equated with being an 'aggressive fighter for women's position' (Trans. IX: 32–3). This is a view shared by Frances Ward, 'I know if I am labelled a feminist it gives people a good excuse for marginalizing me and not listening to me' (in Loudon 1994: 86).

A poststructuralist feminist might be tempted to applaud this as a masquerade designed to further feminist goals. However, this ignores the personal investment subjects have in self-identity labels, especially since this public denial of a feminist stance is not *freely* chosen. If, as poststructuralists like Butler (1990) claim, language is constitutive of our sense of self, then this type of strategic disidentification is likely to be accompanied by a feeling of self-betrayal. This is evident in the following anecdote related by Ward:

> I remember preaching a sermon once and coming down and shaking people's hands at the end of the service and someone came up to me and said, 'You're not one of those feminists, are you?' and I was caught on the hop and said, 'No', which I've always regretted because it felt like a loss of integrity.
>
> (in Loudon 1994: 86)

If women priests are reluctant to be labelled 'feminists', it seems unlikely that they will be prepared to confront the equally hostile reaction engendered by the issue of inclusive language. It is, therefore, no coincidence that the process of strategic disidentification with overtly feminist goals in the post-ordination period appears to have gone hand-in-hand with a relative retreat on the issue of inclusive language (the *Daily Telegraph* 13 July 1994). As noted earlier, from a feminist perspective, not all strategic uses of language are equally valid and some may even be positively reactionary. In this case, the danger is that the subversive power of self-confessed feminists who campaigned for women's ordination is being co-opted and neutralized, leaving the Church's masculinist discursive practices intact.

6.4.4 Celebrating gender difference

Many women priests continue to stress the distinctive nature of their minis-try as *women* priests in the post-ordination period. Priest C claims that the most significant change women have introduced is their different approach to the question of sacerdotal authority. Both she and Priest A say that they are conscious of seeking an alternative to the authoritarian approach to ministry that many men adopt. Although careful not to generalize about *all* men, Priest C argues that the Western conception of masculinity means that 'men are about er dominance leader of the pack erhm going out and fighting their corner achieving that's the male thing it's expected', which in turn means that some male priests are 'into power and relish the thought of being you know erhm emperors of their own little domain absolute rulers' (Trans. IX: 122–9). The more egalitarian concept of authority promoted in MOW and the St Hilda Community may account for the preoccupation with re-visioning modes of authority evident amongst my interviewees and numerous other women priests. Priest A, for instance, resignifies 'authority' as 'leadership' and expresses the ideologically creative idea that 'vulnerability' is an integral feature of any leadership role. She goes on to contrast the self-assuming nature of authority with the self-effacing nature of leadership, when this is properly exercised (Trans. VII: 47–50).

Priest C's focus is less on practical leadership skills, and more on moral leadership. She seeks to disentangle the responsible exercise of 'moral authority', which she conceives of as context-dependent, and being morally 'authoritarian', which she feels relies on abstract reasoning and an appeal to moral absolutes (Trans. IX: 64ff). She tentatively suggests that these two approaches to moral authority may be gendered, 'women meet people more where they are than men do . . . men do intellectualize an awful lot' (ibid.: 46–57). This accords with, and may have been influenced by, Gilligan's (1982) work on women's tendency to draw on an 'ethic of care' and men's tendency to rely on an 'ethic of reason'. However, perhaps because of her legal training, Priest C employs much more cautious modality than Gilligan when making this claim. Hence, she uses a series of hedging devices to mitigate the illocutionary force of her utterances, including, 'that's a sweep-ing statement', 'generally speaking', 'now I have to qualify that' and 'I may be entirely wrong' (ibid.: 39, 46, 47, 51). Contrary to the assumption that a high density of hedges renders women's speech weak and uncertain (Lakoff 1975), in this instance, the effect produced is to make Priest C's propositions appear more authoritative, *because* carefully weighed. This impression was reinforced during the interview by the extremely confident tone in which her assertions were delivered, something that is difficult to capture using transcription conventions. As Holmes notes, 'It is often important in terms of *accuracy* to qualify a proposition or indicate that it cannot be asserted with complete confidence' (1995: 79; italics in the original). Nowhere is this more important, perhaps, than when making claims about the correlation between gender and language use. Significantly, Priest C was also careful to refute the idea that her context-sensitive approach to moral reasoning absolves her from what she perceives to be her moral obligation to challenge people (ibid.: 61).

Related to the issue of authority is the interactional style favoured by women priests. Once again, Priest C contrasts this with the tendency of some male vicars to adopt an 'exceedingly patronizing' and paternalistic mode of address, thereby infantalizing lay people and fostering a culture of dependency within the parish (Trans. IX: 43–4). In her experience, women priests, on the other hand, employ a self-consciously empathetic interactional style and are more 'feely' (ibid.: 49ff). Priest A claims that she consciously tries to give a 'feminine slant' to the content of her sermons, in order to make female listeners feel included, but says she prefers interacting with people in small groups to formal preaching. She is committed to a collaborative approach to ministry, devolving leadership roles to others, especially to other women (ibid.: 35–6). Priest B expresses her regret that her role as priest-in-charge of a small parish denies her the opportunity to work cooperatively with others as part of a ministry team, something she values (Trans. VIII: 35). None of the three priests interviewed regarded these feminine/feminist discursive norms as either 'natural' or inevitable; instead, they consciously employed them as alternatives to dominant masculinist norms. In fact, Priest C claimed that so-called feminine norms go against the grain of what she believes to be her 'naturally' more assertive speech style (Trans. IX: 135ff).

In terms of its impact on theological issues, Robins (1996: 71) believes that women's ordination to the priesthood has helped the Church to move closer to the feminist ideal of embodying spirituality and sexuality together. Although the Act of Synod has revived the 'doctrine of taint', taboos surrounding women's sexuality are challenged every time a woman, especially a pregnant woman, performs sacred priestly rites. Whereas Priest C consciously eschews marked signifiers of femininity, Rev. Joy Carroll, a priest-in-charge in a parish in London, habitually foregrounds such signifiers, by, for instance, wearing short skirts and striking earrings. In an article in the *Sunday Times* she manages to make a symbolic link between the work she does on her body and a central tenet of feminist theology when she says, 'I don't think you should hide your sexuality in the same way that you shouldn't hide your spirituality' (25 June 1995). The body/spirit dualism is also troubled by the marked tendency among some women priests to employ bodily and familial tropes when discussing their ministry. Rev. Penny Martin (1996: 94), for instance, compares the pain engendered by the ordination debate to the pangs of childbirth, while the resistance she has encountered since is alluded to metaphorically in terms of the problems faced by mothers with difficult offspring. She also explains cooperative ministry in terms of the relationship between different parts of the body (ibid.). Such tropes blur the boundary between private and public language, in that they revaluate language associated with women's private sphere activities by deploying them in descriptions of activities that are both public and sacred. But, as noted above, when recontextualized in punning media headlines such tropes tend to reinforce women's connection with the private sphere and/or with certain subordinate roles within the public sphere. This reveals the way in which oppositional discursive strategies employed by women can have unintended effects when appropriated by others, especially by the media.

There is a surprising degree of consensus among those who have been ordained and other commentators in the book *Crossing the Boundary* (Walrond-Skinner, ed., 1994) about the gifts women bring to their sacerdotal role. The question arises as to whether this type of uniformity about women's sacerdotal ministry will serve to inscribe a new set of orthodoxies which may inadvertently lead women to collude in their own marginalization. For instance, some women explain the distinctive gifts they bring to ministry in essentialist terms. Wakeman (1996: 5–6), herself a priest, reproduces the idea that 'for biological reasons [women] have innate pastoral and nurturing skills'. Such essentialist claims may help to reinforce women's supposed suitability for low status roles within the Church, replicating *within* priesthood the separate spheres of ministry that operated in the pre-ordination period *between* female deacons and male priests. This is a point also made by Schüssler Fiorenza (1993: 191): 'The categories of "service" or "selfless", "sacrificing" love have always allowed society and the church to exploit women and to "keep them in their place" and in low-status, low-pay, servant-type occupations.' Citing her own experience, Priest A fears that women who place too much emphasis on the distinctively 'womanly' gifts they bring to priesthood will be assigned to failing parishes (Trans. VII: 56–8). Prior to her appointment, the parish where she is currently priest-in-charge was on the verge of closure, mainly because her male predecessor had neglected his pastoral duties. Unusually, those parishioners remaining requested a *woman* priest on the stereotypical grounds that women are more likely than men to prioritize the pastoral side of their ministry.

6.4.5 Reactions to women's ministry

The acceptance, or otherwise, of women's priestly ministry depends on how it is received by male colleagues and by those in the pews. Bentley (1998) points out that approximately 2,000 women have been ordained as priests since 1994, and that many of these have been successfully integrated into clergy teams and warmly welcomed by parishioners. However, Susan Cooper, one of the organizers of WATCH, makes the pertinent observation that, 'However favourable men are to the idea of women priests, if they've been involved in the Church for a long time they have no experience of working with women as equals' (*Church Times* 23 September 1994). Rev. Mary Robins (1996), a priest at St James parish in Piccadilly, records a number of anecdotes revealing the stereotypical expectations of male colleagues who believe women priests are mainly ex-school marms whose chief function is to patch up other people's problems. She argues that the attitudes of hostile male peers range from control by ridicule, to a misplaced chivalrous attentiveness. The undermining effect of the latter is referred to by one of my respondents:

> another friend I can't remember what the actual words were but she'd been she'd preached and she came down from the pulpit and the vicar who's been sitting in one of the other desks behind and who'd got up and then spoke to the con~congregation and made some remark which I suppose he thought was complimentary but it was devastatingly patronizing she was *furious* ... they've still got this thing about being chivalrous it's all very nice but there's times for chivalry and it's not in front of the congregation

> (Priest C, Trans. IX: 147–54)

When asked in various surveys to evaluate the ways in which women's skills as priests differ from those of their male counterparts, parishioners have done so in largely stereotypical terms. Negative stereotypes include the view of women priests as scheming, manipulative and vain. Among the many trivializing comments was that made by one male respondent who said, 'The effect of our new curate is most noticeable for we have girlish giggles, yes, but no firm direction' (cited in Wakeman 1996: 11–12). Wakeman also notes that comments about the 'natural weakness' of women's voices have been used as grounds for objecting to their ministry (ibid.: 16). In her study of women in the media, Macdonald (1995: 45) argues that 'Attitudes to male and female voice pitch have ... been a peculiarly powerful tool in determining where and when men and women might be granted speaking rights'. Positive reactions are also framed in stereotypical terms. Wakeman (1996: 4) records the comment of one man who was impressed by their 'tremendous sensitivity' which, he claimed, enabled women to enter situations difficult for most men; their 'gentleness' in bereavement work was singled out for special praise. He also reproduced the folklinguistic belief that women are 'better listeners' than male colleagues (ibid.).

Lakoff (1995: 28) highlights the potency of non-response as an mechanism of control in discourse, '[it is] annihilating in that it signifies that the speaker does not exist, that the utterance did not happen'. *The Windsor Consultation Document* (September 1995) reveals that women priests have been subjected to various mechanisms of discursive control, including silence, back-turning and the slur of tainting of altars. In relation to the latter, a strategy of outright avoidance is recommended by the organization R' which circulated a 'Good Church Guide', listing churches throug country where women priests have not ministered. A few reactions h. been extreme, resulting in some women priests being audibly hissed by members of the congregation (Wakeman 1996: 19), and one priest, Rev. Suzanne Fageol, being severely bitten while offering a cup to a communicant (cited in Dowell and Williams 1994: 72). All of these practices have occurred without official censure. Rees is not alone when she expresses her unease about the absence of official monitoring by the Church of the reception of women's ministry, 'a lot of journalists who phone me just can't believe that that wasn't built into the system because you know you start something that big and that new and usually there is someone you know surveying it researching it and just monitoring it in an official way and there's no-one doing that' (Trans. X: 24–8). It was partly to remedy this situation and to provide a support network for women priests that WATCH was set up.

6.4.6   Strategies for overcoming prejudice

There is plenty of evidence of those who campaigned for women's ordination engaging in playful and creative uses of language in order to subvert the Church's dominant belief system. Throughout her book, *A New Strength, A New Song*, which records the history of MOW, Margaret Webster selects for special praise women supporters who mobilized a sense of humour to further their cause (1994: 54, 73, 110, 116, 120). She suggests that an important function of humour is its cathartic potential; it acted as a safety valve for women's sense of anger and frustration at having been denied the right to fulfil their vocations as priests (ibid.: 202). This emphasis on the ability of proponents to exhibit a sense of humour also seems to have been calculated to refute the prevailing view of MOW campaigners as humour*less* feminists, in the knowledge that charges of humourlessness have often been used to rationalize women's exclusion from male-dominated institutions (Gray 1994: 139).

The belief that humour can be used strategically to counter prejudice has carried over into women's exercise of their priestly ministry. Rev. Penny Martin, a vicar of a three parish benefice in Durham, records how she playfully resignifies the 'business agenda' of the priestly fraternity in numerous meetings she has attended as 'gossip' (1996: 80), thereby deftly challenging the stereotypical assumption that women have a monopoly on trivial speech. She also provides examples of occasions when she has used humour to disarm critics, 'Once, twenty-five of us planned a day out . . . I rapturously announced I had all I needed; a drink of water, a lipstick and a change of earrings' (ibid.: 81–2). She claims that this pre-emptive statement seemed to silence the anxiety of those who felt uncomfortable in her presence.

However, as in the case of the Vicar of Dibley's use of self-deprecating humour, it is difficult to assess the extent to which such strategies challenge gender stereotypes, and the extent to which they help to reinforce them. As Cameron (1992: 225) points out: 'Questions of how to express one's ideas in language without being marginalized but also without compromising them are particularly hard, because language is interactive: its effectiveness depends to a large extent on the attitude of the hearer.'

6.5   A creative dialectic between structure and agency?

As is evident from the previous section, women are not passively positioned in relation to the institutional and societal constraints that operate on them. An important strand in the feminist critique of the Church has been a commitment to challenging the power asymmetry of the clergy/lay divide. There is no doubt that the relative insecurity of *some* women priests has led them to appear even more clericalized than male colleagues, but the majority claim to minimize status differences between themselves and lay members of the Church. The irony is that, having struggled to achieve powerful subject positions as priests, the majority of women who have been ordained feel obliged to emphasize the egalitarian concept of the 'priesthood of all believers'. In an address to members of WATCH, before the 1998 Lambeth Conference, Penny Jamieson, Bishop of Dunedin in New Zealand, set out the ideal of 'Mutual Ministry' as one that all women priests should actively strive towards. She defines it as 'a style of leadership that shifts the relationship between the ordained and lay to one of partnership rather than privilege' (*Outlook* 1998, No. 5: 12). However, the ability to realize this goal in practice in the Church of England is, of course, a prerogative of the newly acquired institutional status of women priests. Dowell and Williams (1994: 73) point to independent factors that are likely to facilitate this goal: 'Recession and falling numbers have brought about a decline of the old parochial system . . . So there is simply no way, even if they wanted to, that women priests can be seen to be buying into the kind of clerical status many people (particularly urban dwellers) associate with the Tory shires.' This illustrates the complex interplay between structure and agency that is often difficult to disentangle, but which, in this instance at least, has helped women priests to put into practice, in their everyday relations with those to whom they minister, a central tenet of feminist theology.

As in other contemporary institutions, the Church of England has been moving increasingly towards a business model in order to modernize its structures and improve its mode of operation. For instance, an article in *The Times* (February 1 1996) reports the Church's commitment to using Total Quality Management (TQM) techniques to improve its efficiency. Medhurst

(1999: 289) has referred to the Church's 'preoccupation with managerial structures', which has led to the setting up of the Archbishop's Council to facilitate strong centralized decision-making. As a result, the strategic discourses of bureaucracy and professionalism have for some time been in the process of expanding at the expense of the more communicative discourse of ministry. Women's entry into the priestly ministry has led to a reclamation of the communicative discourse of ministry since, for some of the reasons outlined above, they have come to be identified with collaborative styles of ministry based on the foregrounding of interpersonal goals. The task of reclamation has, in turn, been facilitated by the increasing importance of team ministries and by the growing emphasis on the social and pastoral functions of priesthood as a result of the decline of the welfare state. In this context, male priests are more likely to move in the direction of a stereotypically feminine discursive style than vice versa. The likelihood of this is increased by the fact that the discourse of professionalism is itself changing. According to Baisley (1996: 108), the increasing emphasis on adaptability has led to a new evaluation of the multi-skilled approach she claims women bring to ministry and which was formerly denigrated. Again, rather than being undermined by discursive shifts taking place at the institutional and societal levels of discourse, the goal of promoting a more communicative discourse of ministry, advocated by organizations like MOW, has been facilitated by these shifts.

6.6 Conclusions

What I hope to have shown in this chapter is that a question which seeks to establish whether women priests have challenged, or colluded with, the dominant masculinist discursive norms that prevail in the Church of England is too simplistic. What *is* clear is that their language and behaviour is more likely than those of male colleagues to be fractured by competing, and often contradictory, norms and expectations. From the outset, stereotypical assumptions about what their ministry would mean has constrained the subject positions available to women priests, leading some to adopt feminine norms that are at odds with their preferred discursive style. Their officially sanctioned subordinate status within the Church has led others to distance themselves from feminism in the post-ordination period, while nonetheless covertly pursuing feminist goals. The issue of whether these subject positions are compliant or oppositional is contingent upon a number of factors, including the context in which they are assumed and, crucially, upon how they are perceived and evaluated by others, however playful and subversive the 'performance' is *intended* to be. This offers an important corrective to those who emphasize the performative aspect of the theatrical metaphor of identity construction, while downplaying the critical role of the audience. This is particularly important, since, as my study of women priests suggests, such critical judgements are often differently gendered.

It is often assumed that there are only two possible relationships between dominant and dominated discourses: either the latter can continue to function oppositionally as a reverse discourse, helping to challenge the legitimacy of the former, or it can simply be incorporated and its subversive power neutralized. However, my research into all four communities of practice investigated in this study reveals that a creative dialectic can exist between institutional structures and the ability of individual agents to subvert and transform these. In the case of the Church, the acceptance of so-called 'feminine' styles of leadership and discursive practice has been facilitated by independent changes in its structures and social role as an institution. In order to influence the discursive norms that operate in the public sphere, feminists need to identify and exploit the areas of potential convergence that exist between these norms and the independent discursive shifts that are occurring at the institutional and societal orders of discourse. This applies to all four of the communities of practice investigated in detail in this study. In the concluding chapter, I intend to draw out the global implications of all four case studies for feminist linguistic theory and praxis.

Notes

1. Despite their reputation for conservatism on issues of gender, Low Church denominations have been much more accepting of women's ministry. For instance, the Congregationalists have had women ministers since 1918, while the English Presbyterian Church ordained its first women ministers in the 1950s. The Church of Scotland followed suit in 1969, as did the Methodist Church in 1974. The first ordinations of women within the Anglican Communion took place in the diocese of Hong Kong in 1971, thereby opening the floodgates for other Provinces to follow. Three Anglican Provinces, New Zealand, Canada and the US, also have women bishops, and in another six Provinces, as far apart as Ireland and Burundi, women bishops are canonically possible, although none has yet been elected.

2. One obvious exception to this subordination was the pioneering work women performed as missionaries. The area of missionary work, especially work abroad, permitted women an unprecedented degree of autonomy and licence to teach and instruct the deprived and 'the heathen' (Armstrong 1993: 173).

3. Lehman (1993) derives the criteria for a 'feminine' style of ministry from the research of what he terms 'maximalist' feminists, 'the feminine stance incorporates personal communities, holistic relationships, egalitarianism, empowerment of lay people, democratic decision making, co-operation with nature, open and flexible theology, existential ethics of responsible sharing, and inclusion of women and minorities' (ibid.: 4).

4. In 1995, Dr David Hope, Bishop of London and a leading opponent of women's ordination, was appointed to the archbishopric of York. He was replaced in the see of London by the Right Rev. Richard Chartres, Bishop of Stepney, another vocal opponent of women's ordination.

5. Byrne has since been suspended from her post, having lost the support of her bishop, Neville Chamberlain, despite the fact that a new vestry committee gave her *its* full support. Commenting on Byrne's removal in a recent article in the *Guardian*, a senior church official is quoted as saying, 'This has put the cause of women priests back decades' (13 January 2000).

6. In the US, and to a lesser extent in the UK, this has given rise to a male spiritual backlash. The Promise Keepers, over a million of whose members gathered at a rally in Washington in 1997, is a particularly reactionary organization committed to creating an environment of 'godly masculinity'. The UK branch is a much smaller grassroots movement which has none-theless attracted support in a range of towns and cities around the country (the *Guardian* 1 November 1997).

7

Conclusions and Overview

The question I set out to answer in this book is whether women's entry into previously male-dominated institutional spaces and organizations has made a difference to the hegemonic discursive norms that prevail in these communities of practice, as well as to the ways in which the identities of, and interpersonal relations between, social actors are constructed. I have argued that, at the very least, the increasing presence of women has called into question the unproblematized status of the implicitly masculinist belief systems, values and discursive practices that predominate in these domains. In some cases, however, this has led to the defensive strengthening of traditional fraternal networks, that are often productively competitive, rather than purely cooperative, in terms of their mode of operation. The fact that these networks often transcend the boundaries of institutional discourses is one factor that has helped to ensure that women do not participate as equals within state institutions and grassroots organizations.

Women have responded by developing counter-networks and, in some instances, by establishing women-only groupings, based on alternative discursive structures and norms. Indeed, I hope to have shown that access to civil and public sphere roles has afforded women new opportunities for self-fashioning and that, rather than simply replicating masculinist interactional norms, the public rhetoric of feminist-identified women in particular is often ideologically creative. The findings from my research suggest that even a small number of women can make an impact on dominant discursive norms if they pursue a 'critical difference' approach, whereas the voices of larger numbers of women can be assimilated, if they choose to adopt a policy of accommodation to pre-existing norms and practices. Whatever strategy they employ, women have to negotiate with the many competing and contradictory expectations that exist about how they *should* perform occupational roles differently, including those generated by both women themselves, and by the mainstream media. For instance, on the one hand, they are constructed as problem insiders, with the result that their language and behaviour are more likely than the language and behaviour of male colleagues to be perceived as contradictory and/or at odds with the roles they perform. On the other hand, they are often constructed as agents of much-needed change, capable of civilizing traditionally male-gendered institutional domains, which means that they carry an additional burden, over and above that normally associated with the successful fulfilment of a particular occupational role.

This raises a question about how women's empirically attested tendency to shift strategically between masculine and feminine discursive styles should be interpreted. I have argued that, rather than being conscious attempts to disrupt the symbolic meanings attached to the normative gender ideologies that circulate in the public domain, such discursive shifts are often a means of managing socially ascribed expectations that pull in opposite directions. In other words, not all of the performative shifts women engage in are freely chosen, and some are undertaken at considerable personal cost. Likewise, while differences *between* women within a given community of practice undoubtedly arise as a result of the differing negotiations they make with institutionally and socially ascribed expectations, these differences are sometimes exaggerated, or even manufactured, by vested interests. Hence, the media-generated Blair's babe is placed in opposition to her equally caricatured older socialist feminist sister in the Parliamentary Labour Party. This does not do justice to the wide range of subject positions occupied by women in the PLP. Such reductive and divisive stereotypes abound in media coverage of women in the public domain. The power of mediatized public sphere discourse to produce, as well as reproduce, homogenizing identities for women is illustrated by the way in which the 'Blair's babe' became 'Dewar's dolly' and 'Michael's moll' as she crossed the border into Scotland and Wales respectively.

The metadiscursive and material constraints that operate on women in civil and public sphere roles mean that some of the more utopian accounts of the performative theory of gender need to be qualified. Such accounts tend to underestimate the extent to which the process of interpretation is a site of discursive struggle, including struggles over gender. For instance, I have pointed to the metadiscursive gap that often exists between the way women in the public domain intend their speech to be interpreted and the way it is perceived and evaluated by others, especially after it has been recontextualized and framed in media texts. Hence, women who have uncritically embraced professional norms have been accused of mimicking men, a clear illustration of what Montgomery (1999) refers to as the 'performative paradox'. I agree with Montgomery's view that linguists therefore need to pay more attention to the criteria by which interpreters evaluate the speech acts of others. Following Montgomery, I have tried to show how the validity claims of speakers are often judged on the basis of paralinguistic traces and cues, as well as linguistic ones, and that attention also needs to focus on these. Perhaps inevitably, validity criteria such as 'appropriacy' and 'sincerity' are likely to be contested in cross-sex interaction. Following Cameron (1998: 447), I have argued that what some 'difference' feminists term 'miscommunication' is, in fact, often the result of 'strategic misunderstanding'.

The analytical model set out in Chapter 2 is designed to foreground the way in which texts, including media texts, are often riven by competing and contradictory ideologies of gender. This requires a shift away from a focus on the linear ordering of surface textual features to a more dynamic intertextual model for feminist text analysis that can take account of the complex ways in which texts interact with prior texts and with elements in, or presupposed in, the context of use. In common with a number of other feminist sociolinguists, I have emphasized the centrality of language in constituting social identities and relations, but I have called into question the tendency to assume that other-orientated interaction is invariably collaborative. I hope to have shown that cooperative discursive strategies can exclude, as well as include, others. Likewise, the fact that certain speech acts are intended to be egalitarian does not mean that this is how they will be perceived by addressees.

I have also suggested that the concept of a 'community of practice' needs to be re-examined to take account of the fact that practices that are deemed normative are just as likely to be subject to contestation and change, as consensus. Likewise, it is often necessary to go beyond the norms and constraints that operate *within* given communities of practice to a consideration of those that cut across the boundaries of different communities, including the global beliefs, ideas, assumptions, and so on, that circulate in the wider society. I would argue that media texts offer a rich resource for investigating the latter. Such texts afford access to shared interpretative assumptions and 'patterns of habituation' (Toolan 1996) by which normative gendered identities and relations are disseminated, recycled and, increasingly, contested. I hope to have shown that limited and limiting gendered news frames contribute to the (re)production of expectations and beliefs that constrain the subject positions available to women in the public sphere. Yet, it is the contradictory nature of media coverage that is perhaps most striking. Thus many media producers are critical of overt gender stereotyping, while at the same time contributing to the perception of women's lack of 'fit' with the public sphere roles they occupy, often through their choice of metaphors and the intertexts they draw upon. This has led many women, individually and collectively, to recognize the value of becoming skilled at media management. However, given the metadiscursive gap alluded to above, even more important are the activities of women's groups which aim to monitor media coverage of women in a systematic way, since media institutions can thereby be rendered more accountable for the often trivializing way in which they report the activities of women in public, and, indeed, in private, life.

I have argued throughout this book for a more socially situated theory of language and gender to account for the constant tension that exists between the freedom of individuals to make choices within discourse and the normative practices that function to limit these choices. For instance, the expectation that women will civilize and/or transform previously male-gendered institutional spaces fails to take account of the many mechanisms by which they continue to be segregated and marginalized within these institutions. In the case of the Church of England in the post-ordination period, the subordinate status of women has been overtly sanctioned, whereas in other institutions and organizations this is achieved by more covert means. Appeals made by others, and sometimes by women themselves, to their putative qualities as good listeners, good communicators and 'fixers' have been used to rationalize their concentration in a narrow range of, usually subordinate, institutional and organizational roles. A central thesis of this book is that, as a result, the traditional gendered division between the private and public spheres has, to some extent at least, been replicated *within* civil and public sphere institutions and organizations. As Pateman notes, 'it is not that women are absent from the paid workplace; it's rather that they are present differently' (in Fraser 1995: 33).

In terms of the macro-level of discourse, I have argued throughout this book that feminist-identified women have contributed to the novel restructuring of traditional discursive boundaries. For instance, women formerly active in grassroots politics have exploited the growing trend towards secessionism to secure places for themselves within the new regional assemblies and Scottish Parliament. All the signs, thus far, suggest that women elected to these devolved bodies are using their influence to ensure that grassroots organizations have a much greater say in the process of political decision-making than is true at Westminster. In their own way, women priests have also contributed to the destructuration of the spheres by minimizing the status differences between themselves and members of the laity. Women activists also predominate in new social movements which have helped to enliven the civil sphere as a space where home, work and community all intersect. Women's involvement in these plural sites of political participation make the continuing masculinist 'habitus' that prevails in state institutions less detrimental to the cause of promoting more equitable gender relations in society than might otherwise have been the case. In all of these domains, women have sought the help of the media to publicize their campaigns, but have also exploited new media technologies to bypass the hegemonic power of the mainstream media and to challenge media misrepresentation.

It is a moot point as to whether this process of destructuration is necessarily a good thing from a feminist perspective. Elshtain's (1993) position is typical of those who argue for a reconstruction of the public–private dichotomy, rather than its dissolution. Her initial premise is that there are dangers inherent in the feminist project of seeking to erode the distinction between the public and private spheres since 'it follows that no differentiated activity or set of institutions that are genuinely political, that are, in fact, the bases of order and of purpose in a political community, exist' (ibid.: 217). This conclusion presupposes an acceptance of what is a narrowly circumscribed definition of the 'genuinely political', a definition that feminist-orientated groups like the NIWC, MOW and WEN have, by contrast, sought to extend. Elshtain's argument that this strategy is also in danger of assisting a process whereby strategic values colonize the private sphere is once again contradicted by the activities of organizations like WEN. Through active involvement in WEN, women can translate their everyday private sphere activities into the kind of political capital which enables them to resist such colonization. Yet, there is some evidence that women previously active in social movements like WEN have succumbed to the danger referred to by Cameron of 'replacing collective politics with an individualized quest for "personal growth"' (1995b: 179). This is by no means an inevitable consequence of a blurring of the boundaries between the spheres, since, as this book illustrates, many more women have kept a clear focus on the *collective* goals of feminism.

A number of feminist theorists (Coward 1999; Young 2000) have called into question the importance of gender as an identity category, given the increasingly heterogeneous and complex nature of most Western societies. What I hope to have shown is that gender remains highly salient, not only in terms of the public identities women and men construct for themselves, but also in terms of how they are perceived and judged by others, including the mainstream media. By investigating women's participation in a number of different communities of practice,[1] I hope to have shown that women's performance of gendered identities and relations is nonetheless contingent upon the nature of the communities of practice in which they find themselves, as well as upon the degree to which they subscribe to the normative practices that prevail in these communities. The complex negotiations in which they engage cannot be accommodated within a dichotomous theory of language and gender.

In practice, many feminist-identified women in institutions and organizations within the public sphere have moved beyond a mere critique of masculinism, a position where 'dominance feminists' tend to stop, to a positive advocacy of more gender inclusive discursive norms. I have characterized this as a 'critical difference' approach to gender. I would argue that this sort of critique of the metadiscursive norms that prevail in communities of practice in the public sphere is a logical extension of feminist verbal hygiene practices that come under the umbrella term of 'political correctness' and that focus primarily on lexical and grammatical features of language. This critique has contributed to a discursive shift, whereby interpersonally orientated language is increasing its importance within the public sphere at the expense of ideationally orientated language. However, this increasingly interpersonal orientation in public sphere discourse has not always resulted in promoting empathy between individuals, or in building solidarities between women and/or between women and men. Instead, it often involves competition and conflict, especially in cross-sex interaction, but also in interaction *between* women. And so, a feminist critical discourse analysis needs to be *critical* also of the so-called women-orientated discursive practices that are being promoted in certain public sphere institutions and organizations, since the value attached to these is contingent upon their context of use and on how they are perceived and evaluated by addressees.

Note

1. A possible area for further investigation would be to consider the gendered identities and relations that arise in communities of practice in which men are in a minority, such as nursing and primary school teaching.

Bibliography

Alderman K and Carter N 1995 The Labour Party leadership and deputy leadership elections. *Parliamentary Affairs*, 48, 3, 439–56.

Aldridge A 1987 In the absence of the minister: structures of subordination in the role of deaconess in the Church of England. *Sociology*, 21, 3, 377–92.

Aldridge A 1989 Men, women, and clergymen: opinion and authority in a sacred organization. *Sociological Review*, 37, 1, 43–64.

Armstrong K 1993 *The End of Silence: Women and Priesthood*. London: Fourth Estate.

Baisley B 1996 Being realistic about feminism. In H Wakeman (ed.) *Women Priests: the First Years*. London: Darton, Longman & Todd, pp. 97–116.

Bashiruddin A, Edge J and Huges-Pélégrin E 1990 Who speaks in seminars? Status, culture and gender at Durham University. In R Clark et al. (eds) *Language and Power*. London: Centre for Information on Language Teaching, pp. 74–84.

Bell A 1991 *The Language of News Media*. Oxford: Blackwell.

Bentley L 1998 At the grassroots: the Act in the parishes. In M Furlong (ed.) *Act of Synod – Act of Folly?* London: SCM Press, pp. 101–14.

Bergvall V 1996 Constructing and enacting gender through discourse: negotiating multiple roles as female engineering students. In V Bergvall et al. (eds) *Rethinking Language and Research: Theory and Practice*. Harlow: Longman, pp. 173–201.

Bergvall V 1999 Toward a comprehensive theory of language and gender. *Annual Review of Anthropology*, 21, 273–93.

Bergvall V, Bing J and Freed A (eds) 1996 *Rethinking Language and Gender Research: Theory and Practice*. Harlow: Longman.

Bing J and Bergvall V 1996 The question of questions: beyond binary thinking. In V Bergvall et al. (eds) *Rethinking Language and Gender Research: Theory and Practice*. Harlow: Longman, pp. 1–30.

Black M and Coward R 1990 (2nd edn) Linguistic, social and sexual relations: a review of Dale Spender's *Man Made Language*. In D Cameron (ed.) *The Feminist Critique of Language: A Reader*. London: Routledge, pp. 111–33.

Bolinger D 1980 *Language the Loaded Weapon: the Use and Abuse of Language Today*. London and New York: Longman.

Bourdieu P 1977 *Outline of a Theory of Practice*. Cambridge: Cambridge University Press.

Brown A 1996 Women in politics in Scotland. In J Lovenduski and P Norris (eds) *Women in Politics*. Oxford: Oxford University Press, pp. 28–42.

Brown A 1998 Women in the Scottish Parliament. In *Parliamentary Affairs*, 51, 3, 435–44.

Brown P 1980 How and why are women more polite: some evidence from a Mayan community. In S McConnell-Ginet et al. (eds) *Women and Language in Literature and Society*. New York: Praeger, pp. 111–36.

Brown P and Levinson S 1987 *Politeness: Some Universals in Language Usage*. Cambridge: Cambridge University Press.

Burstyn V 1983 Masculine dominance and the state. *The Socialist Register*. London: Merlin Press, pp. 45–89.

Butler J 1990 *Gender Trouble*. London: Routledge.

Butler J 1993 *Bodies that Matter*. London: Routledge.

Caldas-Coulthard CR 1995 Man in the news: the misrepresentation of women in the news-as-narrative discourse. In S Mills (ed.) *Language and Gender: Interdisciplinary Perspectives*. Harlow: Longman, pp. 226–39.

Cameron D 1990 Demythologizing sociolinguistics: why language does not reflect society. In JE Joseph and TJ Taylor (eds) *Ideologies of Language*. London: Routledge, pp. 79–93.

Cameron D 1992 (2nd edn) *Feminism and Linguistic Theory*. London: Macmillan.

Cameron D 1995a Rethinking language and gender studies. In S Mills (ed.) *Language and Gender: Interdisciplinary Perspectives*. Harlow: Longman, pp. 31–44.

Cameron D 1995b *Verbal Hygiene*. London: Routledge.

Cameron D 1996 The language–gender interface: challenging co-optation. In V Bergvall et al. (eds) *Rethinking Language and Gender Research: Theory and Practice*. Harlow: Longman, pp. 31–53.

Cameron D 1997 Performing gender identity: young men's talk and the construction of heterosexual masculinity. In S Johnson and UH Meinhof (eds) *Language and Masculinity*. Oxford: Blackwell, pp. 47–64.

Cameron D 1998 'Is there any ketchup Vera?': gender, power and pragmatics. *Discourse and Society*, 9, 4, 437–55.

Cameron D 2000 *Good to Talk?* London: Sage.

Cameron D, McAlindon F and O'Leary K 1989 Lakoff in context. In J Coates and D Cameron (eds) *Women in their Speech Communities*. Harlow: Longman, pp. 74–93.

Carter R and Nash W 1990 *Seeing Through Language*. Oxford: Blackwell.

Chopp R 1989 *The Power to Speak: Feminism, Language and God*. New York: Crossroad.

Chouliaraki L and Fairclough N 1999 *Discourse in Late Modernity: Rethinking Critical Discourse Analysis*. Edinburgh: Edinburgh University Press.

Clack B 1996 God and language: a feminist perspective on the meaning of 'God'. In S. Porter (ed.) *The Nature of Religious Language: A Colloquium*. Sheffield: Sheffield University Press, pp. 148–58.

Clayman S 1990 From talk to text: newspaper accounts of reporter–source interactions. *Media, Culture and Society*, 12, 1, 79–103.

Coates J 1987 Epistemic modality and spoken discourse. *Transactions of the Philological Society*, 110–31.

Coates J 1989 Gossip revisited: Language in all-female groups. In J Coates and D Cameron (eds) *Women in their Speech Communities*. London: Longman, pp. 94–121.

Coates J 1995 Language, gender and career. In S Mills (ed.) *Language and Gender: Interdisciplinary Perspectives*. London: Longman, pp. 13–30.

Coates J 1996 *Women Talk: Conversation Between Women Friends*. Oxford: Blackwell.

Coates J (ed.) 1998 *Language and Gender: A Reader*. Oxford: Blackwell.

Cockburn C 1987 *Women, Trade Unions and Political Parties* (Fabian Research Series 349). London: The Fabian Society.

Coward R 1990 *The Whole Truth: The Myth of Alternative Health*. London: Faber & Faber.

Coward R 1992 *Our Treacherous Hearts: Why Women Let Men Get Their Way*. London: Faber.

Coward R 1999 *Sacred Cows: Is Feminism Relevant to the New Millennium?* London: HarperCollins.

Crawford M 1995 *Talking Difference: On Gender and Language*. London: Sage.

Curran J 1987 *Media Coverage of London Councils: Interim Report*. London: Goldsmiths College.

Dahlerup D 1988 From a small to a large minority: women in Scandinavian politics. *Scandinavian Political Studies*, 11, 4, 275–98.

Daly M 1973 *Beyond God the Father*. Boston: Beacon Press.

Daly M 1978 *Gyn/ecology: the Metaethics of Radical Feminism*. London: The Women's Press Ltd.

Darling P 1994 *New Wine: The Story of Transforming Leadership and Power in the Episcopal Church*. Boston: Cowley Publications.

Dowell S and Williams J (eds) 1994 *Bread, Wine and Women: The Ordination Debate in the Church of England*. London: Virago.

Eckert P 1989 *Jocks and Burnouts: Social Categories and Identity in the High School*. New York: Teacher's College Press.

Eckert P and McConnell-Ginet S 1992 Think practically and look locally: language and gender as community-based practice. *Annual Review of Anthropology*, 21, 461–90.

Eckert P and McConnell-Ginet S 1999 New generalisations and explanations in language and gender research. *Language in Society*, 28, 2, 185–201.

Edelsky C 1981 Who's got the floor? *Language and Society*, 10, 3, 383–421.

Elliot R (ed.) 1995 *Environmental Ethics*. Oxford: Oxford University Press.

Elshtain J Bethke 1993 (2nd edn) *Public Man, Private Woman: Women in Social and Political Thought*. Princeton: Princeton University Press.

Fairclough N 1989 *Language and Power*. London: Longman.

Fairclough N 1992 *Discourse and Social Change*. Cambridge: Polity Press.

Fairclough N 1994 Conversationalization of public discourse and the authority of the consumer. In R Keat et al. (eds) *The Authority of the Consumer*. London and New York: Routledge, pp. 253–68.

Fairclough N 1995a *Media Discourse*. London: Edward Arnold.

Fairclough N 1995b *Critical Discourse Analysis: the Critical Study of Language*. London: Longman.

Fairclough N 1996 Technologisation of discourse. In CR Caldas-Coulthard and M Coulthard (eds) *Text and Practices: Readings in Critical Discourse Analysis*. London: Routledge, pp. 71–83.

Faludi S 1992 *Backlash: The Undeclared War Against Women*. London: Vintage.

Faludi S 1999 *Stiffed: the Betrayal of Modern Man*. London: Chatto & Windus.

Farrington C 1994 Renewing the place. In S Walrond-Skinner (ed.) *Crossing the Boundary: What Will Women Priests Mean?* London: Mowbray, pp. 67–82.

Fearon K 1999 *Women's Work: the Story of the Northern Ireland Women's Coalition*. Belfast: Blackstaff Press.

Fiorenza E Schüssler 1993 *Discipleship of Equals: A Critical Feminist Ekklesia-logy of Liberation*. New York: Crossroad.

Fish S 1994 *There's No Such Thing as Free Speech . . . And it's a Good Thing Too*. Oxford: Oxford University Press.

Fishman P 1983 Interaction: the work women do. In B Thorne et al. (eds) *Language, Gender and Society*. Rowley. Mass.: Newbury House, pp. 89–101.

Footit H 1999 Women and the language of politics. Paper delivered at a one-day conference on Women and Politics: Debating Ways Forward. Middlesex University, 18 June.

Forceville C 1996 *Pictorial Metaphor in Advertising*. London: Routledge.

Foucault M 1984 (2nd edn) The order of discourse. In M Shapiro (ed.) *Language and Politics*. Oxford: Basil Blackwell, pp. 108–38.

Fowler R et al. (eds) 1979 *Language and Control*. London: Routledge & Kegan Paul.

Fowler R 1991 *Language in the News: Discourse and Ideology in the Press*. London: Routledge.

Francis L 1991 The personality characteristics of Anglican ordinands: feminine men and masculine women. *Personality and Individual Difference*, 12, 11, 133–40.

Fraser N 1995 (2nd edn) What's critical about critical theory? In J Meehan (ed.) *Feminists Read Habermas*. London: Routledge, pp. 21–55.

Freed A 1996 Language and gender research in an experimental setting. In V Bergvall et al. (eds) *Rethinking Language and Gender Research: Theory and Practice*. Harlow: Longman, pp. 54–76.

Furlong M 1991 *A Dangerous Delight: Women and Power in the Church*. London: SPCK.

Furlong M 1994 The Guardian of the grail. In S Walrond-Skinner (ed.) *Crossing the Boundary: What Will Women Priests Mean?* London: Mowbray, pp. 17–27.

Furlong M (ed.) 1998 *Act of Synod – Act of Folly?* London: SCM Press.

Gee J 1990 *Sociolinguistics and Literacies: Ideology and Discourse*. Basingstoke: Falmer Press.

Gill AM and Whedbee K 1997 Rhetoric. In T van Dijk (ed.) *Discourse as Structure and Process*. London: Sage, pp. 157–84.

Gilligan C 1982 *In a Different Voice*. Harvard: Harvard University Press.

Goldblatt D 1996 *Social Theory and the Environment*. Cambridge: Polity Press.

Gray F 1994 *Women and Laughter*. London: Macmillan.

Habermas J 1984 (2nd edn) *Theory of Communicative Action vol 1: Reason and the Rationalization of Society*, trans. T McCarthy. Cambridge: Polity Press.

Habermas J 1987 (2nd edn) *Theory of Communicative Action vol 2: The Critique of Functionalist Reason*, trans. T McCarthy. Cambridge: Polity Press.

Habermas J 1989 (2nd edn) *The Structural Transformation of the Public Sphere: An Inquiry into a Category of Bourgeois Society*, trans. T Burger with assistance of F Lawrence. Cambridge: Polity Press.

Hall K and Bucholtz M (eds) 1995 *Gender Articulated*. New York and London: Routledge.

Halliday MAK 1994 (2nd edn) *An Introduction to Functional Grammar*. London: Edward Arnold.

Halliday MAK and Hasan R 1976 *Cohesion in English*. London: Longman.

Harris R 1996 *Signs, Language and Communication*. London: Routledge.

Hearn J 1992 *Men in the Public Eye*. London: Routledge.

Herbert C 1994 A resounding silence. In S Walrond-Skinner (ed.) *Crossing the Boundary: What Will Women Priests Mean?* London: Mowbray, pp. 28–53.

Hewitt R 1997 'Box out' and 'taxing'. In S Johnson and UH Meinhof (eds) *Language and Masculinity*. Oxford: Blackwell, pp. 27–46.

Holmes J 1984 'Women's language': a functional approach. *General Linguistics*, 24, 3, 149–78.

Holmes J 1988 Sex differences in seminar contributions. *BAAL Newsletter* No. 31, 33–41.

Holmes J 1995 *Women, Men and Politeness*. Harlow: Longman.

Holmes J and Meyerhoff M 1999 The community of practice: theories and methodologies in language and gender research. *Annual Review of Anthropology*, 21, 173–83.

Humphreys J 1999 *Devil's Advocate*. London: Hutchinson.

Johnson S and Meinhof UH (eds) 1997 *Language and Masculinity*. Oxford: Blackwell.

Johnson S 1997 Theorizing language and masculinity: a feminist perspective. In S Johnson and UH Meinhof (eds) *Language and Masculinity*. Oxford: Blackwell, pp. 8–26.

Kheel M 1990 Ecofeminism and deep ecology: reflections on identity and difference. In I Diamond and G Feman Orenstein (eds) *Reweaving the World: The Emergence of Ecofeminism*. San Francisco: Sierra Club Books, pp. 128–37.

Kiesling SF 1997 Power and the language of men. In S Johnson and UH Meinhof (eds) *Language and Masculinity*. Oxford: Blackwell, pp. 65–85.

King C 1992 The politics of representation: the democracy of the gaze. In F Bond et al. (eds) *Imagining Women: Cultural Representations of Gender*. Cambridge: Polity Press, pp. 131–9.

Kirkpatrick J 1995 In their own words. In F D'Amico and P Beckman (eds) *Women in World Politics*. Westport, CT: Bergin & Garvey.

Klerk V de 1997 The role of expletives in the construction of masculinity. In S Johnson and UH Meinhof (eds) *Language and Masculinity*. Oxford: Blackwell, pp. 144–58.

Kress G and Leeuwen T van 1996 *Reading Images: the Grammar of Visual Design*. London: Routledge.

Kress G, Leite-García R and Leeuwen T van 1997 Discourse semiotics. In T van Dijk (ed.) *Discourse as Structure and Process*. London: Sage, pp. 257–91.

Kuhn G 1992 Playing down authority while getting things done: women professors get help from the institution. In K Hall et al. (eds) *Locating Power: Proceedings of the Second Berkeley Women and Language Conference*, vol. 2. Berkeley: University of California, pp. 318–25.

Lakoff G and Johnson M 1980 *Metaphors We Live By*. Chicago: University of Chicago Press.

Lakoff R 1975 *Language and Woman's Place*. New York: Harper & Row.

Lakoff R 1995 Cries and whispers: the shattering of the silence. In K Hall and M. Bucholtz (eds) *Gender Articulated*. London: Routledge, pp. 25–50.

Lamb R 1996 *Promising the Earth*. London: Routledge.

Langdon J 2000 *Mo Mowlam: The Biography*. London: Little, Brown and Company.

Lave J and Wenger E 1991 *Situated Learning: Legitimate Peripheral Participation*. Cambridge and New York: Cambridge University Press.

Lee D 1992 *Competing Discourses: Perspective and Ideology in Language*. Harlow: Longman.

Lehman Jr E 1993 *Gender and Work: The Case of the Clergy*. Albany: State University of New York Press.

Leonard G, MacKenzie I and Toon P 1989 *Let God be God*. London: Darton, Longman & Todd.

Loudon M (ed.) 1994 *Revelations: The Clergy Questioned*. London: Penguin.

Lovenduski J 1997 Gender politics: a breakthrough for women? *Parliamentary Affairs*, 50, 4, 708–19.

Lovenduski J and Randall V 1993 *Contemporary Feminist Politics: Women and Power in Britain*. Oxford: Oxford University Press.

McClintock A 1995 *Imperial Leather: Race, Gender and Sexuality in the Imperial Contest*. London: Routledge.

McDonagh R 1996 Integration or independence? In K Fearon (ed.) *Power, Politics, Positionings: Women in Northern Ireland*. Belfast: Democratic Dialogue, pp. 25–32.

Macdonald M 1995 *Representing Women: Myths of Femininity in the Popular Media*. London: Edward Arnold.

McElhinney B 1995 Challenging hegemonic masculinities: female and male police officers handling domestic violence. In K Hall and M Bucholtz (eds) *Gender Articulated*. London: Routledge, pp. 217–44.

MacMahon B 1998 *Women, Men and Politeness* by Janet Holmes. Review article in *Language and Literature*, 7, 3, 276–9.

McNay L 1992 *Foucault and Feminism*. Cambridge: Polity Press.

McRobbie A 1994 Folk devils fight back. *New Left Review*, 203, 107–16.

McWilliams M 1991 Women in Northern Ireland: an overview. In Eamonn Hughes (ed.) *Culture and Politics in Northern Ireland 1960–90*. Milton Keynes: Open University Press, pp. 81–100.

McWilliams M 1995 Struggling for peace and justice: reflections on women's activism in Northern Ireland. *Journal of Women's History*, 6, 4, 13–39.

McWilliams M and Kilmurray A 1997 Athene on the loose: the origins of the Northern Ireland Women's Coalition. *Irish Journal of Feminist Studies*, 2, 1, 1–21.

Maltby J 1998 One Lord, one faith, one baptism, but two integrities? In M Furlong (ed.) *Act of Synod – Act of Folly?* London: SCM Press, pp. 42–58.

Martin JR 1986 Grammaticalising ecology: the politics of baby seals and kangaroos. In T Threadgold et al. (eds) *Semiotics, Ideology, Language*. Sydney: Association for Studies in Society and Culture, pp. 225–67.

Martin P 1996 A different way of working: what women bring to collaborative ministry. In H Wakeman (ed.) *Women Priests: the First Years*. London: Darton, Longman & Todd, pp. 76–96.

Mayland J 1998 An act of betrayal. In M Furlong (ed.) *Act of Synod – Act of Folly?* London: SCM Press, pp. 59–75.

Medhurst K 1999 The Church of England: a progress report. *Parliamentary Affairs*, 52, 2, 275–90.

Meehan E 1999 The Belfast Agreement – its distinctiveness and points of cross-fertilisation in the UK's devolution programme. *Parliamentary Affairs*, 55, 1, 1–18.

Mellor M 1992 *Breaking the Boundaries: Towards a Feminist Green Socialism*. London: Virago.

Merchant C 1980 *The Death of Nature: Women, Ecology and the Scientific Revolution*. New York: Harper & Row.

Merchant C 1996 *Earthcare: Women and the Environment*. New York: Routledge.

Mills S 1995 *Feminist Stylistics*. London: Routledge.

Mills S 1997 *Discourse*. London: Routledge.

Mills S 1998 Post-feminist text analysis. *Language and Literature*, 7, 3, 235–52.

Mills S 2000 Gender, politeness and impoliteness. In *English Studies: Working Papers on the Web*, Issue 1, July 2000. Special issue on Feminist Practice. www.shu.ac.uk/wpw/walsh/htm

Milroy B and Wismer S 1994 Communities, work and public sphere models. *Gender, Place and Culture*, 1, 1, pp. 71–90.

Montgomery M 1986 *An Introduction to Language and Society*. London: Routledge.

Montgomery M 1999 Speaking sincerely: public reactions to the death of Diana. *Language and Literature*, 8, 1, 5–33.

Morley J 1984 The faltering words of men. In M Furlong (ed.) *Feminine in the Church*. London: SPCK, pp. 58–68.

Negrine R 1989 *Politics and the Mass Media*. London: Routledge.

Norris P 1996 Women politicians: transforming Westminster? In J Lovenduski and P Norris (eds) *Women in Politics*. Oxford: Oxford University Press, pp. 91–104.

Norris P and Lovenduski J 1995 *Political Recruitment: Gender, Race and Class in the British Parliament*. Cambridge: Cambridge University Press.

Norris P (ed.) 1997 *Women, Media and Politics*. Oxford: Oxford University Press.

O'Barr WM and Atkins KK 1980 'Women's language' or 'powerless language'? In S McConnell-Ginet et al. (eds) *Women and Language in Literature and Society*. New York: Praeger, pp. 93–110.

Paehlke RC 1994 Environmental values and public policy. In NJ Vig and ME Kraft (eds) *Environmental Policy in the 1990s*. Washington DC: Congressional Quarterly Inc., pp. 349–68.

Pateman C 1989 *The Disorder of Women*. Cambridge: Polity Press.

Pearce L 1994 *Reading Dialogics*. London: Edward Arnold.

Perrigo S 1996 Women and change in the Labour Party 1979–1995. In J Lovenduski and P. Norris (eds) *Women in Politics*. Oxford: Oxford University Press, pp. 118–31.

Petre J 1994 *By Sex Divided: the Church of England and Women Priests*. London: Fount Paperbacks.

Plumwood V 1993 *Feminism and the Mastery of Nature*. London: Routledge.

Plumwood V 1995 Nature, self and gender: feminism, environmental philosophy, and the critique of rationalism. In R Elliot (ed.) *Environmental Ethics*. Oxford: Oxford University Press, pp. 155–64.

Porter E 1998 Identity, location, plurality: women, nationalism and Northern Ireland. In R Wilford and RL Miller (eds) *Women, Ethnicity and Nationalism*. London: Routledge, pp. 36–61.

Powell GN 1993 (2nd edn) *Women and Men in Management*. London: Sage.

Poynton C 1990 The privileging of representation and the marginalising of the interpersonal: a metaphor (and more) for contemporary gender relations. In T Threadgold and A Cranny-Francis (eds) *Feminine/Masculine and Representation*. Sydney: Allen Unwin.

Pujolar i Cos J 1997 Masculinities in a multilingual setting. In S Johnson and UH Meinhof (eds) *Language and Masculinity*. Oxford: Blackwell, pp. 86–106.

Purchas P 1996 From expectations to realities and the future. In H Wakeman (ed.) *Women Priests: the First Years*. London: Darton, Longman & Todd, pp. 117–35.

Puwar N 1997 Gender and political elites: women in the House of Commons. *Sociology Review*, 7, 2, 2–6.

Radford Ruether R 1979 *Mary, the Feminine Face of the Church*. London: SPCK.

Radford Ruether R 1983 *Sexism and God-Talk*. London: SCM.

Ramsey C 1987 An Exploratory Investigation of the Concept of Linguistic Naturalness in Mainstream Written Discourse. University of Birmingham: unpubl. thesis.

Remy J 1990 Patriarchy and fratriarchy as forms of androcracy. In J Hearn and DHJ Morgan (eds) *Men, Masculinities and Social Theory*. London and Cambridge, Mass.: Unwin Hyman, pp. 43–54.

Robins M 1996 Recovering from gender stereotypes: codeines and kite. In H Wakeman (ed.) *Women Priests: the First Years*. London: Darton, Longman & Todd, pp. 59–75.

Robson J 1988 Ministry or profession: clergy doubletalk. In M Furlong (ed.) *Mirror to the Church: Reflections on Sexism*. London: SPCK, pp. 106–23.

Ross K 1995a Skirting the issue. In *Everywoman*. London: Everywoman Publishing, October issue, pp. 16–17.

Ross K 1995b Gender and party politics: how the press reported the Labour leadership campaign, 1994. *Media, Culture and Society*, vol. 17. London: Sage, pp. 499–509.

Ross M 1994 The seven sins of women's ordination. In S Walrond-Skinner (ed.) *Crossing the Boundary: What Will Women Priests Mean?* London: Mowbray, pp. 93–131.

Seager J 1993 *Earth Follies: Feminism, politics and the environment*. London: Earthscan Publications Ltd.

Seaton J and Winetrose B 1999 Modernising the Commons. *The Political Quarterly*, 152–60.

Sedgemore B 1995 *The Insider's Guide to Parliament*. Cambridge: Icon Books Limited.

Sedgwick E Kosofsky 1985 *Between Men: English Literature and Male Homosocial Desire*. New York: Columbia University Press.

Seymore-Ure C 1987 Leaders. In J Seaton and B Pimlott (eds) *The Media in British Politics*. Aldershot: Avesbury Press, pp. 3–24.

Shaw J 1998 Gender and the Act of Synod. In M Furlong (ed.) *Act of Synod – Act of Folly?* London: SCM Press, pp. 14–26.

Shaw S 1999 The rhetoric of women, politics and change: a linguistic analysis of gender, language and debates in the British House of Commons. Paper delivered at the Second Biennial Feminism(s) and Rhetoric(s) Conference, Minneapolis, 7–9 October.

Shiels FL (ed.) 1984 *Ethnic Separatism and World Politics*. New York: University Press of America.

Short C 1996 Women and the Labour Party. In J Lovenduski and P Norris (eds) *Women in Politics*. Oxford: Oxford University Press, pp. 19–27.

Skeggs B 1997 *Formations of Class and Gender*. London: Sage.

Smith D 1990 *Texts, Facts and Femininity: Exploring the Relations of Ruling*. London: Routledge.

Smith FL 1993 The pulpit and woman's place: gender and the framing of the 'exegetical self' in sermon performances. In D Tannen (ed.) *Framing in Discourse*. New York: Oxford University Press, pp. 147–75.

Sorlin P 1994 *Mass Media: Key Ideas*. London: Routledge.

Sperber D and Wilson D 1989 *Relevance, Communication and Cognition*. Oxford: Blackwell.

Spretnak C 1990 Ecofeminism: our roots and flowering. In I Diamond and G. Feman Orenstein (eds) *Reweaving the World: The Emergence of Ecofeminism*. San Francisco: Sierra Club Books, pp. 3–14.

Squires J 1996 Quotas for women: fair representation? In J Lovenduski and P Norris (eds) *Women in Politics*. Oxford: Oxford University Press, pp. 73–90.

Sreberny-Mohammadi A and Ross K 1996 Women MPs and the media: representing the body politic. In J Lovenduski and P Norris (eds) *Women in Politics*. Oxford: Oxford University Press, pp. 105–17.

Starhawk 1990 Power, authority and mystery: ecofeminism and earth-based spirituality. In I Diamond and G Feman Orenstein (eds) *Reweaving the World: The Emergence of Ecofeminism*. San Francisco: Sierra Club Books, pp. 73–86.

Swacker M 1979 Women's verbal behaviour at learned and professional conferences. In B Dubois and I Crouch (eds) *The Sociology of the Languages of American Women*. Texas: Trinity University, pp. 155–60.

Swann J and Graddol D 1995 Feminising classroom talk? In S Mills (ed.) *Language and Gender: Interdisciplinary Perspectives*. London: Longman, pp. 135–48.

Talbot M 1997 'Randy fish boss branded a stinker': coherence and the construction of masculinities in a British tabloid newspaper. In S Johnson and UH Meinhof (eds) *Language and Masculinity*. Oxford: Blackwell, pp. 159–72.

Tannen D 1989 *Talking Voices: Repetition, Dialogue and Imagery in Conversational Discourse*. Cambridge: Cambridge University Press.

Tannen D 1996 (2nd edn) *Talking from 9 to 5 – Women and Men at Work: Language, Sex and Power*. London: Virago.

Thomas L 1996 Invisible women: gender and the exclusive language debate. In S Porter (ed.) *The Nature of Religious Language: A Colloquium*. Sheffield: Sheffield University Press, pp. 159–69.

Threadgold T 1997 *Feminist Poetics: Poiesis, Performance, Histories*. London: Routledge.

Toolan M 1996 *Total Speech: An Integrational Linguistic Approach*. Durham, North Carolina: Duke University Press.

Toolan M 1997 What is critical discourse analysis and why are people saying such terrible things about it? *Language and Literature*, 6, 2, 84–103.

Trudgill P 1988 (2nd edn) *Sociolinguistics: An Introduction to Language and Society*. London: Penguin.

Uchida A 1992 When 'difference' is 'dominance': a critique of the 'anti-power-based' tendency in language and gender. *Language and Society*, 21, 4, 547–68.

van Dijk T 1998 *Ideology: A Multidisciplinary Approach*. London: Sage.

van Zoonen L 1994 *Feminist Media Studies*. London: Sage.

van Zoonen L 1998 One of the girls? The changing gender of journalism. In C Carter et al. (eds) *News, Gender and Power*. London: Routledge.

Vig NJ and Kraft ME (eds) 1994 (2nd edn) *Environmental Policy in the 1990s*. Washington DC: Congressional Quarterly Inc.

Voloshinov VN 1986 (2nd edn) *Marxism and the Philosophy of Language*, trans. L Matejka and IR Titunik. Cambridge, Mass.: Harvard University Press.

Wakeman H (ed.) 1996 *Women Priests: the First Years*. London: Darton, Longman & Todd.

Wakeman H 1996 What difference is women's priesthood making in the pews? In H Wakeman (ed.) *Women Priests: the First Years*. London: Darton, Longman & Todd, pp. 1–26.

Walby S 1990 *Theorising Patriarchy*. Oxford: Basil Blackwell.

Walrond-Skinner S (ed.) 1994 *Crossing the Boundary: What Will Women Priests Mean?* London: Mowbray.

Walter, N 1998 *The New Feminism*. London: Little, Brown and Company.

Ward J 1984 Check out your sexism. *Women and Language*, 7, 41–3.

Waters M 1989 Patriarchy and viriarchy. *Sociology*, 23, 2, 193–211.

Webster M 1994 *A New Strength A New Song: The Journey to Women's Priesthood*. London: Mowbray.

Webster W 1990 *Not a Man to Match Her: The Marketing of a Prime Minister*. The London: Women's Press Ltd.

Weldon F 1999 Women don't deserve to be on top. *New Statesman*, 27 August.

Wicomb Z 1994 Motherhood and the surrogate reader: race, gender and interpretation. In S Mills (ed.) *Gendering the Reader*. Hemel Hempstead: Harvester Wheatsheaf, pp. 99–127.

Widdowson HG 1995 Discourse analysis: a critical view. *Language and Literature*, 4, 3, 157–72.

Widdowson HG 1996 Reply to Fairclough: discourse and interpretation: conjectures and refutations. *Language and Literature*, 5, 1, 57–69.

Wilford R 1996 Women and politics in Northern Ireland. *Parliamentary Affairs*, 49, 1, 41–54.

Wilkinson H 1998 The day I fell out of love with Blair. *New Statesman*, 7 August, pp. 9–10.

Wilkinson H 1999/2000 Devolution is a feminist issue. *New Statesman*, 20 December–3 January, p. 54.

Wodak R and Benke G 1996 Gender as a sociolinguistic variable: new perspectives on variation studies. In F Coulmas (ed.) *Handbook of Sociolinguistics*. Blackwell: Oxford, pp. 127–50.

Young C 2000 Out with the old and out with the new, at http://www.salon.com/mwt/feature/2000/01/26/feminism.

Yuval-Davis N 1996 Women and the biological reproduction of the 'nation'. *Women's Studies International Forum*, 1, 2, 17–24.

Zimmerman DH and West C 1975 Sex roles. Interruptions and silences in conversation. In B Thorne and N Henley (eds) *Language and Sex: Difference and Dominance*. Rowley, Mass.: Newbury House, pp. 105–29.

Additional Sources

Against Nature. Channel 4 broadcast on 7 December 1997.

Are Anglican Women Priests being Bullied and Harassed? A survey by MSF Clergy and Church Workers. London: MSF, February 1998.

Blossom. London: Women's Environmental Network, December 1994.

Common Cause: The Story of the Northern Ireland Women's Coalition. Belfast: Public Communications Centre, May 1998.

Forests, Paper and The Environment. London: Women's Environmental Network. Last updated May 1992.

The Greatness of Trust: The Report of the Working Party on Sexual Abuse by Pastors. Oxford: Parchment Ltd, Easter 1996.

Making Women Visible: the Use of Inclusive Language within the ASB. London: Liturgical Commission of the General Synod, 859, C10, 1988.

Numbers in Ministry. London: Advisory Board of Ministry. GS Misc. 476, August 1996.

The Synod Debate: The Ordination of Women to the Priesthood. London: Church House Publishing, 1993.

Outlook. London: WATCH, Issue no. 5, August 1998; Issue no. 7, Autumn 1999.

Putting Breast Cancer on the Map. London: Women's Environmental Network, June 1999.

Real Women: the Hidden Sex. London: Women in Journalism, November 1999.

Recycled Paper. London: Friends of the Earth. Updated by G Green, January 1996.

Relative Values. BBC Radio 4 broadcast on 26 August 1997.

Sanitary Protection: Women's Health and the Environment. London: Women's
   Environmental Network, April 1993.
Test Tube Harvest. London: Women's Environmental Network, December 1996.
Towards Equality. London: Fawcett Society, Winter 1999.
The Vicar of Dibley. BBC1 broadcast on 25 December 1998.
Voices: Turning Listening into Action. London: Central Office of Information,
   October 1999.
Watching Women. London: Fawcett Society, 1999.
WEN Newsletters: No. 1, Autumn 1988; No. 13, Winter 1991; No. 26, Spring
   1995. London: Women's Environmental Network.
Who's Making the News? Women in the Media Industry in Northern Ireland. Belfast:
   Northern Ireland Women's Rights Movement and Downtown Women's Centre,
   1999.
*The Windsor Consultation Document: Women in the Ordained Ministry: The Journey
   Continues*. London: Advisory Board of Ministry, September 1995.
*Working As One Body: The Report of the Archbishops' Commission on the Organisation
   of the Church of England*. London: Church House Publishing, 1995.

Name index

General index